DYLAN AT 80

IT USED TO GO LIKE THAT, AND NOW IT GOES LIKE THIS

Edited by

**Gary Browning and
Constantine Sandis**

imprint-academic.com

Published in the UK by
Imprint Academic Ltd., PO Box 200, Exeter EX5 5YX, UK

Distributed in the USA by
Ingram Book Company,
One Ingram Blvd., La Vergne, TN 37086, USA

ISBN 9781788360456 paperback

A CIP catalogue record for this book is available from the
British Library and US Library of Congress

Bob Dylan Mural by Eduard Kobra, Minneapolis 25 August 2017
(from a photograph by Sharon Mollerus, licensed under the Creative
Commons Attribution 2.0 Generic license CC BY 2.0).

Contents

Bob Dylan performing at the Azkena Rock Festival, 26 June 2010 (photograph by Alberto Cabello, licensed under the Creative Commons Attribution 2.0 Generic license CC BY 2.0).

Dedication

This book is dedicated to Conal Browning.

Things come and go, but some things stay. My son, Conal, is with me most of the time, even if he died over 10 years ago. Paranoid schizophrenia came to possess him in his early teens, and life was a struggle for the next ten or so years until his death. Memories of Conal intersect with memories of Dylan. Life was hard for Conal, but he could tell the inauthentic from the truthful, and he was a good person to be alongside. A half-smile from Conal was worth a lot of the world's laughter.

Conal liked to listen to all sorts of music, and he loved playing the guitar. Late one night when I was rewriting a book that refused to be written, I crept down to the basement kitchen to make another cup of coffee, and I heard Conal playing. The music was gentle and soulful. On another day I came home from work, and he was watching Dylan's 2003 film, *Masked and Anonymous*. I had seen the film, and it didn't seem to add up to much. Dylan's music was powerful, but his acting and the script seemed wooden. Conal liked the film, and he spoke about it clearly, and with conviction. 'It's the truth', he declared. 'There is no way out. There's no outside to political mind control. It's a stacked deck.' I murmured my objection to a political rock concert that takes place in the film, at which, the Dylan character, Jack Fate is enlisted to perform. 'Surely,' I mused, 'the idea of a rock concert to provide funds for a cause is formulaic and unconvincing.' Conal didn't blink. 'Yes,' he said, 'that's the way things go. We can only speak in clichés, protest is as hackneyed as anything else. Nothing works.'

Conal liked Dylan. Above all, he was drawn to the early Dylan. His enthusiasm for the early acoustic Dylan reminded me how much energy and talent the early Dylan possessed. While people of my generation tend to favour Dylan's explosive mid-60s period, where his electric sound and surreal lyrics turned everything around, Conal recognised the vitality of that early music. His favourite song was 'Bob Dylan's Dream', Dylan's elegiac evocation of a preceding convivial time with friends. Just as I found it hard to understand how Dylan could look back wistfully on his earlier years when he was still so young, I was taken aback over how Conal could look back so reverently at a young age. Of course, Dylan was hell bent on moving forward and cutting ties, so perhaps that's what made his looking back so poignant in 1963. Likewise, Conal packed a lot of suffering into relatively few years, so his earlier life appeared dream-like and special. His death was awful. His sister, Eleanor, is not a Dylan fan, yet she chose 'Shelter from the Storm' to be played at the funeral, and listening to the song made sense in the aftermath of the hard rain that had been falling earlier in the day.

Conal had to bear many things; sectioning, arid professionalism, nurses at their wits end, social workers bereft of sociability and parents who seemed to sit on the wrong side of the fence. But near the end he took some philosophy courses at Oxford Brookes University. He had left school early without qualifications, but now, towards the end, he excelled at philosophy and one of his teachers was Constantine, my fellow editor of this book. I did not know Constantine well at the time, but I am grateful that he taught Conal. He remembers Conal in this way:

Conal was in his early twenties when he joined my Introduction to Ethics class as an associate student. I remember the day I first met him well because he had emailed me beforehand to introduce himself and apologise for missing the enrolment deadline. This meant that I had to sign some forms which he brought to class. There was a calm intensity and natural sensitivity to him; a shyness that others might have easily mistaken for aloofness, and a silence for snobbery. Yet I felt I got him straight away. I subsequently got to know him a little bit and he reminded me of myself at his age, in an uncanny number of ways. Conal was much better than I'd been at philosophy, though. He didn't speak often in class, but when he did he asked perceptive questions, with nothing to prove and no axe to grind. He seemed to enjoy the module and was particularly taken by moral particularity, while finding con-sequentialism to be inconsequential. The essays he wrote were thoughtful.

Conal was a bright and likeable kid, one of a handful of memorable students who were far more interested in specific problems and ideas than in how to achieve a particular grade. Sometimes, he'd arrive late to class, or skip a lecture altogether, but was always genuinely sorry to have missed out on whatever we were covering that day. He wanted to make his own way in life and being an associate student gave him the freedom to do it while holding on to some kind of routine and whatever stability might have come with it. In the end, freedom won out and I didn't get to see him during the last months of his life.

Conal Browning is gone, but his spirit's living on and on.

Gary Browning (with Constantine Sandis),
Oxford & London, April 2021

Conal Browning.

Acknowledgements

We would like to thank Universal Music Publishing for permission to reprint from the lyrics to the following songs of Bob Dylan:

'A Hard Rain's A-Gonna Fall'; 'Abandoned Love'; 'Absolutely Sweet Marie'; 'Ain't Talkin''; 'All Along the Watchtower'; 'Are You Ready'; 'As I Went Out One Morning'; 'Ballad in Plain D'; 'Ballad of a Thin Man'; 'Ballad of Hollis Brown'; 'Black Rider'; 'Blind Willie McTell'; 'Blowin' in the Wind'; 'Buckets of Rain'; 'Can't Escape from You'; 'Can't Wait'; 'Changing of the Guards'; 'Cross the Green Mountain'; 'Crossing the Rubicon'; 'Cry a While'; 'Dark Eyes'; 'Desolation Row'; 'Dignity'; 'Every Grain of Sand'; 'False Prophet'; 'Forgetful Heart'; 'From a Buick 6'; 'Gates of Eden'; 'Gonna Change My Way of Thinking'; 'Goodbye Jimmy Reed'; 'Got My Mind Made Up'; 'Highlands'; 'Honest with Me'; 'I Contain Multitudes'; 'I Pity the Poor Immigrant'; 'It's Alright Ma (I'm Only Bleeding); 'I've Made Up My Mind to Give Myself to You'; 'Joey'; 'Key West (Philosopher Pirate); 'Knockin' on Heaven's Door'; 'Last Thoughts on Woody Guthrie'; 'Let Me Die in My Footsteps'; 'Love Minus Zero/No Limit'; 'Make You Feel My Love'; 'Masters of War'; 'Mississippi'; 'Mother of Muses'; 'Mr. Tambourine Man'; 'Murder Most Foul'; 'My Back Pages'; 'My Own Version of You'; 'Narrow Way'; 'Nettie Moore'; 'Never Say Goodbye'; 'North Country Blues'; 'Not Dark Yet'; 'Odds and Ends'; 'One Too Many Mornings'; 'Only a Pawn in Their Game'; 'Pledging My Time'; 'Positively 4th Street'; 'Queen Jane Approximately'; 'Red River Shore'; 'Restless Farewell'; 'Seeing the Real You at Last'; 'Shelter from the Storm'; 'Shooting Star'; 'Song to Woody'; 'Soon After Midnight'; 'Stuck Inside of Mobile with the Memphis Blues Again'; 'Subterranean Homesick Blues'; 'Sugar Baby'; 'Summer Days'; 'Tangled Up In Blue'; 'Tempest'; 'The Death of Emmett Till'; 'The Lonesome Death of Hattie Carroll'; 'This Dream of You'; 'Tin Angel'; 'To Ramona'; 'Tombstone Blues'; 'Tomorrow is a Long Time'; 'Tryin' to Get to Heaven'; 'Unbelievable'; 'Under Your Spell'; 'Wedding Song'; 'When I Paint My Masterpiece'; 'When You Gonna Wake Up'; 'With God on Our Side'; 'Working Man's Blues #2'.

We would also like to thank a few people who helped make this project happen: Bob Dylan for keepin' on. Jeff Rosen for his help and encouragement at the outset. Graham Horswell and Keith Sutherland at Imprint Academic have been terrific. Likewise, Marc Cimino and Joy Murphy at Universal Music Publishing. All of the contributors have been fantastic in getting their writing done, even with all the tired horses in the sun. Raia and Louise have given us terrific personal support. We just couldn't make it by ourselves…

Notes on Contributors

James Adams is an independent researcher and writer living in Charlottesville, Virginia. In the world of Bob Dylan, his primary interests are Dylan fans, fanzines and fan culture.

Nicholas Birns teaches at New York University where he regularly teaches a course on Dylan. He is author most recently of *The Hyperlocal in Eighteenth and Nineteenth Century Literary Space* (Lexington) and is co-editing the forthcoming *Cambridge Companion to the Australian Novel*.

David Boucher is Professor of Political Theory and International Relations at Cardiff University, and Distinguished Visiting Professor at the University of Johannesburg (2016–2021). He has published widely on history of political thought, British Idealism, colonialism and cultural studies, including *Dylan and Cohen: Poets of Rock and Roll* (2004); *Bob Dylan and Leonard Cohen: Deaths and Entrances* (2021 with Lucy Boucher). With Gary Browning he edited *The Political Art of Bob Dylan* (Imprint Academic).

Lucy Boucher has a PhD in Creative Writing from Brunel University, UK, and has been a visiting researcher at the University of Johannesburg, South Africa. She writes on popular culture and is currently researching conceptions of health and fitness from the 19th century to the present and their impact on the commodification of the body in modern society. She is the co-author of *Bob Dylan and Leonard Cohen: Deaths and Entrances* published by Bloomsbury.

Gary Browning is a Professor of Political Thought at Oxford Brookes University. He is the author of many books, including *Why Iris Murdoch Matters* (Bloomsbury, 2018) and *A History of Modern Political Thought – The Question of Interpretation* (OUP, 2016), and is co-editor of *The Political Art of Bob Dylan*. His interest in Bob Dylan goes back to the release of *The Freewheelin' Bob Dylan*, when he realised that popular music was a serious business.

Sophie Grace Chappell is Professor of Philosophy at the Open University, UK.

Katharine A. Craik is Professor of Shakespeare and early modern literature at Oxford Brookes University. She has published widely on Shakespeare and his contemporaries, recently edited *Shakespeare and Emotion* for Cambridge University Press, and is working on a book provisionally entitled *Lifelike Shakespeare*. She is co-editor of *Beyond Criticism*, a series of books with the independent Boiler House Press which sets out to explore the spaces between critical and creative thinking. Katharine also writes creatively and is a published poet and librettist.

Anne Margaret Daniel teaches literature and humanities at The New School University in New York. She specialises in Modernism and in Irish literature. The editor of F. Scott Fitzgerald's last unpublished short stories, *I'd Die for You and Other Lost Stories* (Scribner 2017), she is currently at work on a biography of Fitzgerald, and is, with Jackson L. Bryer, editing the collected letters of Zelda Sayre Fitzgerald. Her essays on books, music and culture have appeared for the past thirty years in books, critical editions, magazines and journals including *The New York Times*, *Hot Press*, *No Depression*, *The Spectator*, and *The Times Literary Supplement*. Please visit www.annemargaretdaniel.com or follow her @venetianblonde on Twitter.

Roger Dalrymple is Associate Dean (Student Outcomes) at Oxford Brookes University where he undertakes both literary and educational research. His books include *Language and Piety in Middle English Romance* (2000), *Middle English Literature* (2004) and *Crippen: A Crime Sensation in Memory and Modernity* (2020). An occasional songwriter and guitarist, he has performed Dylan songs for many years including for the University of Cambridge continuing education course, *Songs of Dylan and Cohen*, and at the Oxford Brookes *Think Human* festivals of 2018 and 2020. His original song about Dylan's legendary 1990 concert in a small New Haven club, 'Toad's Place', can be heard online.

Maximilian de Gaynesford is Professor of Philosophy at the University of Reading, formerly a Fellow and Tutor of Lincoln College Oxford, and author of *The Rift In The Lute* (Oxford University Press, 2017). Currently, his work focuses on finding ways to 'attune' philosophy and poetry, which essentially means removing obstacles between them and finding new means for them to genuinely benefit each other.

Alexander Douglas FRSA is an interdisciplinary and portfolio researcher working across music, the humanities and mental health. An active campaigner for social justice, he is currently the EDI Lead for the British Forum for Ethnomusicology. An award-winning jazz pianist, he is also Artistic Director of the Huddersfield Bach Collegium. Having previously been Visiting Lecturer in Theological Aesthetics at the London School of Theology, he is currently a Visiting Lecturer in Music at Cambridge University as well as a researcher in philosophy of religion at the University of Hertfordshire. His blog posts at www.theomusicology.com have been read in 120 countries and in 2021 he focuses on the clarinet.

Natalie Ferris is a Leverhulme Trust Early Career Fellow at the University of Edinburgh. She is the author of *Abstraction in Post-War British Literature 1945–1980* (forthcoming Oxford University Press, 2022), the co-convenor of the public speaker series Radical Notations, and the co-founder of the Christine Brooke-Rose Society. She is at work on her second monograph, on dynamism and deception in 20th-century art, design and letters, and an edited collection of essays exploring women, creativity and intelligence work. She is the Deputy Editor of *The Cambridge Humanities Review* and the English Editor of *SPACE* architecture journal, and a published writer and critic, contributing to publications such as *Frieze, The Guardian, Tate Etc.* and *Word & Image*.

Ray Foulk brought Bob Dylan back to the live stage, after a three-year absence, for the 1969 Isle of Wight Festival. Organised by Ray and his two brothers, the iconic Island festivals also featured in 1970 the last UK performance of Jimi Hendrix. After later staging Art Deco exhibitions and studying architecture in Cambridge, Ray focused research into the invention of modern art. He is the author of books about Bob Dylan, the Isle of Wight Festivals, and Pablo Picasso. He now lives in Oxford, working as an architect and environmental campaigner, near his four grown-up children and grandchildren.

Keith Frankish is a philosopher and writer. He is Honorary Reader in Philosophy at the University of Sheffield, UK, Visiting Research Fellow at The Open University, UK (where he was formerly a Senior Lecturer), and Adjunct Professor with the Brain and Mind Programme in Neurosciences at the University of Crete, Greece. He works in the area of philosophy of mind and is best known for defending 'illusionism' about phenomenal consciousness. He currently lives in Crete with his family and a large number of animals. Bob Dylan's songs have been part of Keith's life as long as he can remember, and they are now guiding him through the lonesome valley of middle age. There is more information about Keith on his website, www.keithfrankish.com.

Mick Gold is a photographer, journalist and documentary film maker. He won an Emmy for *Watergate* and a Peabody Award for *Endgame in Ireland*. *Hostages in Beirut* won first prize at the Pessac History Film Festival. His most recent series is *Cuba: Castro vs the World* for BBC2 (2020).

Michael Gray is a critic and public speaker. He pioneered the serious study of Dylan's work with *Song & Dance Man: The Art of Bob Dylan* (1972), the first such critical book. Born in 1946, he grew up on Merseyside and studied History & English Literature at York University. His books include the massive *Song & Dance Man III* (1999), *The Bob Dylan Encyclopedia* (2006), *Hand Me My Travelin' Shoes: In Search Of Blind Willie McTell* (2007) and *Outtakes On Bob Dylan: Selected Writings 1967–2021*. He gained the higher doctorate of D.Litt. in 2015 and has lived in southwest France since 2008. His website is www.michaelgray.net.

Garry L. Hagberg is the James H. Ottaway Professor of Philosophy and Aesthetics at Bard College. Author of numerous papers at the intersection of aesthetics and the philosophy of language, his books include *Meaning and Interpretation: Wittgenstein, Henry James, and Literary Knowledge*, *Art as Language: Wittgenstein, Meaning, and Aesthetic Theory* and *Describing Ourselves: Wittgenstein and Autobiographical Consciousness*. Editor of the journal *Philosophy and Literature* and eight edited volumes, Hagberg is presently completing a new book, *Living in Words: Literature, Autobiographical Language, and the Composition of Selfhood* and is also working on three other books, one of which is on aesthetic issues in jazz improvisation. He has performed on about a dozen CDs as a jazz guitarist, and is co-author, with Howard Roberts, of the three-volume *Guitar Compendium: Technique, Improvisation, Musicianship, Theory*.

Lucas Hare is an actor. He also co-hosts the podcast *Is It Rolling, Bob? Talking Dylan*.

Harrison Hewitt is a writer from Toronto. He's been a Bob Dylan fan since he was a boy.

Robyn Hitchcock is a rock and roll surrealist. Born in London in 1953, he is an acclaimed songwriter, guitarist and visual artist. He founded the art rock band The Soft Boys in 1976, and since then has released more than 30 albums. In 1996, he was the subject of Jonathan Demme's in-concert movie *Storefront Hitchcock*. He lives in Nashville and London with his two cats, Ringo and Tubby. He nearly met Bob Dylan on a kibbutz in 1971, but decided to have a shower before lunch...

Jessica Hundley is an author, film maker and journalist. She has written for the likes of *Vogue, Rolling Stone* and *The New York Times,* and has authored books on artists including Dennis Hopper, David Lynch and Gram Parsons. Hundley often explores the counterculture in her work, with a focus on metaphysics, psychedelia and magic.

Fleur Jongepier is an assistant professor of ethics at the Radboud University Nijmegen, the Netherlands. Her research interests include self-knowledge and autonomy, feminist ethics, and digitalization. She has co-authored a (Dutch) book on personal identity and regularly writes blogs, philosophy book reviews and op-eds for national newspapers on topics ranging from Covid-19 triage to online manipulation and the value of art. She keeps trying hard, and sometimes fails, to just enjoy and unself with Dylan and not philosophize too much.

Barb Jungr is an award-winning international performer, musician, recording artist, lyricist and writer. Jungr is best known for performances and recordings of Bob Dylan and Leonard Cohen. With performances across four continents and fifteen solo album recordings she appeared on *Talking Bob Dylan Blues: A Tribute to Bob Dylan* for BBC TV and has appeared on programmes about Dylan's work and on singing Dylan. Will Friedwald's *The Great Jazz and Pop Vocal Albums* (2017) has a chapter devoted to her 2002 CD *Every Grain Of Sand* (Linn Records).

Jean-Charles Khalifa has devoted his academic career at the University of Poitiers (France) to teaching and researching English syntax and advanced translation. He is now retired and a full-time translator. In parallel, he has been interested in Bob Dylan ever since he heard him first on the radio in the mid-60s. He is also a musician and singer, performing locally with an acoustic duet/trio.

Lou Majaw is a performing artist from Shillong in North-Eastern India and is renowned for his Bob Dylan tribute shows. The Lou Majaw Foundation was created with the purpose of advancing music among the community at large without discrimination of caste, creed, etc.

KG Miles is co-curator of the Dylan Room at The Troubadour Club in London, where Dylan first played in 1962. He is also the co-author of *Bob Dylan in London: Troubadour Tales* (McNidder & Grace, 2021). His next book, *Bob Dylan in the Big Apple: Troubadour Tales of New York*, is forthcoming with McNidder & Grace.

Ray Monk is Professor Emeritus in Philosophy at the University of Southampton, where he taught for 26 years. He has written biographies of Ludwig Wittgenstein, Bertrand Russell and J. Robert Oppenheimer. In his retirement he has become obsessed with the merits of veganism and the dangers of climate change. Bob Dylan has been an obsession of his for much longer.

Ioanna 'Nana' Mouskouri is a Greek singer. Over the span of her career, she has recorded over 1,500 songs in more than twelve languages, including Greek, French, English, German, Dutch, Italian, Portuguese, Spanish, Hebrew, Welsh, Mandarin Chinese and Corsican. Her latest album is *Every Grain of Sand: Nana Mouskouri Sings Bob Dylan*.

Anupama Ranawana is a researcher, writer and teacher based in the UK. Her interests and expertise lie in religious political thought, feminist religious thought, decolonial theology and faith and international development. She teaches Asian Theology for Catherine of Siena College (Roehampton) and works in a research advisory capacity with Christian Aid. In Autumn 2021 she begins a research project on the feminist religious voices of Asian liberation in the School of Divinity at the University of St. Andrews.

Amy Rigby has been writing, performing and recording her transcendent songs about everyday life for over thirty years. A teenage denizen of CBGB who fell in love with country songwriting, she started bands Last Roundup and the Shams in NYC's East Village before launching a solo career with the album *Diary Of A Mod Housewife*. Her song 'Don't Break

The Heart' was recorded by Laura Cantrell and 'All I Want' was recorded by Ronnie Spector and included on *The Very Best Of Ronnie Spector*. Amy continues to tour and release new music including the 2018 album *The Old Guys*, the single 'The President Can't Read' and 'Vote That Fucker Out' (2020, with husband and sometime duo partner Wreckless Eric). Her first book, *Girl To City: A Memoir*, was published last year.

Constantine Sandis thought of Dylan as a hippy you couldn't trust until — when he was about 16 years old — his friend Mahmoud Kassem showed him the cover of *Highway 61 Revisited* and convinced him that Zimmy was a punk at heart. Four years later, Joan Baez kissed him at a concert in Rome. Constantine is now Professor of Philosophy at the University of Hertfordshire and a Fellow of the Royal Society of Arts. When not tweeting as @csandis he writes books such as *The Things We Do and Why We Do Them* (2012) and *Character and Causation* (2018).

Emma-Rose Sears gained a first-class degree and masters in English Literature at Oxford Brookes University, and has undertaken graduate work at the University of Reading. She is currently planning a PhD proposal on Elena Ferrante. She runs a café and is a Bob Dylan fan.

Stephen Sedley, latterly a judge of the Court of Appeal, worked while studying law in the 1960s as an accompanist and arranger for Trans-atlantic Records, and as *Tribune*'s folk music critic.

Tim Shorrock is a Washington, DC-based writer and guitar player who grew up in Japan and South Korea during the Cold War. He is the author of *SPIES FOR HIRE: The Secret World of Intelligence Outsourcing* (2008). His article 'JFK, Bob Dylan, and the Death of the American Dream', written at the outset of the coronavirus pandemic in response to Dylan's epic 'Murder Most Foul', can be found at TheNation.com, where he is a correspondent. Shorrock posts regularly on Twitter about Dylan, music and US foreign policy under the handle @TimothyS.

Galen Strawson was a failed poet until he was 25. Then a different kind of poetry — philosophy — took over. He taught at Oxford University for twenty years, then at Reading University and the City University of New York Graduate Center. In 2012 he moved to University of Texas at Austin. He has written a number of books including *Freedom and Belief*, *The Secret*

Connexion, Selves, Mental Reality, The Evident Connexion and *Things That Bother Me.*

Emma Swift is an Australian-born songwriter, currently residing in the USA. A gifted singer inspired by Joni Mitchell, Marianne Faithfull and a plethora of dead poets, her sound is a blend of classic folk and indie rock. In August 2020 she released the critically-acclaimed *Blonde On The Tracks*, a Laurel Canyon inspired reimagining of some of her favourite Bob Dylan tunes on Tiny Ghost Records. The album received Best of 2020 accolades from *Rolling Stone, Nashville Scene, No Depression, The Guardian* and more.

Laura Tenschert is the creator of Definitely Dylan, a podcast and radio show that approaches Bob Dylan's work from a fresh, modern, feminist perspective. She's looking forward to a future for Dylan studies that includes more non-white and female voices.

Bob Dylan's childhood home in Hibbing, Minnesota (GNU Free Documentation License 1.2).

Nana Mouskouri

Foreword

It was a wonderful moment when I received this book. It is so unique and I am full of emotion that most of the Dylan songs I ever sung are included.

Bob Dylan came into my life as a singer-songwriter in the very early sixties. I loved his interpretations of life in songs, each one quite different from the other but all enormously touching. They became as symbolic to me as Greek music. Dylan's world was quite unknown at the time, but when he burst onto the scene, everyone was charmed by the quality of his words and the musical accompaniment. How deep and emotionally inspiring he was to everyone. Ever since, I have continued to love and admire his way of writing: sacred and secret but also meaningful and sublime.

Dylan's songs gave me certain answers. He was searching for a truth he needed to live, and went on learning and communicating, though so many answers still remain blowing in the wind. He can reflect the sadness of departure (whether it's fare thee well or farewell Angelina), or the greatness of a father who wishes to his child to remain forever young. His desire to find the truth that is absolute for him teaches us that he is, for sure, a philosopher — born with a need for truth.

Dylan often becomes surrealist; he upgrades reality. He made me discover all that he learned living in traditional America, inspired by love, humanity and peace. He refuses violence. He always tries to find sincerity because it is clear and transparent; he is a great believer in love, peace and justice.

Dylan's writing is full of surprises. He expresses with strength and lyricism the dangers we risk in order to survive. A searcher of justice, he indicates wisdom, neither imposing upon nor judging anyone. He simply awakens the conscience with love and tolerance. Dylan rejects war, preferring love and truth. He will continue to search until he finds it: real, transparent, sincere and free; honest, sensible and human.

There are many emotions and values to discover in his writings. To this end, I have been very fortunate. In the early sixties, when we first heard his songs, my producer and I started to record Dylan's songs, which for us were so original; a treasure of love (at the time, 'Love Minus Zero/No Limit' and 'Tomorrow is a Long Time', and later 'To make You Feel My Love'). Living in France at the time, it was appropriate to sing some of them in French ('Adieu Angelina', 'Le Ciel est Noir', 'Amour Moins Zéro') and others still in German ('Jedes Körnschen Sand')!

Today we are back to the times are-a-changin'. He appeared at times when we were changing, and yet we are back to changing times. 'Every Grain of Sand' is one that his people sent me in the eighties. It is the most precious present I ever received from Bob Dylan and I would like to end with his words:

> I hear the ancient footsteps like the motion of the sea
> Sometimes I turn, there's someone there, other times it's only me
> I am hanging in the balance of the reality of man
> Like every sparrow falling, like every grain of sand

Thank you, Mr. Dylan, for everything you have offered with your truth.

Nana Mouskouri
Athens, 5 July 2021

Gary Browing and
Constantine Sandis

Prologue
In Death You Face Life

Interviewer: Is there a difference between Bob Dylan in the sixties and the Bob Dylan today?

Dylan: I couldn't tell you... You? Is there a difference between *you* in the sixties and you tonight?

Interviewer: I think so, yes. Don't you think that your music has developed from the sixties?

Dylan: Possibly.

—Landvetter airport, 1978

Bob Dylan did not die young. That still seems a surprise.

Dylan himself has reflected a number of times about his cheating of death, toying with concepts of transfiguration and rebirth. From early on, biographers have recorded Dylan's thoughts on his own death, speculating what it might mean for him to grow old. At the close of his landmark 1986 biography, *No Direction Home – The Life and Music of Bob Dylan*, Robert Shelton wondered what Dylan's future career might be like. Would his creativity come to an abrupt end like that of Rimbaud, or would it flourish in late age, like that of Yeats?

If once an open question, the answer has been clear since 1997's *Time Out of Mind*. This book reflects on the evolving creativity across various stages of Dylan's life and career, from a youthful Guthrie jukebox to elderly statesman with the blood of the land in his voice. On his latest album, *Rough and Rowdy Ways*, the Blakean song 'I Contain Multitudes' serves as a piece of retrospective self-reflection upon Dylan's own many-sidedness, in turn refracted into the many songs on the album. Heartfelt love songs, rowdy blues, mournful reflections on the political past and present, and ruminations on the end of things represent and deepen Dylan's repertoire ever since *Another Side of Bob Dylan.*

We can now consider what it means for Dylan to be entering his seventh decade as a recording artist. If this book is about anything, it is about reflecting on Dylan at 80. How is he? How is his art? Does he still embody the themes and styles of his younger self, or has he developed a late style that won't look back? The Dylan who sings about the death of Kennedy in 2020 appears very different from the Dylan who, in 1963, when giving a speech at the Tom Paine Award shortly after JFK's assassination, claimed to despise the old people in the audience. Yet in 2020, as in 1963, Dylan widens responsibilities for political developments. In his recent 'Murder Most Foul', Dylan traces the legacy of the Kennedy assassination in a succession of cultural developments, just as responsibility for the wrongs that he diagnosed in society in the early 1960s pointed to many people, including the singer himself and his audience (see MONK and BROWNING). This theme of widening responsibility is the focus of 'Who Killed Davey Moore?' which was recorded in 1963 but only officially released in the Bootleg Series in 1991. In this song that is designated a masterpiece in Stephen Sedley's essay, Dylan adapts the nursery rhyme, Who Killed Cock Robin? The song asks one insistent question about who was responsible for the death of the boxer, Davey Moore, who died after a world title bout with Sugar Ramos. It poses the question to a series of people who are implicated in the death; the referee, boxing writers, gamblers, the crowd and the other boxer in the ring, Sugar Ramos. There is no definitive answer to the insistent question, but responsibility emerges as shared between all of these people. Dylan's finger pointing songs are to the point precisely because they demand that all of us consider wider notions of political causation, including our own role in the public world. Hence, 'Murder Most Foul' widens rather than narrows responsibility for what has happened to public life in the USA after the Kennedy assassination, going beyond Oswald and the conspirators in the murder.

Dylan urges us to not look back while constantly using the past to create something for the present. Time is central to him. It moves too fast and is an enemy. Yet it also passes slowly and frustrates our moves. It allows for creation and self-creation, with which Dylan has worked since he created himself as Bob Dylan (see D. BOUCHER). Maximilian de Gaynesford concentrates upon 'Pledging My Time' from *Blonde on Blonde*, where the demanding sense of pledging one's time is explored for what it might mean, and where the richness of its possibilities of commitment are pondered. Time is a jet plane and there's no time to think. Bob Dylan said that. Inside you the time moves. Robyn Hitchcock said that. Dylan's younger self was busy being born, yet his first album sees him rehearsing the end-of-the-line songs of the Delta blues, such as 'In My Time of Dyin'. He doesn't sing such songs any more, but when he ponders mortality in his own late songs, he seems to mean it (see FRANKISH). So much for these long and wasted years. Time is relative to space, yet every distance is not near. We are born *in* time and it's been such a long, long time. Dylan wants to turn back the clock, or even have it pushed back for him (see HARE). Yet he was ahead of his time when he sang the names of Emmett Till, Davey Moore, Medgar Evers, Hattie Carroll, Rubin 'Hurricane' Carter, George Jackson and others, long before 'say their names' became a thing. It looks like he's moving, but he's standing still. Time yields no stability. We said that.

Throughout the years, there is a yearning to create an aesthetic world that defies limit and time. 'Mr. Tambourine Man' echoes Dylan's desire to inhabit a world beyond today and tomorrow. 'Johanna' appears to be unreal, though the song itself tells of the mystery and beauty of the White Goddess of poetry. 'Blind Willie McTell' is a song about the impossibility of singing the blues like Blind Willie McTell, and yet its lamentation for the past and present of America is of a piece with the work of the great Delta bluesmen. Likewise, 'Key West (Philosopher Pirate)' at the tail end of Dylan's seventies is somehow unreal and yet aesthetically true (see DANIEL). The ruefulness of his reflection on ageing animates and troubles *Time Out of Mind*. It might not be dark yet, but it is getting there, as Mose Alison not only *might* have said but did, in fact, remind one of us that he really *did* say when we spoke to him about Dylan towards the end of his life. Saying Goodbye to Jimmy Reed, for Dylan, becomes a way of saying goodbye to himself, and goodbye is no longer too good a word to say.

The urgency of the quest to leave behind past selves is still with Dylan at 80, even if he reflects upon the mother of muses (see TENSCHERT) that takes in American generals, who paved the way for Martin Luther King (see DOUGLAS). Moving on is a paradox, as its very celebration brings with it a remembrance of things past that are never simply left behind (as the older Dylan looks back on a self that was younger rather than so much older, then, after all). There is a negativity even within a positive resolution. When Dylan was urging his girlfriend not to think twice about their relationship because he was moving on, he was in that very song thinking twice, just as his later confidence in not thinking about his lost love *most* of the time betrays moments of concern. If he's just walkin' then how is it that he spends eight verses and another eight choruses telling us that he ain't talkin'?

The later Dylan is forever revisiting past landscapes where he pledges to remember a love who made him lonesome when she went, and recalls a world in which he might have held on to the girl from the red river shore had he not thrown it all away. But he was looking back right from the start, in his teenage dream of an idyllic time with friends who seem to have already disappeared a lifetime ago. Lost time that is not found again occupies a mystical landscape in Dylan songs, where he keeps on keepin' on. You can always come back, but you can't come back *all* the way.

Dylan has traversed many musical styles, from crooning to grouchy blues, by way of traditional folk, rock, country, woogie boogie, gospel and more. Moreover, music is only one of the many art forms that he has explored. He paints, sculpts and has directed and appeared in polarising films. He brings to the role of the DJ a dry humour and a philosophy of musical language. In *Theme Time Radio Hour*, Dylan explores our every-day concepts through a deep and palpable love of the byways of popular musical history. His prose, on the back of albums, in *Tarantula* and in his idiosyncratic memoir, *Chronicles: Volume One* (Dylan 2004), stays with you despite its initial throwaway appearance. Again, while he might seem diffident when speaking in public, his speeches (from the Tom Paine Award to Grammy ceremonies and Live Aid) pack a powerful punch.

Dylan's capacity to exert an influence on a multiplicity of spheres and artistic styles explains the diversity of contributors to this volume. There are essays by musical artists, film makers, essayists, philosophers, actors, linguists, jokermen, literary critics, lawyers, theologians, environmentalists, political and social theorists, promoters who nearly fell off the floor and, of course, Dylanologists. The contributors are people of varied genders, ages and ethnicities, whose essays reflect diverse ways of coming across and thinking about Dylan. Many have written on Dylan before, while others are offering a story about Dylan for the first time. Each has a unique tale to tell, which in turn makes this volume original and very different from what has gone before.

Songwriters, like philosophers, have traditionally only interpreted the world, but times got strange and Dylan felt a change comin' on. Harrison Hewitt sees Dylan as a vehicle of metamorphosis. Times change but Dylan doesn't necessarily change with them (see KHALIFA); when something's not right, he is prepared to say it's wrong in songs that go against the grain, such as 'Union Sundown', 'License to Kill' and 'Unbelievable', all of which share a scepticism about "progress": 'they said it was the land of milk and honey / Now they say it's the land of money / Who ever thought they could ever make that stick.' Things *have* changed and change evidently moves within the song, 'Changing of the Guards' (see CHAPPELL). All its stanzas are powerful expressions of changing fortunes and yet the song as a whole resists definitive determination of a meaning that might delimit its spirit of creativity. Transformation is present in every Dylan album; the winds of change blow wild and free even as he croons 'Why Try to Change Me Now?' on *Shadows in the Night*. KG Miles writes as a fan who remains struck by the power of 'Gonna Change My Way of Thinking'. Dylan's Christian songs receive a more critical reading from Anupama Ranawana, who sees Dylan as continuously engaged with religious themes, and shines her light on Dylan's religious thought by observing its relevance to a number of world religions. Everything passes, everything changes and all things become new as old things slip away.

If there is an essential core to the multiplicity of Dylan's art (and perhaps there isn't), it resides in a restless creativity and determination to stick to its truth. This encompasses his musical respect for others: Woody Guthrie, Ma Rainey, Memphis Minnie, Earl Scruggs, Blind Willie McTell, Odetta, Charlie Patton, Victoria Spivey, Jimmy Reed, Dion, Mavis Staples, Nana Mouskouri, John Lennon, Gordon Lightfoot, Elvis Presley, Umm Kulthum, Cisco Houston, Bobby Vee, Sonny Terry and Leadbelly too… even Alice Cooper. Dylan presses on and, even when he does look back, he tends to reflect on the point of not doing so. In *Chronicles* he takes time to reflect on working with Daniel Lanois on the album *Oh Mercy!* It was an uneven experience, but Dylan is not minded to express any regret. He was focused upon creating, and his creativity in song is not to be side-lined by undue reflection that obstructs or kills the inspiration (see SANDIS). 'Sometimes', he observes, 'you say things in songs even if there's a small chance of them being true. And sometimes you say things that have nothing to do with the truth of what you want to say, and sometimes you say things that everyone knows to be true. Then again, at the same time, you're thinking that the only truth on this earth is that there is no truth in it. Whatever you are saying, you're saying it in a ricky-tick way. There's never time to reflect. You stitched and pressed and packed and drove, is what you did' (Dylan 2006).

How can Dylan's creativity be analysed, given its protean character and Dylan's own reluctance to disturb its magic? The cast assembled for this book does justice to the mystery of creativity and follows Dylan's example in forbearing to reduce collective imagination to the aridity of analysis. They find ways of reflecting upon his artistry and to consider its meandering and sometimes accelerating course in the light of a career that spans a number of forms and stretches across six decades and counting. They deal with how it has endured over time and changed shape with changing times (see BIRNS). Some of them bring their own creativity to bear upon Dylan's own sustained creativity.

Robyn Hitchcock revisits Highway 61 in remembering how he survived the regimentation of school to express a surreal imagination, and Galen Strawson captures the spirit of the sixties in his recollections of his own fragile teenage identity and the atmosphere of the age that inhabits the style of his essay; other sides of the same eternal spirit are evoked by Tim Shorrock, who sees the troubadour as a teacher in the schools of life and death and Lou Majaw in the book's Afterword. You can feel it, you can hear it. Amy Rigby details how Dylan's lyrics can inspire by showcasing an attitude that doesn't hide from the truth, and Barb Jungr recognises how singing a Dylan song can open up a new world of darkness and light. Emma Swift celebrates how *Rough and Rowdy Ways* revived her spirits during the pandemic. She speaks for a lot of people, including the Dylan Twitter community that drew together through life in the time of Covid-19.

Is there anything much in a name? Well, there is, when it is invented by an artist who lives with the name that he has imagined. David Boucher devotes his essay to how and why Robert Zimmerman came up with the name 'Bob Dylan'. Creating your own name ('Elston Gunn', 'Blind Boy Grunt', 'Lucky Wilbury', 'Jack Frost') is a commitment to your own imagination, and Dylan's initial surge of creativity in the early 1960s is traced in a number of essays that circle around his early so-called 'protest' songs (better characterised by Tim Shorrock as *empathy* songs), exploring them from the plurality of perspectives that they entertain. Douglas Alexander focuses on how Dylan's songs, both early and late, draw upon black music in countering racial oppression. Ray Monk and Gary Browning look closely at early songs, making opposing judgments on their value while both recognising Dylan's imaginative and disconcerting way of pointing the finger in unexpected and unsettling directions. Stephen Sedley, a historian of folk music who is also an Appeal Court Judge, recalls meeting Dylan in 1962 in The Troubadour on Old Brompton Road, when Dylan made an early trip to the UK. It is now home to The Dylan Room, co-curated by KG Miles, co-author of *Dylan in London: Troubadour Tales*.

Dylan is remembered as possessing an uncanny ability to master new songs and tunes, and to make them his own, a capacity that he continues to display with the use of various names, masks and hats. Lucy Boucher takes seriously how he has been donning masks, long before the expression 'wear a mask' took on a new meaning. Not unlike the dark glasses he wears to cover his eyes, these are worn by the man behind the shades to shield his creative identity from the glare of publicity. But, as his seemingly unmasked self remarks in Scorsese's *Rolling Thunder* film (using Oscar Wilde's words—an activity which forms part of a wider gag), only a person wearing a mask will tell the truth. Most of the time, Robert Zimmerman has his Bob Dylan mask on. He's masquerading in the Shadow Kingdom.

Dylan's break with the folk music revival and early fans was marked by the sound of an electric guitar, and Garry Hagberg devotes his essay to that guitar and everything it means. Emma-Rose Sears focuses on Dylan's wonderful 1963 'Last Thoughts on Woody Guthrie', which was written when he was moving on from an early hero that was still alive (though not in the condemnatory way that, say, Nietzsche moved on from

Wagner). She notes how Guthrie's presence is as elusive as Dylan's in its haunting of the latter's relentless exposure of lies and half-truths.

The prodigious nature of Dylan's creativity is marked by the affinities that contributors in the volume perceive between Dylan and fellow artists as seemingly diverse as Shakespeare, Picasso and Iris Murdoch. Katharine Craik observes how the Bards of Stratford and Minnesota both get on with the practical work of art while framing poetry and song, which recognises and expresses experiential pain and disturbance. Both bodies of work have given rise to spurious authorship questions, put forward by pussies and wussies. Before *Anonymous?* there was *Masked and Anonymous* (a film whose plausibility has increased in a post-Trump world of false prophets that let it all hang out). And before that, Dylan was Alias (see HUNDLEY), Burrough's invisible hombre in search of his own Ithaca, thousands of years after that original Nobody, Odysseus.

Ray Foulk, who brought Dylan to the first Isle of Wight Festival, sees Picasso's periodic shifts of style and fearless expression of his art as resembling Dylan's own willingness to keep changing direction. And Iris Murdoch's commitment to the value of attending to what is not the self, and to practise 'unselfing' so as to see and care for others, is seen by Fleur Jongepier as allowing us to recognise Dylan's own way of delivering us from a preoccupation with the self by inventing a diverse array of selves with which he can engage. Natalie Ferris looks at all the gates Dylan refers to in early songs, such as the 'Gates of Eden', 'Sad-Eyed Lady of the Lowlands' and 'Absolutely Sweet Marie', and the actual wrought iron gates that he makes in later years. Mick Gold considers Dylan's voices and Roger Dalrymple explores their echoes in live performances, such as his much-bootlegged duets with Patti Smith. James Adams considers the future of both the bootleg and its fans. He urges the case for the curation and accessibility of all Dylan's performances, though the artist's concern for the integrity and presentation of their own work remains a counter-vailing consideration. The essays come to a close with Michael Gray's analysis of the different forms of endings in Dylan's songs. How do you end a track? How do you end an album? What words are appropriate? Is an ending signalled? Does Dylan respect conventions? All of these questions are addressed, and Dylan's endings are worth reflecting on just as all the themes explored in this volume add to our understanding of Dylan's ongoing creative energy.

We could have rearranged the order of the essays that follow and given them all another name. But every ordering tells its own story and that of this book is as much chronological as it is thematic. Both skip back and forth. Little about Dylan is linear. His elusive identity, expressed yet also masked by a relentless creativity, is approached by attending to Dylan's recognition of time, change, repetition, renewal, creation, life and death.

At eighty, Dylan reworks old songs, renewing them and thereby also himself in the process. In his sublime *Shadow Kingdom* streaming event, sparse, drumless arrangements with highly articulate vocals and a retro theatrical vibe capture our attention at every turn. The acapella-esque 'Tombstone Blues' is taken at a funeral pace, which allows regret and reverence to supervene upon disdain. New lyrics transform 'To Be Alone with You' from throwaway Jerry Lee Lewis to a renegade's manifesto, while 'Forever Young' is revealed as never before to be a profound and tender prayer.

Dylan did not die young. But may he stay forever so.

Gary Browning   Constantine Sandis

David Boucher

Dylan and the Rimbaud of Cwmdonkin Drive

Robert Allen Zimmerman officially changed his name on 2nd August 1962 to Bob Dylan. Why, has continued to be a perennial question and irritant to him. On occasions he flatly denied that it had anything to do with the Welsh poet Dylan Thomas. He told Robert Shelton, the *New York Times* music correspondent and Dylan biographer, that he should make it clear that the name did not come from Dylan Thomas, and that he wasn't impressed by the Welshman's poetry anyway. It was too romantic and flowery for his tastes. In the *Playboy* interview with Bob Dylan published in 1978, he was asked if it was because of Dylan Thomas he changed his name. 'No', he explained, changing your name was not uncommon, it's liking changing your location, your mannerisms or appearance. A name can hold you back, and adopting another can have certain advantages. After all, names are only labels by which we refer to each other. An adopted name, Dylan asserted, somehow has to fit and you have to feel that person: 'I just chose that name and it stuck' (Cott 2006, 205–6).

He was, of course, familiar with Thomas's poetry. While still a school-boy in Hibbing, Minnesota, he owned a copy of the *Collected Poems*, and he tantalisingly alludes to the Welshman in the pseudonym he adopted when he played piano for Steve Goodman in 1972 on the album *Somebody Else's Troubles*. He called himself Robert Milkwood Thomas, after the Welshman's most famous radio play for voices, *Under Milk Wood*, first performed on stage in New York, 14th May 1953. Thomas played the first voice. Much Later, in 2007, just three years after the publication of

Chronicles in which he admitted he took his name from the Welshman, Bob Dylan recited Dylan Thomas's most anthologised poem in his 'Theme Time Radio Hour' on 'Death and Taxes'. The poem was 'Do Not Go Gentle Into That Good Night', urging his dying father to rage against the dying of the light.

It was in the first volume of his autobiography, *Chronicles*, that the mid-westerner from Hibbing offered an explanation of why he adopted Thomas's Christian name as his surname. He announced that he took the Welshman's name because he liked the sound of it. It sounded a bit like his second Christian name, Allen, which he had considered using, but thought Dylan with a D more emphatic.

There is no evidence, however, that Bob Dylan was directly influenced in writing his own poetry by Thomas. No one has ever accused him of plagiarising Thomas; nor has he, unlike John Cale and Ralph McTell, ever set any of Thomas's poems to music, nor, despite frequently playing venues in Cardiff, did he make a pilgrimage to Laugharne, some eighty miles away, where Thomas is buried. Both Ginsberg and Ferlinghetti paid homage at the graveside, with the latter marking the occasion with his 'Belated Palinode For Dylan Thomas' with the opening lines: 'In Wales at Laugharne at last I stand beside his cliff-perched writing shed' (Ferlinghetti 1994, 42).[1]

What was the allure of Thomas's name in America, that drew Bobby Zimmerman to it? Dylan Thomas was famous in America. The exotic ultra-bohemian Celt took North America by storm with reading tours in 1950, 1952 and twice in 1953. At the invitation of John Malcolm Brinnin, the author of *Dylan Thomas in America* (1956), he criss-crossed the country in an alcohol-fuelled frenzy, on roads, planes and rail, undertaking the most arduous logistically challenging journeys. His candour, wit and outrageous behaviour attracted audiences all over the country, where he would regale them with anecdotes, embellished with rhetorical flourish; mock them for their pretentiousness; and recite poetry with his booming crystal-clear diction. He was the pioneer of the audio book. Barbara Cohen and Marianne Roney persuaded Thomas in the bar of the Chelsea

---

[1]   In this same collection appears a poem 'The Jack of Hearts (For Dylan)', an allusion, of course, to 'Lily, Rosemary and the Jack of Hearts' off *Blood on the Tracks* (CBS 1975).

Hotel in January 1952 to record a short story and five poems, including 'Do Not Go Gentle Into That Good Night'. The recording launched Caedmon Records, and established 'A Child's Christmas in Wales' as a Christmas classic, selling over 500,000 copies in its first decade, reaching millions of children and their parents throughout North America. Subsequently he signed copies to be sold at his readings. He was a literary megastar who perpetrated the illusion that the poet could make a living outside the academy. He could barely make ends meet, and that was why he was in America!

All the young poets, and especially the Beats, as Leonard Cohen remarked in an email to the author, were 'intrigued with his fame, his genius, his drinking, his unconditional sense of social irresponsibility'. They wanted to be as famous and as outrageous as him. In the year of Dylan Thomas's death, Kenneth Rexroth wrote a poem in memory of his self-destructive friend, 'Thou Shalt Not Kill': 'He is dead / the bird of Rhiannon / He is dead.'[2] In Rexroth's view Thomas was one of the great titans of the post-war generation, who deliberately destroyed himself through excess. In poetry, he was the great influence on the Beat Generation. In 1957 Rexroth recalled the last time he saw Dylan Thomas. His self-destruction had gone beyond the limits of the rational and 'assumed the terrifying inertia of inanimate matter. Being with him was like being swept away by a torrent of falling stones' (Rexroth 2001, 495).

In Ferlinghetti's view there was no one quite like Thomas writing at the time. There was a radiance, wholeness and harmony that set him apart. Thomas was responsible for igniting the 'San Francisco Poetry Renaissance' by giving readings to large audiences in the Bay Area, and recording two programmes at Berkeley for KPFA Radio. Dylan Thomas's voice, Ferlinghetti wrote, in *Literary San Francisco*, 'had a singular beauty and richness, in the great Welsh oral tradition; and the excitement he generated was an early inspiration for a tradition of oral poetry here, the subsequent San Francisco poetry movement being consistently centred on the performance of poetry in public' (Ferlinghetti 1980, 166).

Even though Thomas died in 1953, his legend lived on. He was the subject of the highly successful 1956 play 'Dylan', written by Sidney Michaels and based on Brinnin's book. It ran in the Plymouth Theatre,

---

[2]   http://www.bopsecrets.org/rexroth/poems/1950s.htm [accessed 27 Jan 2021].

New York, and Alec Guinness won a Tony for his portrayal of Thomas. William Greenway, a famous American poet, started reading Thomas in about 1960 and commented that Thomas had taken America by storm, 'and it stayed stormed' (Greenway 1995, 45).

Bobby Zimmerman was not the only mid-western folk singer to be struck by Dylan Thomas's name. Howard Nicholas Grooms changed his name to Dylan Todd and recorded a tribute to one of Bob Dylan's heroes, James Dean, who had died in a car crash in 1955. The song was the commercially successful 'The Ballad of James Dean'. Dylan Todd was mentioned in three different articles in *Billboard*, 1st September 1956. In 1958 Dylan Todd brought out an LP entitled *American Folk Songs*, and he made regular appearances on the TV shows of Ernie Kovacs and Gary Moore. Robert Zimmerman could not have avoided coming across the name Dylan from this source in his youth.

It was, however, more than the name that connected Dylan Thomas and Bob Dylan. There is a poetic connection, but it is not one of direct influence. It is more that they share a conception of what it is possible to attain in poetry. They both greatly admired the French symbolist poet Jean-Nicolas Arthur Rimbaud (1854–91), who was one of the major influences on both men's consciousness of what the poet aspires to achieve *in* writing. Just as Dylan Thomas had been the inspiration for the performance poetry of the Beats, infusing it with what Lorca called *duende*, Rimbaud was for both Thomas and the Beat writers the very embodiment of a visionary poet.

Dylan Thomas was the self-proclaimed 'Rimbaud of Cwmdonkin Drive' (Thomas 2000, 548). Thomas, like Rimbaud, struggled with his demons and gave them every opportunity for expression, irrespective of where they lay in the extremes of his consciousness. In a letter to Henry Trees, dated 16th May 1938, Thomas confessed: 'Very much of my poetry is, I know an enquiry and a terror of fearful expectation, a discovery and facing of fear. I hold a beast, an angel, and a madman in me, and my enquiry is as to their working, and my problem is their subjugation and victory, downthrow and upheaval, and my effort is their self-expression' (Thomas 2000, 343–4). This type of poem, Marjorie Perloff argues, has an internal dynamic requiring no external intelligible reality for its meaning. It revels in, rather than resolves, mystery. It is the type of poetry that stems from Rimbaud and is based on the principles of 'indeterminacy and undecidability', and is 'compositional rather than referential', the focus shifting from 'signification to the play of signifiers' (1999, 23). It is the tradition to which Lorca also belonged, and it is certainly the poetry that Dylan Thomas and Bob Dylan strived to produce. Thomas, for example, argued that the poem is 'its own question and answer, its own contradiction, its own agreement... A poem moves only towards its own end, which is the last line. Anything further than that is the problematical stuff of poetry, not of the poem' (Thomas 2000, 344).

Anthony Scaduto argued that Dylan wanted to write poetry for the people of the streets as Rimbaud had done. He maintains: 'There was much of Rimbaud in Dylan' (1996, 135). Pete Karmen remembers Bob Dylan saying to him in Greenwich Village, 'Rimbaud's where it's at. That's the kind of stuff means something. That's the kind of writing I'm gonna do' (Scaduto 1996: 169). In *Chronicles* Dylan declared that his discovery of Rimbaud was 'a big deal'. He was particularly impressed by a letter, addressed to George Izambard, in which Rimbaud said 'je est un autre' — 'I Is Someone Else' (2004, 289; Rimbaud 2002, 365). Rimbaud's letter also expressed the necessity for the extreme disorientation of the senses, which Dylan himself had experienced through his excessive drug taking. Rimbaud exclaimed: 'The suffering is tremendous, but one must bear up against it, to be born a poet, and I know that's what I am. It's not all my fault. It's wrong to say I think: one should say I am thought' (Rimbaud 2003, 364–5). Rimbaud was a permanent inspiration to Dylan. Patti Smith, who wrote the preface to the 2011 edition of Rimbaud's *Season in Hell* (2011), recognised that she and Dylan had been working towards Rimbaud's 'derangement of the senses' to attain the knowledge that comes from 'pain, voyaging, searching' (Shelton 2011, 299).

References

Brinnin, J.M.(1956) *Dylan Thomas in America*, London: JM Dent.

Cott, J. (ed.) (2006) *Dylan on Dylan: The Essential Interviews*, London: Hodder and Stoughton. Bob Dylan interview with Ron Rosenbaum, *Playboy*, March, 1978.

Dylan, B. (2004) *Chronicles: Volume One*, London: Simon & Schuster.

Ferlinghetti, L. (1994) *These Are My Rivers: New and Selected Poems*, New York: New Directions.

Ferlinghetti, L. & Peters, N.J (1980) *Literary San Francisco*, New York: Harper Collins.

Greenway, W. (1995) Dylan Thomas and a contemporary American poet, in *The World Winding Home*, pp. 45–51, Swansea: The Dylan Thomas Society of Great Britain.

Perloff, M. (1999) *The Poetics of Indeterminacy: Rimbaud to Cage*, Evanston, IL: Northwestern University Press.

Rexroth, K. (2001) Disengagement: The art of the Beat Generation, in Charters, A. (ed.) *Beat Down to Your Soul*, London: Penguin.

Rimbaud, A. (2003) *Complete*, Mason, W. (ed. & trans.), New York: Random House.

Rimbaud, A. (2011) *A Season in Hell and the Drunken Boat*, Varèse, L. (trans.), with a Preface by Patti Smith, New York: New Directions.

Scaduto, A. (1996) *Bob Dylan*, London: Helter Skelter.

Shelton, R. (2011) *No Direction Home*, revised and updated ed., Thomson, E. & Humphreys, P. (eds.), London: Omnibus Press.

Thomas, D. (2000) *The Collected Letters*, new ed., Ferris, P. (ed.), London: Dent.

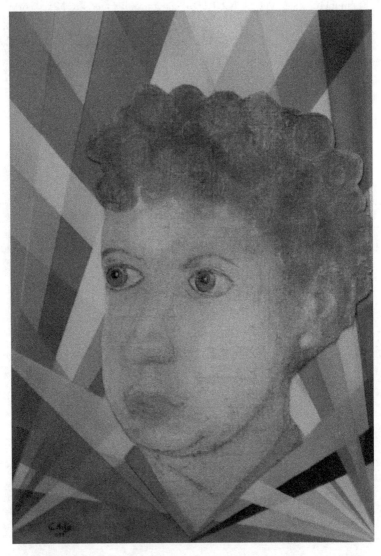

Portrait of Dylan Thomas by Gianpiero Actios, 2013 (licensed under the Creative Commons Attribution-Share Alike 3.0 Unported license CC-BY-SA 3.0).

Stephen Sedley

Brief Encounter, 1962

As ever, it takes longer to explain how it came about than to describe what actually happened. In 1962 I was a law student, living in London and earning an erratic living as a translator and musician. In the last of these capacities I scored some arrangements and played guitar accompaniments for Transatlantic Records, who had signed the songwriter Sydney Carter to make an album of his songs with an upcoming actress, Sheila Hancock. (One track, 'My Last Cigarette', reached 49 in the charts as a single.)

In late October Transatlantic secured a booking for Sydney, with the Honduran singer Nadia Cattouse, to play one of the best folk venues, the Troubadour coffee bar basement in Earl's Court. With my fellow guitar accompanist, Ralph Trainer, we went there from a recording session which had included Sydney's 'Blow the World to Kingdom Come'. At the Troubadour, Sydney and Nadia included another of his anti-nuclear songs, 'I Wanna Have a Little Bomb Like You'.

The reason I recall our doing these two songs is that, unforgettably, the Cuba missile crisis was approaching a climax which was capable within hours of starting a nuclear world war, and everyone was nervously aware of it. This places us in the last days of October 1962 — a little earlier than Dylan's first arrival in London is often dated. But Dylan (who, with no real acting experience, had been brought over by the BBC to appear in a TV play, 'The Madhouse on Castle Street') was definitely at the Troubadour on that geopolitically anxious evening.

What used to happen at the Troubadour was that, after the billed show, the musicians were free to stay on and jam for a while — not what a jazzman would recognise as a jam session, but individual singers starting a song which others would then take up. Usually it petered out within an hour or so, but occasionally further singers and instrumentalists would come by and a good session would take off. This was one such occasion. It included the singer Judith Silver as well as Ralph and me. Others who persist in my memory of the evening, but some of whom may in truth belong to other evenings, include the American banjo-picker and ragtime guitarist Dave Laibman, Scots singer-guitarists Nigel Denver and Jimmy McGregor, and Bert Jansch.

As all events, the audience was packed and the session going well when Judith pointed to a wild-haired youth sitting in a cloud of smoke towards the back of the audience and said to me, 'Isn't that the kid who's just issued his first album in the States?' Evidently it was. Judith beckoned him on to the stage (in reality a wooden platform about 4 inches off the cellar floor). He came up, seemingly diffident and, sounding rather helpless, said, 'I don't have a guitar.' I passed him my Harmony Sovereign, borrowed Ralph's spare Spanish guitar, and the session took off, though not before Dylan had retuned my D string almost to breaking point.

Dylan's musicianship was rapidly apparent. He picked up songs almost instantly and took the lead in many of them. I recall few of the songs that were sung, but they included 'The Leaving of Liverpool' — which turned up on the next album as 'Boots of Spanish Leather'. I also recall Bert Jansch (though this may have been on a different night) doing his trademark version of 'Nottamun Town', the melodic source of 'Masters of War'. Bert, however, would only play solo: rightly, in my view, he wouldn't join jam sessions.

Memory is both fallible and suggestible. Researchers in the past, I think, may have obtained a somewhat different account of that Saturday evening from the late Anthea Joseph, who ran the club and was, as always, on the door upstairs. Where our recollections differ, she is as likely to have been right as I am. I have simply relayed what is now lodged in my memory.

In the years that followed I wrote a folk music column for *Tribune*. In it, I covered Dylan's first London concerts. In May 1964 I find myself writing that Dylan

> has an even better ear than [Woody] Guthrie had for the poetic possibilities of everyday language, together with a feeling for rhetoric that enables him to jolt his audience in its seats. On paper, most of his

songs are riddled with faults—clumsy phrases, absurd rhymes, badly thought-out melodies—and technically neither his guitar nor his harmonica nor his voice are anything more than average. Yet he is a real artist, with his well-timed throwaways and his shy grin, with the pushing intensity of his delivery, and with the seething live images that run through his songs. He often aims too high and comes a cropper; but he barely ever commits the deadly sin of cliché.

Two of his songs I would say are masterpieces. One is 'Who Killed Davey Moore?', a shattering reworking of the old Cock Robin idea. [Davey Moore was a young professional boxer killed by a blow to the head.] The other is 'Don't Think Twice, it's All Right', practically the only outstanding song about love produced by the folk revival.

If he can keep his omnivorous mind off easy pop formulas… and can go on learning from the genuinely popular American tradition, and if the American folk establishment will stop kowtowing to him and bully him occasionally, Dylan may in time become the great figure they are already cracking him up to be. At 23 he still has plenty of time.

A year later Dylan played a packed Albert Hall, where touts were getting £10—half a week's wages in 1965—for tickets. This time I suggested that, in lieu of sensible criticism, he was being killed with kindness.

If Dylan had been intelligently criticised early on by the people he was ready to listen to he would still be trying to write better songs. As it is, he's in effect given up the effort…

I think the real trouble is the universal acclaim that now follows him —the applause drowns the opening lines of half his songs, and the admiration wraps him in cotton-wool. How can you keep protesting hotly when everyone within earshot is busy agreeing with you, especially the people who are making money out of you? The songs sounded different, and Dylan's whole approach was different too, in the days when he had to shout 'For Christ's sake, listen' and didn't know if people were going to.

So Dylan went his way, I went mine, and I still have the guitar I lent him in 1962.

Sir Stephen Sedley's Harmony Sovereign (photographed by Sedley in 2021).

Emma-Rose Sears

Spectres of Dylan
Hauntology in Last Thoughts on Woody Guthrie

'And take me disappearing through the smoke rings of my mind
down the foggy ruins of time...'

'The question of identity has been at the core of Dylan's persona and
career ever since he assumed the alias "Bob Dylan" in a gesture of (re)-
invention' (Hamscha 2015, 105). Many critics have invoked the elusive
identity of Bob Dylan, searching for something consistent in the self-
proclaimed multitudinous music man. As Susanne Hamscha points out,
'to speak of him as a shape-shifter or multiple self has become a standard
approach in analyses' (Hamscha 2015, 99). Todd Haynes' biopic, *I'm Not
There* (2007), has further engaged with the protean nature of the man, Bob
Dylan, and the many personae he inhabits: 'The earnest folksinger, the
mischievous tramp, the indulgent rock star, the fire and brimstone
preacher, the bohemian poet, the country crooner, and the tortured blues-
man', along with invocations of Rimbaud, Verlaine, Ginsberg and the
Beat poets (D'Cruz 2013, 324). Indeed, as Lulewitz and Vernezze contend,
'It's hard to think of anyone more fluid as a performer than Bob Dylan'
(Lulewitz and Vernezze 2006, 113). Yet 'Last Thoughts on Woody
Guthrie' summons not only the mysterious and haunting 'I' of Dylan,
whatever that may be, but a haunting of another kind.

A ghost inhabits Dylan's poem, and that ghost is Woody Guthrie. Yet
Guthrie was not dead in 1963; he was in Brooklyn State Hospital with
Huntington's chorea. Why then does the title echo a requiem or eulogy?

'Last Thoughts on Woody Guthrie' implies not only that no more shall be spoken of him, but also that Dylan is having the final word. With this striking declaration, then, Dylan situates Guthrie in a strange ontological space: he is neither dead nor alive, and fundamentally this is never stated anywhere in the poem's 194 lines.

So where is Guthrie in these pages? Situated in the title and the closing utterance, Woody frames the poem, yet the man as corpus is elusive, only 'appearing' in abstract concepts such as hope, and dramatisations of the non-concrete—the Grand Canyon at sundown. Yet he is undeniably there. Perhaps, like Dylan himself, he is there by not being there? 'The Basement Tapes' recording of 'I'm Not There', with its haunting and crackly refrain, 'I'm not there, I'm gone', seems in fact firmly to place the singer *there*, wherever that may be. Perhaps, as in 'Mr. Tambourine Man', we are meant to understand 'there' as in '*there* is no place I'm going to': not that Dylan is going nowhere—no place—but that *there* IS a no place—*there* is a non-place, and that is where he is going. *There* becomes a present absence, or absent presence.

To make more sense of this we must explore the nature of ghosts, and what haunting can mean. As Hamscha observes, 'ghosts are commonly featured in Dylan's lyrics and are one of his most significant key images, standing for the self outside the self or identity at one remove' (Hamscha 2015, 104). She continues, 'the spectre is a deconstructive figure that is neither absent nor present, neither dead nor alive. Consequently, the priority of material existence and presence is supplanted by an existence that is inherently incomplete and indefinable. Ontology, in other words, is replaced by its quasi-homonym "hauntology"' (Hamscha 2015, 106). I would like to suggest that the Woody Guthrie of 'Last Thoughts' is a spectre/ghost that haunts the narrative, complicating the notion of identity and the material or real, and this can be further illuminated by two critical theories; Jacques Derrida's 'hauntology' in *Spectres of Marx* (1993) and Mark Fisher's concept of the 'eerie' from his work, *The Weird and the Eerie* (2016).

Derrida's concept of 'Difference' had already situated identity in a curious protean guise; endlessly deferred and repeatedly reassessed, it is constantly in motion. Drawing any notion of itself from its 'other', the impossibility of the existence of the 'I' alone rendered metaphysical 'reality' unstable. This is the starting point for complications of origin and reality. Indeed, not only does Derrida confound a solid sense of selfhood, the notion of hauntology then replaces this shaky presence with a deferred non-origin—to speak plainly, nothing is there: a loaded phrase reinforcing Derrida's ubiquitous binaries; on the one hand, nothing is there, as in absence. On the other it suggests 'nothing' IS there, as in there is certainly something there (as we have mentioned in reference to Dylan's 'I'm Not There')—a very eerily present absence, located in an undefined temporal spatiality—the ghost.

In Fisher's *The Weird and the Eerie*, the notion of the 'eerie' in particular fundamentally concerns hauntology; that is, questions to do with existence and non-existence. Whereas Fisher describes the 'weird' as constituted by presence (for example something which does not belong), the eerie constitutes something more akin to Derrida's spectre: 'The sensation of the eerie occurs either when there is something present where there should be nothing, or there is nothing present where there should be something.' A *failure* of absence or a *failure* of presence (Fisher 2016, 61). This takes on the notion of the ghostly in its more ubiquitous sense when we ascribe to it agency, attaching it to Derrida's non-origins. Both these concepts can be seen at work in Dylan's poem.

In 'Last Thoughts' surface identity, or the material real, is exposed like a ghostly horror trope where imagery of masked men made of molasses assault us, with a succession of demands in 'chocolate cake voices' to look, 'look at my skin, look at my skin shine, look at my skin glow, look at my skin laugh, look at my skin cry' (Dylan 1991). These people who, as Dylan reminds us, may not have insides are almost uncanny automatons, their saccharine substance belonging to the unstable and consequently haunting realm of the material. Fisher points out that 'capital is at every level an eerie entity' for it is 'conjured out of nothing' (Fisher 2016, 11), and Dylan's juxtaposition between capitalism/materialism and the spiritual/hopeful that operates throughout the poem is a good example of this. Dylan was a voice of the 1960s counterculture and the beatnik rejection of the masters of war, politicians, corporations and fat cats, whose 'old road' was 'rapidly aging' (Dylan 1964), and in 'Last Thoughts' the things associated with the ruling classes—dollar bills, Macy's windowsill, frat houses, yacht clubs, supper clubs—are thrust into contradiction with hope, which whips around 'some windy corner on a wide angled curve' (Dylan 1991). Material things cannot define hope, which is abstract, yet although it is hope which may be malleable and manipulated, it is capital that seems to become insubstantial and eerie here, taking on ghostly qualities.

The area in which Fisher's eerie and Derrida's spectre can be seen to most effectively converge is in knowledge or, more appropriately, the absence of it. Indeed, Derrida posits that the spectre lies outside of our realm of knowledge; as a non-present presence it does not belong: 'One does not know: not out of ignorance, but because this non-object, this non-present present, this being-there of an absent or departed one no longer belongs to knowledge' (Derrida 2006, 5). Fisher's notion of the eerie relies also on knowledge (albeit a lack of, rather than the spectre which does not belong to the system of knowledge in the first place), but as such the power of the eerie also lies outside of knowing: 'The eerie concerns the unknown; when knowledge is achieved, the eerie disappears' (Fisher 2016, 62). As the nature of the spectre cannot be pinned down or contained, there is an inevitability about it that is troublesome, which is harnessed by Dylan throughout 'Last Thoughts':

> But it's trapped on yer tongue and sealed in yer head
> And it bothers you badly when you're layin' in bed
> And no matter how hard you try you just can't say it
> And yer scared to yer soul you just might forget it. (Dylan 1991)

One cannot speak of it. It seems at once forgotten and unforgettable. Both something and nothing, 'it is some "thing" difficult to name', then. Moreover, the subject's inability to utter and the potential to forget give the most haunting strain to these lines, the ephemeral quality, the always slipping away, 'one cannot control its coming and goings' (Derrida 2006, 11). The fleeting nature of the unknowable spectre 'signifying an always already unrealised and unrealisable ontology' (Hamscha 2015, 106).

Yet another slippery and unpredictable feature of the poem, the rhythm of 'Last Thoughts' is constantly changing. As Dylan recited it in 1963, it is almost an unpunctuated stream of consciousness: though this literary device was used often to illuminate the plot and motivation of a novel through an unfiltered insight into character, here Dylan does something different. We are not simply presented with his own inner consciousness but one that speaks to humanity at large, and in Dylan's zeitgeisty style. Dylan originally addressed an audience in 60s New York but continues to address all of us across time and space. As Derrida remarked on Shakespeare's *Hamlet*, 'the time is out of joint'. This same nod to the dislocation of time, and the notion of being 'out of time', is important. As D'Cruz discusses, being out of time does not simply indicate the convergence of past, present and future of which spectres inhabit, but also evokes a rupture in rhythm, which is apparent in 'Last Thoughts', especially at the moments Dylan questions his actions — 'why am I walking, where am I running, what am I saying, what am I knowing' (Dylan 1991) — interrupting the neater couplets before meandering into free verse and unpredictable rhyme scheme — the 'vague traces of skipping reels of rhyme' mentioned in 'Mr. Tambourine Man' feels appropriate. We feel out of step with the beat as we are never allowed to get comfortable and are constantly cut short by the speaker. Furthermore, being out of time points to an ill-timed delivery of what one says, chiming with the rather uncomfortable atmosphere the poem creates as a whole. We are left with a restless departure and return through juxtapositions, 'a disjointed or disadjusted now' (Derrida 2006, 1) where 'sun-decked desert and evergreen valleys turn to broken down slums and trash can alleys' (Dylan 1991).

Ghosts 'resist mastering and subjection through knowledge, power, action, place or time. Ghosts come to us as effects, as traces of something that has been lost, that has been purposefully repressed or that cannot be properly articulated' (Hamscha 2015, 109). So how does Woody Guthrie feature in the poem? I have tried to show where and how spectres can appear in 'Last Thoughts' and not simply to point out what and where Woody is, but rather that he signifies something more than himself, in line with 'Dylan's own playful and elusive approach to the perils of presuming a coherent and consistent identity' (D'Cruz 2013, 320). As we have suggested, Guthrie only appears as a frame at the start and end of the poem. The rest of the time I would venture he is lingering liminally as a spectre which ephemerally inhabits abstract concepts, predominantly that of hope. Much of the discussion, critical or otherwise about this poem, centres upon Dylan's, and by extension our own, search for hope, and the failure of the material to live up to the conceptual. As in many of Dylan's songs, particularly 'Mr. Tambourine Man', somewhere in the haunted windy curves, the silhouettes and somnambulant wanderings, through memory and trance, hope and authentic identity is out there. Though it might only ever exist as a spectre out of time.

...It's just a shadow you're seeing that he's chasing. (Bob Dylan, 'Mr. Tambourine Man', 1965)

References

D'Cruz, C. & D'Cruz, G. (2013) 'Even the Ghost was more than one person': Hauntology and authenticity in Todd Haynes's I'm Not There, *Film-Philosophy*, 17 (1), pp. 315–330.

Derrida, J. (2006) *Spectres of Marx*, Abingdon: Routledge.

Fisher, M. (2016) *The Weird and the Eerie*, London: Repeater Books.

Hamscha, S. (2015) The ghost of Bob Dylan: Spectrality and performance in *I'm Not There*, in Banauch, E. (ed.) *Refractions of Bob Dylan, Cultural Appropriations of an American Icon*, pp. 98–111, Manchester: Manchester University Press.

Lulewitz, P. & Vernezze, P. (2006) 'I Got My Bob Dylan Mask On': Bob Dylan and personal identity, in Porter, C.J. & Vernezze, P. (eds.) *Bob Dylan and Philosophy: It's Alright, Ma (I'm Only Thinking)*, pp. 124–133, Chicago, IL: Carus Publishing Company.

Bob Dylan performing at St. Lawrence University in New York, 26th November 1963 (public domain, from the 1964 yearbook of St. Lawrence University).

Ray Monk

The Uses of Illiteracy
The Lonesome Death
of Hattie Carroll

The British folksinger and songwriter Ewan MacColl spoke dismissively of the 'cultivated illiteracy' of Bob Dylan's topical songs. Stripped of its intention to disparage a body of work that MacColl considered to be 'tenth rate drivel', the phrase is remarkably apt with regard to at least one of those songs, namely 'The Lonesome Death of Hattie Carroll', which I, and many others, including, it seems, Dylan himself, regard as one of his very best.

The song tells the story of the killing of a poor, black woman in her fifties by William Zantzinger, a wealthy white tobacco farmer in his twenties. The killing took place on 8th February 1963 at the Emerson Hotel in Baltimore, which that night was hosting the Spinsters' Ball, a white tie affair for the local elite. Zantzinger arrived already very drunk and wielding a white toy cane that he used to hit almost everyone who came within reach. Hattie Carroll was working as a barmaid, and Zantzinger ordered a drink. She was busy serving another customer, so did not respond immediately. 'N*****, did you hear me ask for a drink?' Zantzinger shouted, adding, 'I don't have to take that kind of shit off a n*****.' He then struck Hattie hard on the shoulder with his cane. Hattie collapsed, saying to her fellow barmaids, 'That man has upset me so, I feel deathly ill.' She fell unconscious and was taken to hospital. Meanwhile, the police were called and arrested Zantzinger, charging him with disorderly conduct and two counts of assault. The following morning, news came that Hattie Carroll had died in hospital, but by then

Zantzinger was already out on bail. The police issued a murder warrant for Zantzinger and again allowed him out on bail.

Hattie Carroll had several serious health problems, including an enlarged heart, hardened arteries and high blood pressure. She died of a brain haemorrhage, which, the medical examination into her death concluded, had been brought about by the fear and anger caused by the blow she received from Zantzinger. He was found guilty of manslaughter, the maximum sentence for which was ten years in prison. The sentence handed down to Zantzinger, however, was just six months.

The day of Zantzinger's sentencing, 28th August 1963, was a momentous one for the civil rights movement, coinciding as it did with the March for Jobs and Freedom in Washington DC, in which a crowd of around 200,000 heard Martin Luther King's inspirational 'I have a dream' speech. Sharing the stage with King that day was Bob Dylan, who sang two new songs, 'When the Ship Comes In' and 'Only a Pawn in Their Game'. On the way back to New York the following day, Dylan read a short newspaper article about Zantzinger's killing of Hattie Carroll and the sentence he received. Within a few weeks, 'The Lonesome Death of Hattie Carroll' was written.

To appreciate how good the song is and how quickly Dylan was progressing as a songwriter at this time, it is helpful to compare it with two previous songs he had written about the murder of African Americans. 'The Death of Emmett Till' was written in 1962, but never appeared on any studio albums until it was included on *The Bootleg Series Vol. 9: The Witmark Demos: 1962–1964*, released in 2010. Dylan himself described it as 'bullshit' and it is clearly the work of a songwriter who has not fully mastered his craft. It begins:

'Twas down in Mississippi not so long ago,
When a young boy from Chicago town walked through a Southern door,
This boy's dreadful tragedy you should all remember well,
The colour of his skin was black and his name was Emmett Till.

It then depicts the horrors of Till's killing at the hands of two brothers, and the subsequent trial of the murderers at which they were found not guilty (a year later, they cheerfully admitted their guilt). 'If you can't speak out against this kind of thing', Dylan admonishes his listeners, 'a crime that's so unjust / Your eyes are filled with dead men's dirt, and your mind is filed with dust.' It ends:

> But if all of us folks that thinks alike, if we gave all we could give,
> We could make this great land of ours a greater place to live.

The sentiment, the outrage at the cruelty and injustice, is genuine, but its expression is hackneyed and lacking linguistic inventiveness. This song, one might safely say, was not uppermost in the minds of the members of the committee who awarded Dylan the Nobel Prize for Literature.

Considerably more sophisticated is 'Only a Pawn in Their Game', one of the songs Dylan played at Washington, which was written about a year later. It is about the killing of Medgar Evers, a black civil rights activist and the Mississippi state secretary of the NAACP (the *National Association for the Advancement of Colored People*). Evers was assassinated by the white supremacist and Klansman Byron De La Beckwith. Dylan, however, chooses to play down Beckwith's role in Evers' death. He does not even mention his name. Rather, the song presents Evers' killer as himself a victim of a pernicious system. When he dies, Dylan's last verse says, his grave will have:

> Carved next to his name
> His epitaph plain
> Only a pawn in their game.

Every previous verse ends (with a slight variation in the first):

> But it ain't him to blame
> He's only a pawn in their game.

The leaders of society, the politicians, soldiers, governors and the heads of the police, Dylan suggests, use the poor white man 'like a tool'. They tell him that he is better than his black neighbours, whom they teach him to hate and to kill. This is very far from the previous exhortations to 'speak out against this kind of thing' and to 'make this great land of ours a greater place to live'. Just as 'Only a Pawn in Their Game' refuses to blame the killer, so it avoids urging any particular response. What it presents is not a moral judgment, an imperative, or an expression of revulsion, but rather a largely impersonal analysis.

The song is without doubt an advance on 'The Death of Emmett Till', but, to put it mildly, there is something uncomfortable about a white, middle-class, university-educated young man telling a large group of black people who had gathered to protest against, among other things, their poverty and their exclusion from university (an injustice against which Medgar Evers had fought hard) how to understand the system that oppresses them and that they should not blame the man who killed one of their leaders. And this, I think, leads us to something important about 'The Lonesome Death of Hattie Carroll' and its use of 'cultivated illiteracy'.

All three are 'finger pointing songs', but in very different ways. 'The Death of Emmett Till' points its finger at the murderers and asks us to stand up to them. 'Only a Pawn in Their Game', on the other hand, points to the unequal and racially unjust society that creates such people. In 'The Lonesome Death of Hattie Carroll', Dylan takes aims at both these types of target, but he adds a third, which, oddly, seems to include some of the people on his own side of the civil rights struggle.

The song has a satisfyingly clear structure. The story of the killing is given in the first verse, the background of Zantzinger's life in the second, the life and character of Hattie Carroll in the third, and in the fourth and final verse we hear about the trial and the light sentence Zantzinger received. After each of the first three verses, Dylan sings this refrain:

But you who philosophise disgrace and criticise all fears
Take the rag away from your face
Now ain't the time for your tears.

After the final verse, the last two lines of this refrain are changed to 'Bury the rag deep in your face / For now's the time for your tears.' The usual interpretation of this is that Dylan is suggesting that we should weep, not for the death of Hattie Carroll, or for the inequality highlighted by the comparison between her and Zantzinger, but rather for the injustice of a legal system which hands out such a paltry sentence to a rich white man for murdering a poor black woman.

But there is another, to my mind more satisfying, interpretation that hangs on solving the song's great puzzle: who are these people who 'philosophise disgrace and criticise all fears'? Neil Corcoran in his contribution to the collection of essays *Do You, Mr Jones?* has suggested that they are 'the armchair *philosophes* of the liberal-left'. This is surely right as far as it goes, but sheds no light on what is really puzzling, namely, what does it mean to philosophise disgrace and to criticise all fears? Christopher Ricks in *Dylan's Visions of Sin* has suggested that Dylan has in mind those 'who hold forth and who spin philosophical excuses for what is simply disgrace'. But who has ever done this? What examples are there? Simon Armitage gets us close, I think, when, in his lecture 'We Need to Talk About Robert: Bob Dylan and the Nobel Prize for Literature', he accepts Corcoran's suggestion about the *philosophes* but adds that it might include Dylan himself.

Where does Dylan philosophise disgrace and criticise all fears? Well, in 'Only a Pawn in Their Game'. Addressing a crowd of people who had every reason to fear people like Byron De La Beckwith, Dylan had told them that he was not the problem. And, rather than empathising with their horror at the disgraceful act that Beckwith had committed, Dylan had urged them to accept that he was not guilty. In place of empathy, he had offered a rather lofty and distancing analysis.

In 'The Lonesome Death of Hattie Carroll' Dylan seems determined to reverse this. The problem with the usual interpretation of the song is that it suggests that we should withhold our tears, our emotional engagement, until we hear about the light sentence that Zantzinger received, but one of the most striking things about the song is that it is clear that Dylan's own emotions are engaged from the very beginning. In contrast to 'Only a Pawn in Their Game', in which Beckwith's name is never given, William Zantzinger's name—or rather, a corruption of it—is the first thing we hear. Dylan seems so insistent that that name *is* the first thing we hear that the song has no musical introduction, not even a couple of bars of guitar strumming. In a move that seems designed to give the opening line further emotional impact, Dylan leaves out the 't' in Zantzinger's name, so the song begins: 'William Zanzinger killed poor Hattie Carroll.' Changing the name in this way allows Dylan to pronounce it with maximum sneering. 'William Zzzanzzinger', he hisses, leaving us in little doubt that this is a man he holds in great contempt. Equally, we know straight away how he feels about Hattie Carroll. Simon Armitage has criticised Dylan's use of the word 'poor' in this first line as being redundant because of what we subsequently learn about Hattie Carroll in the song. What he misses, I think, is that Dylan's purpose here is not to describe Hattie, but to express sympathy with her.

Dylan is determined to separate himself from the kind of intellectual who offers the sort of cold, impersonal analysis that he had himself offered in 'Only a Pawn in Their Game'. At every turn, he expresses, and invites us to share, an emotional identification with the victims of injustice, inequality and prejudice. And this is the use to which he puts his 'cultivated illiteracy'. For me, the most powerful line in the song comes at the end of the verse about Hattie, when he sings, 'And she never done nothing to William Zanzinger', his voice dripping with outrage and indignation. Think how much more affecting this is than the more grammatically correct 'And she never did anything to William Zanzinger.' The language Dylan uses in this song is chosen not for its precision or its poetic compression, but rather to identify with the people on whose behalf he is singing. Armitage criticises the redundancy in the phrase 'rich wealthy parents' that Dylan uses in the verse about Zantzinger, but its purpose is to put Dylan on the side of those who use phrases like that, i.e. almost everybody *except* the university educated philosophers and critics.

'The Lonesome Death of Hattie Carroll' is a *much* better song than its two predecessors, and one of the things that makes it so great is the way it uses ordinary, 'illiterate' language, not only to protest against the injustices of society, but also to arouse in us anger and indignation at people like William Zantzinger, and pity, empathy and solidarity for people like 'poor Hattie Carroll'.

References

Armitage, S. (2017) *We Need to Talk about Robert: Bob Dylan and the Nobel Prize for Literature*, lecture at Oxford University, 8th March, [Online], http://podcasts.ox.ac.uk/we-need-talk-about-robert-bob-dylan-and-nobel-prize-literature?fbclid=IwAR1va0jLmugub4MVwKd2TL88oR7J k_bll9CH8UDDTjCLrG2cUxR0ijNRUZA

Corcoran, N. (ed.) (2017) *Do You, Mr Jones? Bob Dylan with the Poets & Professors*, London: Vintage.

Ricks, C. (2011) *Dylan's Visions of Sin*, London: Canongate Books.

Bob Dylan performing at St. Lawrence University in New York, 26th November 1963 (public domain, from the 1964 yearbook of St. Lawrence University).

Alexander Douglas

Bob Dylan and the Story of Black America from 1865-1965
Theology? Aesthetics? Culture?

A spectre lurks in the house of music, and it goes by the name of race.
(Radalno and Bohlman 2000, 1)

In hindsight, it makes sense that the first two Bob Dylan songs I ever heard were on jazz compilations by virtue of their popularity. In the case of the first—Joshua Redman's version of 'The Times They Are A-Changin'' from *Timeless Tales (for changing times)*—it was a cue to track down that particular album and listen to the whole thing really carefully. With the second—Cassandra Wilson's version of 'Shelter from the Storm' from *Belly of the Sun*—the main desire was to replay the song, followed by a broader interest in anything Wilson had recorded. At that point, there was no desire to track down the original versions. For me personally, the earlier release of Herbie Hancock's *The New Standard* (especially 'Norwegian Wood' and 'Scarborough Fair') had offered an authoritative masterclass in how a black musician could take music by white artists and turn it into something that spoke to a whole new audience without denying the importance of the original. There were far less black jazz musicians in the UK who could actually play the music back in the late nineties than is the case at this time of writing, and so as a young aspiring jazz musician I had a special interest in artists who looked like me. It became convenient to assume that I would not like Bob Dylan's original performances as much as I liked these arrangements.

Perhaps none of these instances of black musicians reimagining songs by white songwriters is as important as Sam Cooke performing Dylan's 'Blowin' in the Wind' – and irrespective of all those who have wished to accuse Dylan of negative forms of cultural appropriation, there is no real doubt that 'Blowin' in the Wind' was the inspiration for Cooke's 'A Change is Gonna Come'. Despite what many have taken to be the hope espoused by the lyrics of that song, Cooke had not missed – nor misinterpreted – the nascent ambiguities of 'Blowin' in the Wind'. With barely comprehensible surgical precision, Dylan had put his finger right on the fact that the problems of American society were in fact insoluble, and Cooke knew it. 'A Change is Gonna Come' was always going to be leveraged for a type of saccharine hope across multiple cultural and ethnic constituencies both then, now and in the future – but there is a darkness hidden in the yearning of both the music and lyrics in this song that is arguably best understood in light of the darkness that hid within the hope espoused by Dr. King ('I may not get there with you') and the darkness that shrouded the last years and months of Malcolm X's life ('I live like a man who is dead already' – a sentiment that, despite their many differences, eerily corresponds to King's assertion that 'a man who is not prepared to die is not prepared to live').

It has been easy to ignore connections between Dylan and Malcolm X due to the latter's well-known disenchantment with the non-violent protest espoused by King. It remains a surprise that more scholarly attention has not been given to the question of quite how Malcolm X's diagnosis of the precursors and ramifications surrounding John F. Kennedy's assassination ('chickens coming home to roost' as an ascription for the unregulated violence at the heart of a so-called 'civilised' society) could have gotten him in so much trouble with his brothers at the Nation of Islam. But given King's death at the hand of white dissidents ('supremacists') and Malcolm X's death at the hands of black dissidents ('rebels') – to say nothing of J. Edgar Hoover's persecutions during that same period – when Dylan asks what a person must do before they can be recognised as a human being and indicates that the answer to that question – and others like it – is 'blowin' in the wind', we may be sure that he had understood what many Americans of all ethnicities had not.

The murder of George Floyd finally forced significantly more Americans to face the fact that assimilation and integration are not 'social experiments' that can be said to have succeeded.

The historical genesis of Bob Dylan's music emerges from much more substantive musical and cultural hybridity than is generally acknowledged. Such an acknowledgment should not be understood as constituting an erasure of the seminally important contributions Black Americans have made to the cultural landscape of the US. Just as it is important to not turn an account of Dylan's work into an unremitting hagiography, it is equally important to avoid rewriting history to create binary formulations detailing the important cultural contributions of African-Americans at the cost of a rather more nuanced historical understanding. Perhaps we have enough evidence to take the position that no genuine historiographical framework for understanding Dylan's output can afford to depend too much on Dylan's own testimony, which at times does appear to have had a rather 'interesting' relationship with historical facts that we can ascertain. And after all of the sociological analysis and speculation, Dylan's actual music is the most important witness in this conversation.

Since Jamestown (1607), music on the North American continent has exemplified multiple hybridities. There are in fact two canons of spiritual: African-American (we no longer use the word 'Negro') and 'white' (Jackson 1933; Yoder 1961). And as Goff (2002) explains: 'it is an indictment of American history that black and white gospel developed as separate—and parallel—traditions… [I]n segregated America, gospel music provided only a small component of the overall music market for white America while it played a much larger role in the black community' (Goff 2002, 4). However, in numerical terms, the sales figures for white (later 'Southern') gospel music dwarfed that of black gospel. In addition, white gospel music was hand-in-glove with country music and a very significant part of the white popular music imaginary. Practices of musicking were imbricated across black and white long before 'Emancipation', and from 1865 onwards there is effectively a post-spirituals, pre-20th-century-gospel canon of what were in fact known as 'gospel songs' that can legitimately be taken to exemplify the so-called 'Second Great Awakening' (the white 'singing evangelist' Ira D. Sankey is arguably the most prominent name in this regard). Given that the heritage of gospel music is not the sole provenance of African-Americans and that white gospel music is significantly under-researched, it is a fallacy to assume that when Dylan turns to the gospel music tradition, a singular 'Black' mode of aesthetic production is all that he has 'in his ears'.

Things are further complicated when we understand that while it is impossible to identify exactly when the blues comes into existence, Amiri Baraka has been justifiably recognised for his argument that the question of how the American Negro transitions from being a slave to being a citizen is of critical importance for understanding not just 'the blues' as a cultural product, but the make-up and identity of a 'Blues People' (the title of his book) — without whom this music could not exist. Indeed, '[t]he one peculiar referent to the drastic change in the Negro from slavery to citizenship is his music' (Jones/Baraka, 1963, x). However, one thing that late 19th-century blues and late 19th-century gospel song have in common is that both were practised by both white and black musicians. And so when W.E.B. Du Bois writes in *The Souls of Black Folk* (1903) that 'the problem of the twentieth century is the problem of the color line', he is in effect arguing that liberal Enlightenment humanism has in fact done nothing to ameliorate the dehumanisation of diasporic b/Black people — but perhaps this book can make some contribution to a re-envisioned humanism in which b/Black people are not anthropologically inferior. Du Bois does not believe that this can be achieved by an appeal to rationality and so the 'andragogic' strategy he employs in this work focuses on affective and emotive domains. It can be argued that Dylan's songwriting was an even more effective medium for the disbursement of very similar aspirations.

The chronological period covered in this narrative begins and ends with presidential assassinations. White America was simply not ready to afford equality to black people when Abraham Lincoln was killed. Ninety-nine years later when John F. Kennedy was assassinated, the paradox is that while much had changed, nothing had changed — and in this year that we celebrate Dylan's 80th birthday, he would likely be amongst the first to attest to the fact that this is still the case. The essential message of 'Blowin' in the Wind' is eerily prescient regarding the future of both America and Black America even as it documents the (then) present. It may only be coincidence that our timeline herein also corresponds to the entire life-course of W.E.B. Du Bois, who can only have been horrified to see the enlightened German society he experienced and believed in at the turn of the 20th century capitulate to the unspeakable evils dispensed by the Third Reich, and who died in exile from his homeland and his people in the same year that Dr. King spoke of 'having a dream' and Bob Dylan sang a song for Medgar Evers—an event Malcolm X watched silently and disapprovingly from the sidelines. (Perhaps one of the most poignant moments from the film footage of Dylan's performance of 'Only a Pawn in Their Game' that day in the nation's capital is the site of a black man taking off his hat at the moment when Dylan calls Medgar Evers' name; it could just be because he was hot at that precise moment, but with other hat-wearing black men in the same shot who do not remove their hats, the timing is certainly interesting and the gesture feels more 'intentional'.) There is much more to say about Du Bois' historical legacy but it is an unfortunate fact that his ideas are now better understood—and by more people from more back-grounds—now that he is no longer with us. Although it would be absurd to suggest that this was his specific intention, with these songs of protest —added to his media interviews—Dylan manages to achieve a huge part of what Du Bois aspired to achieve but ultimately would not live to see for himself—an argument that gains traction when one considers the narrative journeys of 'The Times They Are A-Changin'' and 'When the Ship Comes In' (both of which leverage an understanding of hope in ways that seem strange until we remember Dylan's identity) in that they prefigure a type of protest that is not only remarkably reminiscent of the Old Testament 'minor prophets' (Habbakuk and Amos being but two examples which come to mind) but also exemplify a subtlety, depth and acknowledgment of the necessity of 'acceptance' (as explicated by Joseph Campbell's 'sorcerer' who learns how to 'accept' (Campbell 1949) and by the chapter 'The Coming of John' in Du Bois' *The Souls of Black Folk*). Both men knew the power of music to move hearts and minds.

With the rise of secularism in western societies, it has become much easier to assume that it could not have been possible for enslaved black peoples to have become true proponents of Christianity. Although this chapter has not been able to accommodate a discussion of Dylan's so-called 'gospel trilogy', one more explicitly theological dimension to the story of Black America from 1865 to 1965 starts with the fact that white gospel music became renamed 'Southern' gospel music as part of a bid to preserve this music as a conservative bastion of Southern WASP identity. In light of the fact that white Southern Christians not only ignored the plight of their black brothers and sisters but were actively complicit in much of the grotesque violence that was perpetrated, it is interesting to note that Dylan was not the first musical thinker of Jewish identity and heritage to write the Black American experience in song. Albert Meeropol had already blazed that trail in writing 'Strange Fruit'. But well before his turn to evangelical Christianity, Dylan knew that these black Americans were his brothers and sisters and did not need the apropos of gospel music to find a theology superior to that of the entirety of white Southern Christianity in the US—so when he took the step of adding the New Testament to the Old, he followed Dietrich Bonhoeffer in hearing something in the Black Sacred Music traditions of the earlier part of the last century that actually expressed the *evangelion*—the 'gospel'—in music in ways that he might not always have heard in more 'contemporary' gospel traditions.

Forty years after Sam Cooke's death, Dylan takes to the stage to play 'A Change is Gonna Come', and not for the first time, a guitarist switches to keys later in their career. It's far from a technically ideal vocal performance but, at the same time, it is impossible to think of anyone who understands this song better. What we know is not as important as what we understand.

References

Du Bois, W.E.B. (1903) *The Souls of Black Folk*, Chicago, IL: A.C. McClurg & Co.

Campbell, J. (1949) *The Hero with a Thousand Faces*, New York: Pantheon Books.

George Pullen Jackson, G.P. (1933) *White Spirituals of the Southern Uplands*.

Jones, L. & Baraka, A. (1963) *Blues People*, Chapell Hill, NC: University of North Carolina Press.

Radano, R. & Bohlman, P. (eds.) (2000) *Music and the Racial Imagination*, Chicago, IL: University of Chicago Press.

Yoder, D. (1961) *Pennsylvania Spirituals*, Lancaster, PA: Pennsylvania Folk Life Society.

Alexander Douglas.

Gary Browning

Dylan and the Political
– Then and Now

Dylan reaches 80, and a question worth asking is how the 'old' Dylan
relates to the younger one. His revisiting of the Kennedy assassination in
the song 'Murder Most Foul' allows for its examination, even if the
question defies a definitive answer. Dylan's early fame was bound up
with his expressive response to the mood of the times. The folk revival
and the civil rights movement inspired countless singers and activists.
Joan Baez testifies to how Dylan encapsulated the times in his scruffily
authentic demeanour, writing songs which 'seemed to update the concepts of justice and injustice' (Baez 1988, 92). Dylan's songs evoked, but
were not exhausted by, the particular incidents that they related. If Dylan
sang finger pointing songs, the finger pointed in many directions, and
often to himself and his audience. Dylan's songs were hard to pin down,
yet they expressed a mood and sharpened sensibilities (Boucher and
Browning 2009, 1–12). In 'Murder Most Foul' Dylan reconsiders the
assassination in November 1963 of President John F. Kennedy. Kennedy
represents both the promise and the demise of the 1960s, in his
ambiguous and fleeting incarnation of the cause of civil justice. 'Murder
Most Foul' conveys the foulness of the assassination, and the continuing
reverberations of an untimely end of an era and a popular movement. It
serves as a requiem for a President, a movement and for Dylan's early
political songs.

   Dylan's second album *The Freewheelin' Bob Dylan* was released in May
1963, and its mix of tender love songs and allusive political songs established Dylan's eminence in the idiom of popular song. In 'Blowin' in the
Wind' a series of rhetorical questions challenges listeners to respond to

the imperatives of moral and political progress. 'A Hard Rain's A-Gonna Fall' addresses a young man, who incarnates the possibilities of a new generation. Questions are posed on what he might do to avert an apocalyptic future, which is anticipated by multiple images of disturbance and devastation. This power of this song, as in so many Dylan songs, turns on the predicament that it insists upon for the singer himself and his audience. At a rally in Greenwood Mississippi in July 1963 and at the March on Washington in the following month, Dylan sang 'Only a Pawn in Their Game'. This song recounts the murder of the civil rights leader Medgar Evers at the hands of a white man. Unlike Phil Ochs in his 'The Ballad of Medgar Evers', Dylan widens responsibility for the killing to encompass the entire culture of white oppression, which deploys poor whites as attack dogs for the maintenance of white supremacy. For Dylan, the blame for Medgar Evers' death lies with the system of race hatred rather than with a lone killer.

> The deputy sheriffs, the soldiers, the governors get paid
> And the marshals and cops get the same
> But the poor white man's used in the hands of them all like a tool
> He's taught in his school
> From the start by the rule
> That the laws are with him
> To protect his white skin
> To keep up his hate
> So he never thinks straight
> 'Bout the shape that he's in
> But it ain't him to blame
> He's only a pawn in their game.
>
> — 'Only a Pawn in Their Game'

The narrative is delivered in a murderous rattle of short, sharp, bullet-like words, which emphasise the automatism of the assassin. The song is designed to make its listeners, notably its white listeners, think hard about what has happened and their role in an oppressive system. Likewise, 'The Lonesome Death of Hattie Carroll', which was also recorded in 1963 for Dylan's 1964 album *The Times They are A-Changin'*, rehearses the death of a poor black woman, Hattie Carroll, in a Baltimore hotel at the hands of a rich white tobacco farmer, William Zantzinger. Dylan indicts Zantzinger (the song refers to him as Zanzinger), yet the song focuses its anger upon the injustice of the lenient sentence that is handed out to Zantzinger. It is not so much the casual racism of Zantzinger himself, but the racial oppression of the entire system of justice that is castigated. Listeners are challenged to recognise their participation in a corrupt political and legal system, and blame stretches beyond Zantzinger to the judge, liberal excusing of wrong-doing and a wider public indifference to injustice. The blackness of Hattie Carroll is not referred to expressly, just as the singer's whiteness is mentioned neither in this song nor in 'Only a Pawn in Their Game'. This silence is questionable, but eloquent in serving to intensify the questions to be asked of themselves by a white singer and his primarily white audience.

Dylan's early political songs are provocative. Hard questions are asked, and answers involve an acceptance of responsibility on the part of the singer and his audience. The March on Washington marked a significant moment for prospects of radical political change. Yet the gathering political progress, chorused in Dylan's 'The Times They Are A-Changin'', was subverted abruptly by the assassination in Dallas of President John F. Kennedy in November 1963 by Lee Harvey Oswald. Dylan responded publicly to the assassination in a speech at the Emergency Civil Liberties Committee's Bill of Rights dinner on 13th December, where Dylan was awarded the annual Tom Paine Award. Dylan was young and nervous, and he began drinking in the afternoon of the event. The atmosphere was formal, and attendees were mostly older and of a different generation, including many notables of the old left, whose liberalism had been forged in a different atmosphere. Dylan's speech was inflammatory. He talked of his youth, and how he wished the old people in the room were not there. He declared that it wasn't an old people's world, and he did not feel comfortable with their suits and lack of hair. He spoke approvingly of radicals who had gone to visit Cuba in opposition to a government ban on so doing. His then girlfriend, Suze Rotolo, attests to his concern and confusion, remarking, '...Bob was in a heady place. And his speech reflected that, not to mention what he'd been imbibing beforehand to calm his nerves' (Rotolo 2009, 264). Things got worse when he spoke about Lee Harvey Oswald. Dylan declared that he had to admit, 'I saw something of myself in him' (see Shelton 1986, 201). In response to the commotion caused by the speech, Dylan sent an open letter to the

Emergency Civil Liberties Committee, explaining his inexperience in giving speeches. Yet he did not apologise, and maintained that a wider responsibility for crime should be embraced instead of mere lip-service being paid to the idea.

Dylan's speech reflects his youthful uneasiness at being expected to conform to an old left political line. The disconcerting edginess of his speech reflects his youth, and yet aspects of the speech and his immediate reaction to Kennedy's death retain significance. Dylan felt uncomfortable in merely idealising Kennedy, whose regime had banned visiting Cuba, and in his characteristic concern to widen responsibility for a disturbed political culture, he recoiled from pinning all the blame for the murder and ensuing political confusion upon a lone assassin. Subsequently Dylan disavowed the rigid world of the folk revival and the constrictions of political movements, insisting upon speaking for himself rather than any group. Soon he would upset the crowd at the Newport Folk Festival and beyond by going electric, and performing in a way that was true to himself rather than confirming a presumed identity.

Dylan retreated from a wider political world and settled in Woodstock, composing and performing songs that evoked 'the old weird America' of traditional American music with his band, *The Band* (see Marcus 1997). In his 1967 album *John Wesley Harding* Dylan delivered a collection of songs which was stripped of the complex production techniques that the Beatles and progressive bands were pioneering, and steered clear of a counterculture that would be celebrated at the Woodstock Festival. The album critiqued conventional American mythologies while stepping back from the political arena. The second song begins, 'As I went out one morning / To breathe the air around Tom Paine / I spied the fairest damsel / That ever did walk in chains' ('As I Went Out One Morning'). Dylan imagines Tom Paine, whose civil liberties award he had accepted in 1963, to be warning of the compromised spirit of liberty that once animated the fledgling Republic. 'I Dreamed I Saw St. Augustine' rehearses the tune of 'The Ballad of Joe Hill', but that song's encomium to the radical Joe Hill is transformed into a confession of weary political quietism. Other songs on the album underscore the bankruptcy of the political present by deconstructing dubious American myths, such as the steadfastness of the original migrants and the virtue of the cowboy hero and affiliated maverick outsiders of American folklore. In the shadow of

Watergate, Dylan, like many of his contemporaries in the 1970s, turned to intimate personal relations in the wake of a disillusionment with politics.

An idiot wind is blowing, and nostalgia for the revolution that had been in the air informs the intense stories of love lost, found and lost again on *Blood on the Tracks*. Political critique is revived in songs such as 'Hurricane' and 'Clean Cut Kid', where individuals are held to be victims of an oppressive and racist political culture. But Dylan did not return to the political world of the early 1960s and the dissolution of political hope and ambition in the aftermath of Kennedy's assassination until his recent album, *Rough and Rowdy Ways*. In the song 'Murder Most Foul', which was released ahead of the album, Dylan devotes nearly 17 minutes to reflecting upon the death of Kennedy. On the face of things, 'Murder Most Foul' is very different from Dylan's youthful speech about the assassination at the Tom Paine Award ceremony. 'Murder Most Foul' is a work of an old man looking back, rather than a young man, fired up and angry. It was written on the verge of Dylan entering his eightieth year, and in the shadow of the Trump presidency. Its meandering narrative of the death of Kennedy and subsequent cultural developments covers a lot of ground. The assassination is held to imply a wider conspiracy beyond Oswald, and the subsequent evocation of assorted events and cultural achievements follows no evident pattern as it winds around the brutality of the assassination.

Intermittently, the narrative assumes the perspectives of Kennedy himself, his assailants and the watching TV audience, so that the listener is forced to think through how things appeared to Kennedy, his murderers and the watching millions. In tracing the cultural aftermath of the assassination, Dylan relates the ascent of British popular music in the guise of the apparent innocence of the Beatles and Gerry and the Pacemakers. The hedonistic and countercultural extravagance of the Woodstock Festival substitutes for political radicalism, and Dylan's association of it with an Aquarian age conveys his ironic dismissal of its presumed significance. The relatively innocent, if overblown, Woodstock Festival gives way to Altamont, and the violence at a concert of the British bad boys, the Rolling Stones, conjures up their 'Sympathy for the Devil', in which 'you and me' figure as the Kennedys' killers.

As 'Murder Most Foul' progresses, Dylan imagines Wolf Man Jack, the legendary DJ, playing songs that convey a truthfulness and underlying integrity, which persists despite the foulness of the political murder and the innocent and devilish hedonism that followed. The final lines refer back to 'Murder Most Foul' itself, which, in reimagining the foul political murder that has disrupted the political world, inspires those who listen to the song to see it as offering continuing hope that awful events can be survived and creative possibilities reimagined:

Play Deep in a Dream and play Drivin' Wheel
Play Moonlight Sonata in F sharp
And Key to the Highway by the king of the harp
Play Marchin' Through Georgia and Dumbarton's Drums
Play Darkness and death will come when it comes
Play Love Me or Leave Me by the great Bud Powell
Play the Blood Stained Banner – play Murder Most Foul

Just as the young Dylan's political songs posed questions for his listeners and spread responsibilities for what was happening, so Dylan in this late political song sees the possibilities for sustaining a common cultural world in the wake of political defeat to lie in a shared world of cultural creation that is to be accessed by all of us in listening to the song itself. If we live in a world of political defeat, it is an honourable defeat. Dylan's renewed commentary on the political world, and the need to combat the continued injustice of racism, were evidenced in an interview for the *New York Times* that followed the release of *Rough and Rowdy Ways*. In the interview, Dylan describes George Floyd's awful death as 'beyond ugly. Let's hope that justice comes swift for the Floyd family and for the nation' (Brinkley, *New York Times* 2020).

References

Baez, J. (1988) *And a Voice to Sing With – A Memoir*, London: Century.
Boucher, D. & Browning, G. (2009) *The Political Art of Bob Dylan*, Exeter: Imprint Academic.
Brinkley, B. (2020) Bob Dylan has a lot on his mind, *The New York Times*, 12 June.
Marcus, G. (1997) *Invisible Republic*, New York: Henry Holt.
Rotolo, S. (2009) *A Freewheelin' Time*, London: Aurum Press Ltd.

Shelton, R. (1986) *No Direction Home: The Life and Music of Bob Dylan*, London: New English Library.

Joan Baez and Bob Dylan at the Civil Rights March on Washington, DC, 28th August 1963 (photograph by Rowland Scherman, public domain).

Garry L. Hagberg

Dylan's Stratocaster

What an instrument is, is no simple matter. One can think of it as a special kind of prosthetic device—an extension of volitionally controlled embodiment. Arms, legs, fingers and—under the influence of this analogy—instruments go together. Or one can think of it as a surrogate voice. This brings the instrument closer still into the living body—the singer sings not with any extension of the body, but with an instrument granted by nature already within it. On this analogy, instruments are not grouped with arms and fingers, but with larynx, tongue and breath. Or one can think of an instrument as inner-to-outer transducer, expressing the contents of the heart. Here the instrument goes not with body parts, but with human experiences—love, loss, heartbreak, reconciliation. Finally, one might think of an instrument as an artefact that has its own character or soul. So conceived, part of the player's task is to bring out what the instrument carries within, voicing what the instrument 'wants' to say.

We can picture the nature, character and identity of instruments in any of these four ways (or any combination thereof) explicitly in language; but this is rare. More common is the intuitive subscription to such models, without verbal expression; the pictures exert a submerged influence on our thinking, reactions, interactions and expectations.

On the evening of 25th July 1965 at the Newport Folk Festival, Bob Dylan walked onstage, not, as expected, a solo act with harmonica and a round-hole flattop acoustic guitar—the definitive instrument of folk musicians since the emergence of the genre, but with an electric, solid-body Fender Stratocaster—the definitive instrument of rock musicians. Woody Guthrie, Pete Seeger, Leadbelly, Doc Watson, Joan Baez, Judy Collins, Willie Nelson—all flattop acoustics. Eric Clapton, George Harrison, Jeff Beck, Jimi Hendrix, Stevie Ray Vaughan—all Stratocasters. Dylan had a band with him—another electric guitar, electric bass, drums and organ, all amplified to the hilt. The company one keeps, as an instrument, is no small matter. But why should that matter erupt, with deep and strong feelings, as a moral issue?

The audience of seventeen thousand shouted, yelled and booed as Dylan's band performed their first number, 'Maggie's Farm'. By the time of their second number, 'Like a Rolling Stone', the jeering was so loud and widespread that much of the highly amplified sound was inaudible. A general sense of dismay, disappointment or aesthetic disorientation does not usually emanate loudly; the sense of betrayal does.

Seeger was backstage, saying that if he had an axe he'd cut the power cable. Audience members were shouting 'Sellout!' and 'Get rid of that band!' The emcee, Peter Yarrow (of Peter, Paul and Mary) pleaded with Dylan to get his acoustic and play solo. Audience members near the stage shouted, 'We want the old Dylan.' Understandably, Dylan was badly shaken by the experience. He was playing Newport, a place essential to his meteoric rise in recognition, for the third year in a row; after 1965 he didn't return for 37 years.

Dylan was perceived in the press to have sold out folk authenticity for the fame and fortune of pop-rock stardom. Although world fame did ensue, what Dylan was doing was nudging politically-directed protest songs toward more personal, introspective writing, simultaneously expanding the traditional sonic palette to include the textures of electric instruments. It was, in its distinctive way, early fusion music, soon to be developed further with The Band.

That Stratocaster, strapped around Dylan's shoulder as he stepped out from backstage, has been insufficiently explored. Angry fans surely thought it didn't belong on that body. Surely the historical relations surrounding it were not only ill-fitting to Dylan, but *antithetical* to him. So they asked themselves: do we believe this person we thought we knew, or do we believe the instrument that is telling us something new and destructive to our previous understanding.

If they believe Dylan, they demand the removal of his distorting, ill-fitting prosthetic, replacing it with one ensuring a consonance between the inner life of the songwriter and the outward associations of the instrument. If they believe the instrument, the outrage is deeper: Dylan is presenting a persona incompatible with what they thought they knew.

Their fury becomes directed at a duplicitous person rather than at a misaligned prosthetic.

Here a third layer of fit surfaces: audience members came to Newport to see an external, mimetic, reflection of themselves—their political interests, social causes and related protests. *All* of Dylan thus becomes the prosthetic. With that guitar strapped to him (along with his all-black leather garb, polished and pointed Beatle boots, and wholly new superstar look in place of the work clothes in which he had always appeared), they felt a sudden, aesthetically vicious, severance of their own prosthetic.

What, then, of the surrogate voice model? If an instrument is of a kind that goes with the larynx, the sense of outrage deepens further, the audience member ventriloquised as the dummy of an unknown master ventriloquist. Those who had crowned Dylan 'The Voice of a Generation' took it personally. In hearing the Stratocaster's 'voice' as a mismatch of one's entire sensibility, the direction of fit is violently reversed: rather than speaking truly for a generation, the 'voice' is now, without consent, co-opting audience members, saying what it wants in their name. The natural reaction to shout against this ventriloquial takeover in one's own, reclaimed, voice would reach its apotheosis in the infamous 'Judas!' accusation of 17th May 1966.

The third way of construing an instrument was as inner-to-outer transducer that conveys the contents of the human heart. The move from hand-me-down flattop to new Strat was—at least for those unaware that Dylan's first guitars were Silvertones—not unlike that from poetry to mail-order catalogue. A hollow body makes its own acoustic sound through its own resonant 'speaker'. A solid-body electric has a barely audible sound of its own—sending its electrical signal from steel strings to magnetic pickups through a cord to an amplifier with loudspeakers. Everyone in the audience knew this fundamental difference. Decades before, when Segovia was asked what he thought of the electric guitar, he replied, 'It cannot last—it has no soul'—a sentiment that Dylan's audience shared. The Stratocaster was spewing out their heartfelt utterances in an alien language they couldn't understand. Yet they criticised it, unawares of the irony of doing so whilst treating the fourth verse of 'The Times They Are A-Changin'' as gospel. 'We want the old Dylan!' was an encapsulation of this. While he finally returned on stage with an acoustic, Dylan ended the affair with 'It's All Over Now, Baby Blue'.

What of the fourth way of construing an instrument? If it is an artefact that possesses its own character, the player's obligation is to recognise, appreciate and bring this out. No one in Dylan's audience that night cared for the soul of a Stratocaster (contra Segovia, it does have one). For them, it was not just the wrong tool for the job; the job itself was wrong. Whatever that instrument wanted to say, they didn't want to hear it. Yet they complained that the poor quality of sound system made it hard to listen to what they did not want to hear; it literalised a metaphorical distortion.

Video recordings show that Dylan did not play the Stratocaster as a Stratocaster but as if it were an acoustic flattop (using mainly open chords in or near first position—the standard harmonic language of the idiom; when he changed keys, he used a capo). Mike Bloomfield, an experienced electric guitarist as part of the Paul Butterfield Blues Band and a guitarist with whom (unbeknownst to his fans) Dylan had already recorded, played all the highly skilled lead. Bloomfield's guitar, inserting powerful blues-rock lead riffs between Dylan's sung phrases, was so loud that Dylan's chordal-accompaniment playing became impossible to hear, thereby multiplying the offence.

Dylan is a guitar player in the singer-songwriter school. No one in the genre cares about, or should be measured against, the knowledge and ability of, say, Wes Montgomery in jazz, Jimmy Page in rock, Julian Bream in classical or Chet Atkins in country. The instrument is used, and powerfully so, as needed, with most of the writing composed on guitar with that standard elementary harmonic vocabulary (usually, E major, C major, D major, A minor, D minor, E minor and perhaps B major and F major), all without going past the first few frets up the fingerboard. But on a Stratocaster there are twenty-two frets. That upper fingerboard is a harmonic, melodic and rhythmic world crying out for expression. In response, a wonderful and aesthetically powerful transformation occurred.

Jimi Hendrix had been working though some new possibilities for material, and the newly released 'All Along the Watchtower' kept coming back to him. Unsatisfied with a number of takes in London, on return to New York he layered overdubs over the basic tracks and discovered, or released, the piece's true voice. Dylan's *John Wesley Harding* original was straightforward, with three main chords moving from A minor, down to G major, down to F major, back up to G major, returning up to the starting point of A minor, repeating throughout the song. Between the sung choruses he interposed his characteristic harmonica passages. This rough schematic packed up and moved into Hendrix's intricate musical imagination, as if Dylan's Strat was calling out to its true master. (One wonders if any Dylan song would have rattled Hendrix's mind if it weren't for his going electric.) Hendrix's version, released in 1968, is one of the greatest achievements in classic rock.[1] The song became a massive hit for both him and Dylan. Hendrix uses the same chord progression, with rhythm guitar, bass and drums as backing for his singing and his Stratocaster soloing and chording. But it isn't just soloing in the style of, say, Clapton. It's a carefully layered part-playing, with different sounds and voices emanating from it at different times. The result brings us back to the four conceptions we began with.

The fourth we have already seen: it was as if the instrument had a soul calling to express itself. No instrument literally does that, of course. It is a matter of the creative relations between the instrument and its player, bringing to the surface submerged possibilities that are otherwise invisible. Hendrix achieved all this to such an extent that Dylan exclaimed: 'It's Jimi's piece; I just wrote it.' Dylan only began to play it live in 1974 (four years after Hendrix's death) and each of the 2,268 times he has done so (it is the song he has performed the most by a long shot), it has been in Hendrix's style: 'ever since he died, I've been doing it that way. Strange how when I sing it, I always feel it's a tribute to him in some kind of way.'

The flattop, like the classical, guitar has tonal variation possible as a result of the distance of the fingernails to the bridge (brighter if closer, mellower if farther, fuller if rest-stroke, thinner if free-stroke). The Stratocaster has a five-position switch and three knobs; the former controls the selection, the latter the master volume and tone. (In Hendrix's time it was a three-way switch, with players setting it to positions between the three official ones to achieve blends that were later formalised.) The result is an

---

[1]   On release in 1968 it quickly became Hendrix's highest ranking American single, receiving massive radio play. It is number 48 on *Rolling Stone*'s 500 Greatest Songs of All Time; in 2000 *Total Guitar* named it number 1 of the Greatest Cover Versions of All Time; Hendrix's solo (the four within the song are ranked as one solo) is number 5 on *Guitar World*'s list of the 100 Greatest Guitar Solos. Countless rock guitarists, including Steve Lukather, have quoted Hendrix's lines in their solos.

instrument with many expressions, all clearly of the same face. Hendrix let it speak in its varying dialects. The result is a powerful example of what can happen when the fourth model is in play, but is inexplicable in those terms alone.

The third, transducer model, captures another aspect of Hendrix's achievement. Like the harmonica breaks between Dylan's choruses, there are four separate guitar lead solos. In his second, Hendrix employs two devices that give it an expressive gestural character, as if someone were gesturing emphatically with their arms, swaying in a full-upper-body gesticulation. The first device is the slide, so that the pitch shift on the strings of the Stratocaster is not controlled step-by-step with frets. With a metal slide depressing the strings to near the frets, Hendrix creates a long pitch change (using almost all of the fingerboard), moving like a glissando on a fretless violin. The sound is mimetic of embodied physiognomy. Added to this is a considerable delay on the slide guitar signal, the gestural sweep literally resonating within the piece, expanding the width of its sonic footprint. It is the kind of playing that renders the third model of how an instrument works plausible.[2]

The second model was that of the surrogate voice. Hendrix himself is here the surrogate for Dylan. But the instrumental surrogacy is captured by the way he plays his third solo, employing a wah-wah pedal. The wah (functioning like a plunger mute on a trumpet) changes the tone colour of the pitches dramatically, giving the instrument the sound of a speaking human voice. Through these shifts of darkness and light, the solo's humanity becomes discernible.

The first model, of a prosthetic extension, manifests noticeably in Hendrix's first solo. The lead tone at the beginning is sharp, loud and slightly distorted, achieving a longer sustain. One can feel the aggressive

---

[2]   There is another moment in the song that shows the transducer-of-the-heart model powerfully. When Hendrix sings Dylan's line 'who feel that life is but a joke', he changes the F major chord, for the one and only time, to a D minor chord below it. It makes musical sense, because D minor is the relative minor of F major, so there is no sudden disjunct key change by brute force. But there is an abrupt sense of the bottom falling out: the D minor removes the floor of the expected F major and suddenly we are in a kind of freefall. This effect, called 'word painting', is strengthened by the momentary cessation of rhythmic definition—we hear continuing rhythm in the mind's ear, but are momentarily cast into the void like nothing matters.

muscular attitude towards the fingerboard and strings. As soon as the sung verse begins, the tone becomes less distorted, the volume lowered, and the hand picking softened. These are differing human movements through a prosthetic (Hendrix's 'outro' solo makes the guitar neck seem like his arm).[3] It is as if Hendrix is correcting what he takes to be the over-loud and non-listening playing of Bloomfield with Dylan in Newport. His recording is not only *of* Dylan, but *about* him. When Dylan walked onstage with that Stratocaster, he (knowingly or otherwise) created a line of implication concerning the fecundity of his songs; what they could call for and what they could come to mean. Presenting the four models of an instrument simultaneously, Hendrix redeems that Newport night forever; everything that was wrong is here made right. Every possibility implied is herein realised, every suggested direction explored. Of his very first hearing of Hendrix's version, Dylan later said, 'It overwhelmed me, really. He had such talent; he could find things inside a song and vigorously develop them. He found things that other people wouldn't think of finding in there.'

Although he played all the most audible and memorable parts on his Stratocaster, Hendrix built it all over his playing A minor, G major, F major, G major on an acoustic flattop. Dylan's instrument-as-surrogate was there, as the foundation over which the Stratocaster would sing; the instrumental voice of a generation.[4]

---

[3] In *Renegades Born in the USA*, Bruce Springsteen tells Barack Obama: 'When I hold a guitar, I don't feel like I'm holding anything. It's just a part of my body, you know. It's just another appendage. That's how it feels, you know. When I strap it on it, it's like that feels like my natural state.'

[4] In 2013, Christie's auctioned a Strat authenticated as Dylan's Newport guitar for a record-breaking $965,000. Dylan claimed he still possessed the original and that this was a different, stolen, guitar, requesting its return. The dispute was settled in undisclosed terms.

Jimi Hendrix with Fender Stratocaster, 10th May 1968 (photograph by Steve Banks; licensed under the Creative Commons Attribution-Share Alike 4.0 International license CC-BY-SA 4.0).

Maximilian de Gaynesford

Pledging My Time

'I'm pledging my time to you / Hopin' you'll come through, too.' The refrain has had the run of my skull for over thirty years, circling around the many occasions where it seems to apply, back to this celebration, where it may have something to say about the complex relationship built up over decades between a song-and-dance man and his audience.

There has been much pledging of time, after all, one way and another. The time it takes to compose and to listen, to perform and to respond, to think and to re-think. A time to do these things and a time for these things. But all this remains a little mysterious when put in the context of a sung pledge. What does it mean to pledge one's time? What is it to pledge anything in the context of singing a song? What does it take and (slightly different) what does it cost? Trying to get a little clarity about this, or at least to give a little more edge to the questions, is what I shall try to do.

'I'm pledging my *time* to you.' What is being pledged here is quite unusual. One's heart, one's love, one's belongings, one's life; these are all things one hears pledged merrily away, in and out of love songs (perhaps most interestingly in out-of-love songs). But pledging one's time—that is a different matter.

Time matters when Dylan sings of it. 'Precious time'; there is a cost to wasting it, one we inevitably think twice about when told not to think twice about it. But time is an unstable thing in ways that make a pledge of time unstable too perhaps. At times, 'time is an enemy', at times a jet plane which 'moves too fast', at times it does not move at all but 'passes slowly', in the mountains, when lost in a dream.

We do talk of 'giving our time' to someone, of course, and perhaps that is essentially what is going on in pledging it. But when we say this, what we generally mean is that we will give someone our attention, that we will expend effort on their behalf. What we offer, and what the other expects, is the attention, the effort. Time itself seems to slip out of the picture rather. Imagine saying, 'Well, I didn't expend any effort on your behalf or attend to you in any way, but I did what I promised: gave you my time.' The wit in offering such an excuse would be more than matched by the annoyance in receiving it. What then are we offering when we offer time?

Taking time seems easier to understand than giving it. Try to imagine yourself pledging just that: bare time. Is it even possible? And of what use would it be? What comes to mind is a Faust-like bargain with the devil, a theme Dylan keeps close to hand. 'Satan will give you a little taste, then he'll move in with rapid speed.' Each pledges their time to the other, so it is a reciprocal arrangement—as reciprocal, perhaps, as between a singer and their audience. 'Tell me what you're gonna do / When the devil calls your cards.' It is just that, since both take Faust's soul to be immortal, the devil gets the far better deal. From the moment that Faust's time runs out, the devil's time begins. 'The devil can have you, I'll see to that.' And this will not simply be in the continuous present—'I'm pledging my time to you'—but in an *eternally* continuous present.

Such a present is not much of a present, perhaps, even when what is on offer is the very opposite of damnation. Or at least that is what we may fear when 'voices echo, this is what salvation must be like after a while'. Still, one can conceive of moving calmly to that doom, and with a certain lilt: 'The promised hour was near... All the lords and ladies / Heading for their eternal home.' See how such a scene is also backed by a pledge and one in the process of being redeemed. It may give us insight into the notion of bare time. But how revealing it is, and how simultaneously disconcerting, that pledging one's time puts us in mind of a time out of mind—a distant past beyond anyone's remembering and an eternal future beyond anyone's imagining.

'I'm *pledging* my time to you.' It is not just what is pledged that is unusual but the very act of pledging it. Promisings there are aplenty in Dylan's songs, but this is the only occasion I can think of where he explicitly uses the heightened notion of a pledge. And until its recent re-pledging in *Shadow Kingdom*, Dylan had only performed the song live twenty-one times, all within the twelve years 1987–99. More a blip than a bleep for a long-distance operator.

'I'm pledging my time to you.' That might simply be describing what is going on. But one gets the sense that the act of pledging itself seems to be taking place, here and now, in the very producing of the words. Widening from pledge to promise, it recalls that undertaking to the Tambourine Man, made here and now: 'cast your dancing spell my way / I promise to go under it.' The sense of going under a certain spell points directly to what is peculiar about the relationship between singer and audience: how organised, voluntary, premeditated it is. Usually, people have no choice about what spells they go under; they are passive objects of the magician's powers. But here the person has leave to undergo the spell voluntarily, and in that most active of ways: in making a promise to do so, here and now.

But hold on; here and now? When Dylan sings 'I'm pledging my time to you', does the pledging really happen where and when we hear it? If so, doesn't it take place wherever and whenever we hear it, indeed whenever each of us hears it? Or if that seems wrong, perhaps we should take ourselves out of the picture. Say it happened just once, where and when Dylan sang it before the microphones. But there were several takes of the song, in March 1966. Was there only one pledging and—somewhat miraculously, because Dylan could not have known at the time—it was the one contained in the recording that was eventually released? But several of those takes have now been released. And there are those twenty-one live performances of the song—a relatively poor number but any riches here are potentially an embarrassment. Which 'I'm pledging' is the real pledging, where is the here and now of it?

It is tempting under these difficulties to retire and say that all this is fiction: whatever the words seem to say, there was no actual pledging, not then and there, not here and now, not even now and then. So with all pledgings, a cynic might say: only ever a fiction, of one sort or another. And not just a cynic either. Even—or perhaps especially—those romantics who 'carry roses' may 'make promises by the hours', where that little twist into the plural ('hours') embeds its barb more deeply.

And here we go down in the flood. Where promising is at issue, what Dylan's songs would often have us hear is a sad complaint—not a whine or a grumble or a moan, and not a mere murmur either, but a straightforward charge. 'With all your promises you left for me / But where are you tonight, sweet Marie?' Promises 'left for me' suggests tangible objects, things left to stand surety for an obligation, 'pledges' in an original sense of the word. So there is the insult on top of the injury: not only do you not keep your promises, but you leave me to keep the pledges which were meant to guarantee your promising. Where promises are tangible elsewhere, they are often just as disposable: 'She promised this a-lad she'd stay / She's rolling up a lotta bread to toss away.' And tangible need not mean solid: pledges can be as fluid as the errant promise-makers themselves: 'You break your promise all over the place / You promised to love me, but what do I see / Just you comin' and spillin' juice over me.'

Promises are hard to keep, so the honest thing to do may be not to make them. But that is easier said than done, we may feel tempted to say, there being so many enticements to make promises. For example, what if the person we are interested in urges us to make them? 'You say you're lookin' for someone / Who will promise never to part.'

And that temptation to think 'easier said than done' has its own enticements to go wrong, with its over-easy contrast between words and deeds. When we promise, our words *are* deeds, and to contrast the two is precisely the trick of the promise-breaker, squirming off the hook. Better then: the honest thing with promising is neither easily said nor easily done.

There is of course the divine option: 'God don't make promises that He don't keep.' But what we may wake up to here is that a comforting reassurance may just as easily seem like an ominous threat. And in keeping with such higher matters, there is another complication to which Dylan's songs are alive: if a promise is made but not seriously, insisting on keeping it willy-nilly may itself be death-dealing: 'Uttering idle words from a reprobate mind / Clinging to strange promises, dying on the vine.' That is the sign of the Dead Man.

Hearing that phrase now—'I'm pledging my time to you'—is like stepping back from song to song until we reach the one in which it is sung. And whatever we are to make of the now and here, it is a pledging that we hear differently as the songs build up between the now and the then. Therein lies the heart of what is given and what is taken in this pledging of time between singer and audience. That pledging has much to do with worrying over the songs themselves. This song for example.

It tells a complex story as I hear it, in marked contrast to the breezy 'Well' with which it starts (as four of its five verses do). That 'Well' suggests the song is trying to keep a certain company on *Blonde on Blonde*: like 'Rainy Day Women §12 & 35', 'Leopard-skin pill-box hat' and 'Absolutely Sweet Marie' and quite unlike the lamenting 'Oh's' of 'Stuck Inside of Mobile' or the straightforward recountings of 'Fourth time around' or the simple entrance of 'Ain't it just like the night' in 'Visions of Johanna'. The pose is measured, unruffled, a rocking on one's feet, a balanced way of getting around to the point. But it is a pose. The story it tells is evidently desperate, though that only breaks through clearly at one point, with the impersonal form 'they sent for an ambulance'.

What marks the stations along the way are the changes to the hoped for reciprocity. 'I'm pledging my time to you / *Hopin' you'll come through, too.*' At first the phrase seems to mean 'hoping you will deliver, do something for me'. Then it moves to 'hoping you will appear, become present, come to me, join me'. And finally it seems to mean 'hoping you will recover, revive, pull through, survive'. Or perhaps not finally, depending on one's interpretation. In the final verse, there is perhaps one movement left: from 'hoping you survive' to 'hoping you endure', where the pledging is in part some sort of commitment to support that enduring into the future.

It is the addition of 'Now…' in *The Lyrics: 1961–2012* — 'Now I'm pledging my time to you' — which suggests this last possibility: that there has been some significant change of attitude, one that is being marked here and now, a new pledge. But the omission of 'now' in the 1964 release makes me feel uncertain. Sometimes I hear that new pledge and sometimes I do not. In the absence of further words, much depends on the instrumental passage following the final verse, what may be implied by its tone.

Much of the song is a pose, perhaps, and that also plays both ways at once. Take what we make of 'Somebody got lucky'. The studiedly impersonal form, together with the third-personal 'they sent for an ambulance', may suggest an appalling nonchalance — that someone might happily re-use a phrase for sexual triumph to describe surviving a medical emergency (particularly if there is an implication, as there seems to be, that the emergency came about as a result of the very nonchalance that is vaunted). But if we are prepared to think that there is indeed a significant change of attitude here, a pledge of enduring commitment, then 'Somebody got lucky' may be a parody of that pose precisely in order to fix it, to focus clearly on it, the better to reject it.

Perhaps. But there are, thankfully, many ways of pledging one's time. Thinking about these things is just one.

Portrait of Bob Dylan 2008 (XIART.at, published under the terms of the GNU Free Documentation License, version 1.3).

Nicholas Birns

Keepin' On
Bob Dylan's Path Forward

Dylan has always been forthright about the deliberate mystery of 'Tangled Up In Blue'. The multiple rewordings and revisions, the ambiguity between the song being one story and many stories, the switch between first- and third-person experience that is embedded in the song but also present in every tweak to the lyrics Dylan made, and the way any attempt to make fully cohesive sense of the action fades before it crystallizes into a pattern make it a song both exhilarating and, at its core, impossible to pin down.

At a certain point in the song, though—the end of the second-to-last verse on the album version—the speaker describes living on 'Montague Street', renting a basement from a couple who fall out with each other. At the beginning of the stanza, there was 'revolution in the air'. But the couple breaks up. The man gets involved in profitable but demeaning financial skulduggery. The woman, perhaps, objects to this. She thereby 'had to sell everything' and 'froze up inside'. Rather than reacting to this imbroglio emotionally, though, the speaker's response is kinetic and dynamic, projecting forward. He moves on. But it is not just in space. It is also in time. Moreover, whereas moving on would connote a certain callousness or lack of compassion, the speaker clearly continues to care about situations he has nonetheless had to leave behind. Therefore, he does not just move on. He *keeps on*:

And when finally, the bottom fell out
I became withdrawn
The only thing I knew how to do
Was to keep on keepin' on

Like a bird that flew
Tangled up in blue

Given the temporal variations of 'Tangled Up In Blue' from the lyric past of 'thirteenth century' to the conjectural future of 'some day on the avenue', that 'keepin' on' though necessarily meaning to keep on through time, is so spatial is notable. A bird that flies continues in time. But it does not necessarily know it is doing so. In its own mind, it moves forward only in space. 'Keepin' on' is akin to persevering, enduring, persisting, lasting, but not quite the same as any of these. The other terms are laden with both a metaphysics and an affect that 'keepin' on' forswears. They are also highfalutin and in the traditional language of eloquence while 'keepin' on' is workaday and naturalistic. In verbal terms, 'keepin' on' is a valuable counterweight in a song that, as Timothy Hampton has pointed out, alludes to Petrarch not only in content but in form. 'Keepin' on' jettisons the grand unpretentious to maintain itself in motion. If 'keepin' on' were to make any claims, it would not actually keep on. Indeed, 'keepin' on' does not always keep on in the song's own revision history. In the *Real Live* (1984) version, the speaker decides to 'be me. And get on that train and ride.' Even in this rephrasing that eliminates the actual words, though, the essence of 'keepin' on' is retained. There is a going forward, but also a passivity, a lack of declarative, unfolded intention. Much like Jacob after he wrestles with the angel, survival and continuity comes at the implied cost of a certain loss of primal inspiration.

For me as a listener, there have always been three major signposts in 'Tangled Up In Blue' that I use to thread my way interpretively through the song. I claim no particular authority for these (except the protean nature of the song probably makes most listeners to unfurl such a spool). But they do help explain how 'keepin on' is an act of willpower yet makes few substantive claims. In the second stanza, where the speaker—who I prefer here as using first-person pronouns—tells the tale of the married woman with whom he 'used a little too much force', there is a sense of violation, of guilt, of being out of control. Yet in the next stanza, where— here I prefer to see the speaker as part of a collective, rather than editorial 'we'—'we' obtain, for an unhappy man, a job on a fishing boat 'outside of Delacroix'. This gesture—particularly meaningful in a working-class, honky-tonk, dog-eat-dog, paddle-your-own-canoe American south—is an altruistic one. that balances the tendencies towards anomie and dis-affection in the other stanzas.

What the speaker—in my improvised through-line thread—wins from this altruism is the freedom he gains in the second-to-last stanza. There is an inference (bolstered by later revisions) that the speaker is involved in a love triangle with the couple on Montague Street, perhaps a situation not unlike that chronicled by Leonard Cohen in 'Famous Bleu Raincoat'. The man gone, the woman desolated, the speaker has an opportunity. But (inferentially) to seize that opportunity would be to be drawn too much in a web not of his own making and from which he might not be able to free himself. There is also, perhaps, an anxiety about the homoerotic here. Being involved with the woman would also mean, metaphorically, being involved with the man whose epic fall from grace still casts such a long shadow over the woman's state of mind. To con-template this would only ensnare the protagonist in a self-analysis that is not his métier. So he chooses to 'keep on keepin' on' out of a sort of insensate duty to himself. He avoids being defined by anyone else's circumstances. Having helped a friend get a job down south, he has gained a self-distancing that is not narcissistic or even necessarily autono-mous. 'Keepin' on' is a mode of not being entangled in other people's scripts or expectations. This is always an imperative for Dylan (and perhaps one of the reasons he revised this song so much). Keepin' on is nothing but being kinetic, ongoing: like a bird that flew.

Blood on the Tracks is an album that, notwithstanding the many twists in Dylan's career, established him as a creative figure who outlasted the era in which he first gained popularity. As Dylan's career lengthens, 'keepin' on' becomes more positive. The escape from the imbroglio on Montague Street was simply a solo going-forward. The potential of a more collective 'revolution in the air' having vanished by the time the fateful choice had to be made. By the time of 'Not Dark Yet', over two decades later, 'keepin' on' has become more of an inspirational mantra.

Vocabularies of potentiality have always had a place in Dylan's most storied songs. 'The Times They Are A-Changin'', 'Blowin' in The Wind', or, far more pessimistically, even 'A Hard Rain's A-Gonna Fall', potential is something that hovers in the air as a kind of unused reservoir of prophecy. By 'Not Dark Yet' the uncertainty has to do not with potential but postponement. The speaker has been all around the world, and has an even wider, more cosmopolitan, more fully lived range of experience than the presiding intelligence of 'Tangled Up In Blue'.

> Well, I've been to London and I've been to gay Paris
> I've followed the river and I got to the sea
> I've been down on the bottom of a world full of lies
> I ain't looking for nothing in anyone's eyes
> Sometimes my burden is more than I can bear
> It's not dark yet, but it's getting there

Experience has not satisfied this figure. But it has given them a saving disillusion, a lack of attachment, a disinclination to want anything from anyone else. But there is not the sense of freedom, even if a somewhat nihilistic freedom, present at the end of 'Tangled Up In Blue'. There is the reverse of potential: an accumulation of negative energy, of sad wasted time. But why this is not simply depressing is that there is still an ongoing process, of getting there. If getting there is a roadmap for the ultimate destination of darkness, it is also a delaying tactic, a way of staving off the end. It's getting there is not the same as it will get there or it's on the way there or, certainly, it's going to get there. It is a movement-towards, likely an irreversible one, but not inevitable or deterministic. The getting there is saved from such a fate by an inheritance of 'keepin' on', whose kinetic qualities view with and even outweigh the temporal direction in which it is headed. 'Keepin' on' is not pushing towards a goal, striving for a prize. Indeed, being drawn towards a goal or an end is virtually absent from the idea of 'keepin' on'. This is so even as 'keepin' on' clearly denotes *converging* on a goal or an end. There seems to be a path forward. But it is also a path *sans* destination. 'It's not dark yet / but it's getting there.'

These lines from 'Not Dark Yet' build on the accumulation presented by sheer existence. They have mortality in mind. But they nonetheless zigzag and pirouette in order to both predict and avoid mortality. The shadows lengthen, yet the lengthening is precisely a way of avoiding the looming shadows.

The purport here is less about endings than sustainability. Sustainability, in turn, has been the preoccupation of the latter half of Dylan's career. He has explained the formative mode of his Never Ending Tour as being remised on sustainability, the capacity to be reiterated in multiple times, contexts and occasions. As mooted in some of his post-1988 concerts' contrary reception, the most sustainable art is not always the best art. But if sustainability is truly the imperative it may not want to be the best art. Part of the suggestive of 'keepin' on' is one of perseverance, but another is one of preservation, of protection, even of maintenance. To go back to 'Tangled Up In Blue', to escape from being drawn into the separating couple's drama the protagonist does not assert any superior morality or any demanding aesthetic intent. He simply says: I have to get out in order to keep on, to be on the move, to sustain myself.

Dylan's 2020 album *Rough and Rowdy Ways* arrived during the height of the Covid-19 pandemic in the US, and served as a kind of insensate witness to events it did not foresee. The first song released, and ultimate song on the album, 'Murder Most Foul', was particularly fortuitous in its application to time. Written as a dirge about the 1963 assassination of President John F. Kennedy, it became, in application, a litany for those who were dying even as the video was watched and the song was down-loaded. A searing indictment of America as a pseudo-civilisation, a chant across time lamenting an instance of time whose violence is still not exhausted. Yet, despite these vistas of the calamitous present and the distant past, it is the sideways moments in the song, those where Dylan refers to his own contemporaries. That are the most poignant. The fore-most these are to the Eagles:

> Play Don Henley — play Glenn Frey
> Take it to the Limit and let it go by

And to the Who:

> Tommy can you hear me, I'm the Acid Queen

These acknowledgments of counterparts who had rival artistic visions make the song dynamic and were what spur its acts of memory into being meaningful in its present articulation. Here, 'keepin' on' becomes a catalysing agent. Another song on *Rough and Ready Ways*, 'Crossing the Rubicon', testifies to 'keepin' on' by inversion. 'Crossing the Rubicon' is a declarative, decisive action. The song is full of metaphors of this kind of decisiveness: 'I poured the cup'; 'I turned the key'; 'I lit the torch'. Yet 'Crossing the Rubicon' is as anthological and amorphous as 'Tangled Up In Blue'. It alternatively seems to endorse classical and Christian

worldviews, optimism and pessimism, possessiveness and renunciation.
The song's final assertion —

> I looked to the east
> And I crossed the Rubicon

has a finality 'keepin' on' lacks. But that sense of continuing, without fear
of expectation, promise or reward, remains. There is a direction. A path
forward. But no goal. No end.

Barcelona, 1984 (photograph by F. Antolín Hernandez, licensed
under the Creative Commons Attribution 2.0 Generic license CC BY
2.0).

Sophie Grace Chappell

Beyond Communication
'Changing of the Guards'
as a 'Non-coalescent' Artwork

Art is good art just insofar as it is good psychic nutrition, good soul food. One important way for it to be good soul food is for it to exemplify the archetypal patterns of human life, and to do so in a way that scores highly by the three measures of *pleasure, interest and reality*: it is fun (or otherwise a positive experience); it is fascinating or arresting or intriguing; it tells the truth, or some important truth. (These three measures can of course be traded off against each other.)

There are many ways for literary and other cognitively loaded art to be bad. Often the work is bad because it *doesn't* exemplify the archetypal patterns, or at least not in any way that scores at all highly by these three measures. It doesn't have any pleasing or interesting or revealing plot, or the plot is an inchoate mess, or perhaps it doesn't have any plot at all. The writer, as we say, 'didn't know what she was doing' when she wrote it. (Or more exactly, no part of her psyche knew what it was doing. Creative processes don't have to be conscious, and sometimes, as Coleridge reminds us, are all the better for not being. There is a reason why Homer, and Teiresias, are blind.)

Again, a work of literature can be bad because it *does* exemplify the archetypal patterns, but too unpleasantly, or too unrealistically, or too uninterestingly. It's more horrifying or nihilistic than we can cope with; or it lacks the ring of truth or credibility, so that it fails to get taken seriously, and so does not really get a hearing; or it's boring or cliched or mechanical or predictable in how it exemplifies the symbols—and/or, it exemplifies too few of them.

At one limit of this last range of possibilities—from exemplifying too many symbols at once to exemplifying too few—lies simple mechanical allegory, where each thing in the allegory stands for something in the world, and the interactions in the real world and in the allegory world run strictly in parallel. The simpler and more mechanical an allegory is, the likelier it is to fail artistically, because, quite literally, it doesn't leave enough to the imagination.

Yet even quite mechanical allegory does not *always* fail as art, nor fail to be psychically nutritious. Generations of English minds were nurtured on Bunyan's *Pilgrim's Progress*, one of the most heavy-handedly allegorical books there has ever been. The *Pilgrim's Progress* is an odd book, to 21st-century tastes, but certainly not an artistic failure. Why not, given its continuous and very unsubtle allegorising? I think the answer is that Bunyan is at his best precisely when the allegories cease to be *mere* allegories, when the Giant Despair, Vanity Fair and the Slough of Despond are no longer mere functioning cogs in the simple-minded mechanics of evangelical 'salvation', and become true symbols, pointers towards something deeper, more mysterious and more psychic.

I would say the same about the best-known 20th-century English Christian allegorist. C.S. Lewis's deeply flawed, yet deeply engaging, *The Lion, The Witch, and the Wardrobe* series is at its best not when Lewis is preaching, in thin disguise, that the traitor Edmund (i.e. any one of us sinners) is saved by the blood of the Lion (i.e. the Lamb), but when Narnia becomes a place of distant castles and shadowy forests and nigh-infinite oceans.

Of both Bunyan and Lewis I would also say what Lewis's friend and critic J.R.R. Tolkien said, that it is precisely when they undergo this sea-change[1] from mere allegory into imaginative and 'mythopoeic' freedom that Bunyan and Lewis are at their most truly Christian. As Tolkien himself described this change:

> I cordially dislike allegory in all its manifestations, and always have done so since I grew old and wary enough to detect its presence. I

---

[1]   For once, I hope, this allusion rises above the level of pointless automatic cliché. Given that Ariel's song—like the whole play—is about the transubstantiation of contingent arbitrary loss into the necessary beauty of art, the idea of 'sea-change', as Shakespeare actually meant it, is actually relevant here.

much prefer history, true or feigned, with its varied applicability to the thought and experience of readers. I think that many confuse 'applicability' with 'allegory'; but the one resides in the freedom of the reader, and the other in the purposed domination of the author... Every writer making a secondary world wishes in some measure to be a real maker, or hopes that he is drawing on reality: hopes the peculiar quality of this secondary world (if not all the details) are derived from Reality or are flowing into it... So great is the bounty with which [the Christian writer] has been treated that he may now, perhaps, fairly dare to guess that in Fantasy he may actually assist in the effoliation and multiple enrichment of creation.[2]

With Bunyan and Lewis, and with Tolkien himself too, it is when their stories stop being (or being understood as) mere allegories that they begin to have a real psychological power. For then they start to be free to communicate to us in the language of the symbols; and the whole point of that language is that it goes deeper than the articulate. (Cp. Jung on dogma in religion and therapy: 'Were psychology bound to a creed it would not and could not allow the unconscious of the individual that free play which is the basic condition for the production of archetypes.')[3] Each symbol, or at least each of the great symbols, stands for something that is intensely significant to us, but in ways that cannot be made fully explicit: the power of the symbol lies precisely in its direct communication with the deeper and less articulate parts of our minds. Something like this seems to have been what both Tolkien and Lewis had in mind when they talked about 'myth': a highly-charged word for both of them, by which they seem to have meant roughly, in my terms, *story that embodies the archetypes, the symbols.*

The thinness of allegory is then one way for art's interaction with the symbols to fail to be psychically nutritious, and so to fail as art; yet art can sail very close to this wind, and still succeed. The opposite way to fail is for the interaction to be, as it were, too fat: for too many symbols to be

---

2   My quotation merges two sources, both of which use Tolkien's own words verbatim. Up to the ellipsis the words quoted come from Carpenter (1977, 189–90). After it, they are from Tolkien (1939).

3   Jung (1953, 16). On the free play of the unconscious cp. T.S. Eliot (1920, 153) on Blake: 'the idea, of course, simply comes.'

deployed at once, all in a crowd, a confused rabble of images, with none of them given the space it needs to breathe or develop or signify properly.

Yet narrative art—and non-narrative art—can succeed when it courts this extreme too. Here is Maritain (1953, 314) on what he calls 'modern', as opposed to 'classical', poetry:

> [In modern poetry,] in the preconscious life of the intellect, the image, instead of being used for the birth of ideas in the process of abstraction [as it was in classical poetry], are moved and quickened by poetic intuition, under the light of the Illuminating Intellect: and the uncon-ceptualisable intelligibility involved in poetic intuition passes through them in an *intentional*[4] or immaterial manner, so that they are made into the vehicle of an intelligible meaning, which will never terminate in a concept, and can remain implicit, even sometimes undetermined, but still is an intelligible meaning, capable of obscurely touching and moving the intellect.

Good art may not only involve what I have called the interplay of symbols that are to some extent indeterminate in their content; further-more, good art may sometimes be *so* indeterminate in its use of a multi-plicity of symbols, that it does not actually ever coalesce into any fixed propositional content at all—and yet is good art for all that, indeed is good art precisely *because* it is indeterminate in this way.

Maritain's example of a non-coalescent modern lyric is T.S. Eliot's 'The Hollow Men'. Since in this case I have the advantage of the flow of time over Jacques Maritain, and also because it is actually a better example than 'The Hollow Men' of what Maritain calls non-coalescence, I'll talk about something from a more recent Nobel Prize for Literature laureate: Bob Dylan's 'Changing of the Guards'.

Sixteen years
Sixteen banners united over the field
Where the good shepherd grieves
Desperate men, desperate women divided
Spreading their wings 'neath the falling leaves

---

4   Scholastic sense of 'intentional', as in Descartes.

Fortune calls
I stepped forth from the shadows to the marketplace
Merchants and thieves, hungry for power, my last deal gone down
She's smelling sweet like the meadows where she was born
On midsummer's eve near the tower

The cold-blooded moon
The captain waits above the celebration
Sending his thoughts to a beloved maid
Whose ebony face is beyond communication
The captain is down but still believing that his love will be repaid

They shaved her head
She was torn between Jupiter and Apollo
A messenger arrived with a black nightingale
I seen her on the stairs and I couldn't help but follow
Follow her down past the fountain where they lifted her veil

Sixteen years
Sixteen banners united over the field
Where the good shepherd grieves
Desperate men, desperate women divided
Spreading their wings 'neath the falling leaves

Fortune calls
I stepped forth from the shadows, to the marketplace
Merchants and thieves, hungry for power, my last deal gone down
She's smelling sweet like the meadows where she was born
On midsummer's eve, near the tower

The cold-blooded moon
The captain waits above the celebration
Sending his thoughts to a beloved maid
Whose ebony face is beyond communication
The captain is down but still believing that his love will be repaid

They shaved her head
She was torn between Jupiter and Apollo
A messenger arrived with a black nightingale

I seen her on the stairs and I couldn't help but follow
Follow her down past the fountain where they lifted her veil

I stumbled to my feet
I rode past destruction in the ditches
With the stitches still mending 'neath a heart-shaped tattoo
Renegade priests and treacherous young witches
Were handing out the flowers that I'd given to you

The palace of mirrors
Where dog soldiers are reflected
The endless road and the wailing of chimes
The empty rooms where her memory is protected
Where the angels' voices whisper to the souls of previous times

She wakes him up
Forty-eight hours later, the sun is breaking
Near broken chains, mountain laurel and rolling rocks
She's begging to know what measures he now will be taking
He's pulling her down and she's clutching on to his long golden locks

Gentlemen, he said
I don't need your organization, I've shined your shoes
I've moved your mountains and marked your cards
But Eden is burning, either brace yourself for elimination
Or else your hearts must have the courage for the changing of the
guards

Peace will come
With tranquillity and splendor on the wheels of fire
But will bring us no reward when her false idols fall
And cruel death surrenders with its pale ghost retreating
Between the King and the Queen of Swords

People often say vaguely that this song is 'about the Tarot', though I can
see no clear evidence of that except in the very last line; anyway, to say
that it is 'about the Tarot' is not very informative, even if it is. Every
stanza in the song offers us at least one beautiful or striking image, some
characters, and the beginnings of a story; then each successive stanza

disrupts the last by starting the story again.[5] Or should that be 'by starting *another* story'? How many stories are there in the song? And whose stories are they? Not even that is clear. We can discern perhaps four main characters—'I', 'she', 'the captain' (who seems by his (?) hair colour to be emphatically white), 'the beloved maid' with the 'ebony face'… or is it two, each of them seen from two diffracted perspectives? These main characters are set against a shifting background of often-hostile others (the 'desperate men', the 'merchants and thieves', the 'they' who 'shaved her head', the 'renegade priests' and 'treacherous young witches'). It looks like race, war, certainly romantic betrayal, possibly rape, and revolution are all in the air somehow. Narrative continuities, or apparent continuities, are achieved by anaphora and cross-reference ('She wakes him up'), by reference back to an assumed shared past ('The flowers… that I'd given to you') and, at a more material level, by the background beat of a vaguely stable rhyme-scheme (but with some internal-rhyming crosscurrents, and with no true rhymes at all in the final stanza). Above all, what is constant throughout is of course the powerful momentum of the music to which the words are set. Yet there is no narrative coalescence. Despite its apparent allusions both to Dylan's own life, and (to my ear at least) to the American Civil War, there is no one historical or even autobiographical story that the song tells. Dylan himself has said of 'Changing of the Guards' both that 'It means something different every time I sing it', and also that 'Changing of the Guards' is 'a thousand years old'.

I think he's right on both scores. The song means no one complete thing, and an indefinite number of different fragmentary things, precisely because it is not a clear one-dimensional narrative, but a multidimensional array of symbols that arrange themselves into all sorts of possible, but incomplete, narrative shapes. Here, as elsewhere in Dylan's lyrics, the power of the lyric comes from the power of the symbols that it puts before us—and those symbols are, most of them, a good deal more than a thousand years old. Dylan's writing very often exemplifies what I

---

5   In the next song on the same album, 'New Pony', Dylan seems to take this trick of starting a story then immediately tossing it aside to the point of self-parody: the very first line of the song introduces a pet pony called Lucifer, the second tells us laconically that 'she broke her leg and needed shooting'.

have called non-coalescence, and 'Changing of the Guards' is perhaps the perfect example of that.

References

Bunyan, J. (1678) *The Pilgrim's Progress from This World, to That Which Is to Come*, London: Nath. Ponder.

Carpenter, H. (1977) *Tolkien: The Authorized Biography*, London: Allen & Unwin.

Eliot, T.S. (1920) 'William Blake', *Athenaeum*, 13 Feb.

Jung, C.G. (1953) *Psychology and Alchemy*, Hull, R.F.C. (trans.), London: Routledge & Kegan Paul.

Lewis, C.S. (1950) *The Lion, The Witch, and the Wardrobe*, London: Geoffrey Bies.

Maritain, J. (1953) *Creative Intuition in Art and Poetry*, New York: Pantheon Books.

Tolkien, J.R.R. (1939) On fairy stories, as published in Lewis, C.S. (ed.) *Essays Presented to Charles Williams (1947)*, Oxford: Oxford University Press.

Bob Dylan performing in Rotterdam, 23rd June 1978 (photograph by Chris Hakkens, licensed under the Creative Commons Attribution-Share Alike 2.0 Generic license CC-BY-SA 2.0).

Anupama M. Ranawana

'What More Can I Tell You? I Sleep with Life and Death in the Same Bed'

Ineffability, Memory and Dylan's 'Religious' Thought

'I, I shall be released...' Nina Simone's sweet hoarseness transcends the material, imbuing Bob Dylan's words with yearning, and with liberatory hope. The song, a classic of early Dylan, is itself heavily influenced by gospel music, and pregnant with images of religious redemption.

My first real memory of Bob Dylan is a religious one. I am in church, ten years old, a hot Sunday in Sri Lanka, standing at the front of the youth choir, in an itchy dress, determinedly vocalising the truth that the answers were blowin' in the wind. My father, a 60s teenager who also embraced the social justice movements of the 70s, played Dylan sometimes, in the evenings, but not in a religious way. The product of a 'secular Buddhist' home, Dylan spoke to his spiritual soul, in much the same way as Lennon's later works did. Within my own unidentifiable, hybrid anarcho-spiritual practice, the lyrics of the anguished ballad 'Every Grain of Sand' draw me back always to love, to community, to my ancestors, to hope (however fractured).

> I hear the ancient footsteps like the motion of the sea
> Sometimes I turn, there's someone there, other times it's only me.
> — 'Every Grain of Sand' (1981)

As my musical experiences deepened and matured, I sometimes wondered how Dylan would react to his music being a frequent go-to as a Communion hymn, sung by middle-aged aunties arrayed in scapulars and rosaries. I also marvelled at how Dylan's lyrics could speak so clearly, so spiritually and so equally to — *inter alia* — pious Catholics, a secular Buddhist and an agnostic. Both the early and latter Dylan resists any one religious definition. There are many worldviews to Dylan's music and lyrics, a steeped religiosity, a yearning for understanding the ineffable. There is a Protestant Dylan, a Catholic Dylan, a Zen Master Dylan, a Jewish Dylan, a mystical poet Dylan. Much like his fellow poet Leonard Cohen, we are also presented very often with contemplations of grace — but grace that exists in a fractured sense.

Listening last year to the album *Rough and Rowdy Ways* I once again asked myself about the 'religious' Dylan. Is there a religious Dylan? In his review of the same album, Religious News Service reporter Jeffrey Salkin formulated the question in a different way. Briefly mapping out Dylan's journey from his Jewish roots to his brief and controversial embrace of evangelical Christianity in the 1970s, Salkin is moved by the song 'Goodbye Jimmy Reed' to ask, 'what religion is Dylan now?' (Salkin 2020).

> You can bring it to St. Peter
> You can bring it to Jerome
> You can bring it all the way over
> Bring it all the way home.
> — 'My Own Version of You' (2020)

Salkin, of course, is referring to the multitudes of Dylan's work, as well as the spiritual transformations of the artist's own faith journey. Dylan's Christian conversion in the 1970s is deemed controversial because it seemed out of step with the cultural battles for equality and radical justice that liberals were involved with at the time. When Dylan became a Christian, he did not initially embrace the Jesus as radical movement or the Christian traditions of civil rights activists. Instead, he found a temporary space in a reactionary Christianity that blamed liberalism for economic and moral decline, as evidenced by the lyrics of 'Slow Train' and 'When You Gonna Wake Up'. Dylan's Christian evangelical moment was a brief one, but, as Sanchez (2019) notes, it left its mark in that he performed a popular remaking of an old-time religion, foreshadowing much of the younger celebrities of American Evangelism today.

There is significant evolution from this brief explicit Christian moment, and the density and multiplicity of themes in 2020's *Rough and Rowdy Ways* rather defy any single religion, with strong themes of spirituality, the afterlife, mortality and the mystique of 'eternity'. So much of the album's craving for, and understanding of, freedom also runs parallel—to my mind at least—to the written poems of the *Therigatha*:

> She's a three-knowledge woman who's left death behind; freed from slavery, debtless, a nun with developed faculties, set loose from all ties, her task done, fermentation-free. (Thig 13.5, in Buswell et al. 2017)

> I ain't no false prophet, I just know what I know… Can't remember when I was born and I forgot when I died… I ain't no false prophet—I just said what I said. ('False Prophet', 2020)

In the *Therigatha*, the writings of the first Buddhist women, there is a disruption of the idea of liberation seen not as one watershed moment but of ongoing confrontation and struggle. Indeed, the text contains fifteen different words and phrases for freedom. They are at once texts of confession, as well as craving for deliverance. There is so much of this in Dylan's writing, in the religiosity of his phrasing, his seeking for liberation, for the understanding of the life that is to come and, in the album *Rough and Rowdy Ways*, his exploration of the death of the Self—a fundamental aspect of Buddhism. Underlining these notes of transition and contemplation that are in Dylan's corpus as well as the text of the *Therigatha* is no new insight—although thinking through Dylan's themes of seeking freedom and truth against the same themes in a feminist Buddhist text may be a site for further exploration. In *Bargaining for Salvation*, for example, Steven Heine picks up the Buddhist tendency in Dylan's writing, arguing that Dylan has a great affinity with the Zen worldview, even as he zig-zags between various proclamations of truth throughout his career. Heine, indeed, is trying to make sense of—as many religious studies scholars who think through with Dylan—where the poet places himself. Is he always Bobby Zimmerman? Is he always the Dylan of the great evangelical turn? Is it just brilliant ethnicity? Is he nothing but a restless pilgrim? Is he a prophet raging against American suffering? Or is Dylan an unpindownable changeling on whom we can all simply reflect our own needs to have music 'save our mortal souls'?

Aasgaard (2019), discussing Dylan's existential themes in 'Señor (Tales of Yankee Power)', draws our attention to the cruciality of the period 1961 to 1973 in understanding Dylan's religious thought. Aasgaard notes that, in this period, Dylan uses the Bible primarily in the service of social and economic criticism, much like spirituals and blues in 'The Times They Are A-Changin'', 'Masters of War' and 'Señor (Tales of Yankee Power)'. In the latter part of this period, Aasgaard notes that Dylan develops a deeper understanding of biblical ideals and concepts of Jewish and Christian traditions more generally. By this time, the Bible serves as a reservoir for interpreting life and the world more generally. Dylan's use of biblical motifs, figures and events becomes more varied and multivalent in his later period, with different motifs often being woven together.

This weaving and syncretism are important also for Taylor (2013), who notes the Christian perspective runs like a thread throughout Dylan's songs, all the while also drawing from the ancient Jewish prophetic tradition, the Jesus Movement of the 1970s, as well as the Christian roots of folk-country-and-blues music. For Taylor, this is how Dylan can search for truth whilst staying apolitical and anarchist, arguing that his embrace of Christianity only deepened the latter via an embrace of Christian anarchist sentiments (Taylor 2013). He cites a 1986 *Rolling Stone* interview in which Dylan remarks:

> Well, for me, there is no right and there is no left. There's truth and there's untruth, y'know? There's honesty and there's hypocrisy.
> (Gilmore 1986, cited in Taylor 2013, 6)

Spargo and Realm (2009) underline that to engage with Dylan's religious thought is to converse with an artist who purposively pulls together a variety of religious traditions and attitudes and then yokes them together into a larger syncretistic imagination. In short, he seeks to function like a prophet, a new Jeremiah (Spargo and Realm 2009, 88). For them, the song I sang in church so many years ago is imbued with prophetic rage. They also identify elements of Dylan that one could compare to the writings of mystical saints, in the way that Dylan sometimes infuses erotic love with the passion of Christ (Sparge and Realm 2009, 93). Spargo and Realm note

that Dylan's spiritual influences like the Carters and the Staples Singers
are bound together by one theme—that of finding oneself immersed
within an otherworldly feeling whilst trying to square this with a lived
experience of mortals reaching for as well as railing against the sacred.
The epitome of this, they find, is 'Oh Mercy', which renders the singer as
a quiet, relentless prophet (Spargo and Realm 2009, 99).

But how does it square, man? Michael Gilmour, who has written
extensively on Dylan's religiosity, points us back to revelation and sub-
version. Gilmour would agree with other scholars that the Bible is a key
text for Dylan's writing, but that Dylan works not in a univocal way but
in 'prophetic pastiche'. This, then, is not a systematised form of religiosity
but one that is open to receive the sacred and which encourages the
audience to embrace 'an openness to whatever nourishes' (Gilmour 2011,
128). Attenuative approaches, argues Gilmour, would 'inevitably involve
speculation, exaggeration, selectivity, and distortion' (Gilmour 2004,
2000). Dylan's religious thought cannot be easily defined and contained.

Perhaps the best way to conclude these brief notes on Dylan's
religious thought is to recognise that we bring to Dylan our own desire to
discover, our own desire for spiritual significance. What we discover in
Dylan, as he converses with anarcho-spiritualists, Christian evangelicals,
rosary clutching aunties, Buddhist women, Hebrew prophets and a host
of others, is, in fact, an obscure prophet, one who looks for and sketches
an alternative worldview to the material culture of this world. He uses
this steeped religiosity to move past it to argue for something more
universal (Morgan 2020).

> If I do it upright and put the head on straight
> I'll be saved by the creature that I create
>
> —'My Own Version of You'

What is most vividly foregrounded, perhaps, is an aspect of interbeing,
where Dylan absorbs, and also encourages us to absorb, a variety of
alternative worldviews that point us to a greater, universal truth. To
encourage a dismantling, a rending of our known kinship narratives, to
die to our one self and, instead, pick up circular, multiple selves.

References

Aasgaard, R. (2019) *'Señor (Tales of Yankee Power)': A Window into Bob Dylan's Existential and Religious World*, Oslo: Cappelen Damm Akademisk.

Buswell, R.E. & Lopez, D.S. (2017) *Therīgāthā: The Princeton Dictionary of Buddhism*, Princeton, NJ: Princeton University Press.

Gilmour, M. (2004) *Tangled Up in the Bible: Bob Dylan and Scripture*, London: Bloomsbury.

Gilmour, M. (2011) *The Gospel According to Bob Dylan*, Louisville, KY: Westminster John Knox Press.

Heine, S. (2009) *Bargainin' for Salvation: Bob Dylan, a Zen master?* London: Continuum.

Morgan, R. (2020) Bob Dylan's *Rough and Rowdy Ways* contains religious multitudes, *Religion Unplugged*, [Online], https://religionunplugged.com/news/2020/9/2/bob-dylans-rough-and-rowdy-ways-contains-religious-multitudes [21 February 2021].

Salkin, J. (2020) What religion is Dylan now?, *Religion News Service*, [Online], https://religionnews.com/2020/06/23/dylan-album [21 February 2021].

Sanchez, A. (2019) Bob Dylan's overlooked Christian music, *Sojourners*, [Online], https://sojo.net/articles/bob-dylans-overlooked-christian-music [21 February 2021].

Spargo, R.C. & Ream, A.K. (2009) Bob Dylan and religion, in Dettmar, K.J.H. (ed.) *The Cambridge Companion to Bob Dylan*, pp. 87–99, Cambridge: Cambridge University Press.

Taylor, J. (2013) Bob Dylan and antithetical engagement with culture, *Pro Rege*, 41 (4), pp. 16–26.

Bob Dylan at Massey Hall, Toronto, 18th April 1980 (Photograph by Jean-Luc Ourlin, licensed under the Creative Commons Attribution-Share Alike 2.0 Generic license CC-BY-SA 2.0).

KG Miles

Apocalypse Soon

When Bob Dylan was inducted into the Rock n Roll Hall of Fame in 1988, Bruce Springsteen said that the loud snare drum 'shot' at the start of the song 'Like A Rolling Stone' in 1965 kicked open the door to our minds. Fast forward to 1979 and the crash of a cymbal at the start of the song 'Gonna Change My Way of Thinking' is an attempt to kick open the door to our souls. This time around, however, this opening salvo is not the beginning of unbridled pop success and critical acclaim. That cymbal crash marked the beginning of what fans and critics alike would refer to, in largely hushed tones, as the 'Christian' era.

'Gonna Change My Way of Thinking' is Track One on Side Two of the first of a trilogy of albums, a Holy Trinity of *Slow Train Coming*, *Saved* and *Shot of Love*. Released on the 20th August 1979, at the start of three years, 1979–81, where the music would be dominated by an evangelical zeal. A time when Dylan was on a mission from God and where Dylan would preach on vinyl and on stage so vehemently that hardly anyone really noticed how divine the music really was.

When released in 1979, the album 'Slow Train Coming' was a relative chart success for Dylan. It got to Number 2 in the UK and went Platinum in the US. Yet another in a long list of 'return to form' album moments for him. The critics were mostly enthused also. Jann Wenner in *Rolling Stone* magazine of September that year is particularly taken by 'Gonna Change My Way of Thinking', saying that the track is 'Set in a tough, relentless rhythm, is a fire and brimstone sermon stripped of subtlety, though not of poetry.' Lyrically Dylan reaches back into his Bible but with a directness born of his recent evangelical classes with the Vineyard Fellowship. There is no mere allusion here, there is Dylan at his most religious finger pointing. Quoting pretty directly from the Gospel of Matthew, Dylan says, singing out from the vinyl like a fervent TV preacher, that 'Jesus said, Be ready for you know not the hour in which I come / He said "He who is not for Me is against Me", Just so you know where he's coming from.' Dylan wouldn't be pussy footing about for the next three years.

This classic 12 bar blues number is not just a religious rant though. Dylan really chucks the blues kitchen sink at this one and Dylan is possibly never better than when he is reaching back into the history of the blues or when he is passionately ranting. Here he is very much doing both. With this song we get pulpit thumping blues but with a pure secular eroticism. Dylan sings of the 'Georgia Crawl', an extremely erotic dance that in all honestly you can imagine being the go-to floor filler for the unfortunate Delia or the 'charcoal dusky maidens' of the song 'Blind Willie McTell'. As Jann Wenner remarks, it is 'as close as anything to matching' the blues eroticism of the Rolling Stones in 'Brown Sugar'. In a moment of clairvoyance, Wenner says it is 'As good as it gets'.

Interestingly, Wenner sees the song as a 'direct descendant' of 'With God On Our Side', with Dylan giving the warning that it will be the 'Apocalypse soon if you don't watch out'. Dylan has taken the general tone of 'With God On Our Side' but 'now the idea is developed with a stridency that makes for maximum discomfort and maximum rock n roll'.

The musical path taken by Dylan has from the very start been scattered with not only biblical references (e.g. the Witmark demo 'Long Ago, Far Away', later covered by Odetta), but with very stark allusions to personal and at times global demise. As early as 1962 and the writing of 'Let Me Die In My Footsteps' Dylan is both contemplating and mentally preparing for his own death. Not always the harmonic musings of a young man barely out of his teens. Throughout his career Dylan will look to biblical language, even stories, but he will also, through songs such as 'Desolation Row', 'A Hard Rain's A-Gonna Fall' and—more optimistically—'When The Ship Comes In', focus his songwriting mind to the end of days. By the end of the 70s Dylan is focused fully upon the Bible and its message, and with the ability to summon the biblical power of such forceful musicians and singers, his finger is fully pointing at the listener. Our own personal salvation is no longer a lyrical conversation piece. It is a straightforward question… Saved, yes or no? 'I'll see you, maybe, on Judgment Day', he answers in 2020's 'My Own Version of You'.

The album version of 'Gonna Change My Way of Thinking' had the benefit of an exceptionally strong musical line up behind Dylan, notably the English guitarist Mark Knopfler and the backing of the Muscle Shoals horns that were a fabulous backdrop for Dylan. There was also the most harmonious of gospel singers in Carolyn Dennis, who was to crop up later in the story as Mrs. Dylan, Helena Springs and Regina Havis. However, as with most of the songs from this three-year period, the story really began when they were taken on the road.

When the tour of 1979 was due to begin, Dylan had two rather critical choices. Firstly, Mark Knopfler had other commitments so couldn't play guitar. Dylan was fortunate enough to be able to get the criminally underrated Fred Tackett, who is best known for his work with the band Little Feat. Tackett was able to reproduce the Knopfler guitar sound where needed but also brought a classy, understated sound which suited many of the songs. The second choice was brought about due to lack of resources... Dylan couldn't take both the horns and the girls on tour. He very wisely chose the girls.

With one of the finest Dylan musical ensembles, Tim Drummond on Bass and Jim Keltner on drums forming one of the best possible rhythm sections, Willie Smith or Spooner Oldham on keyboards and the exquisite gospel chorus of, at various times, Carolyn Dennis, Helena Springs, Regina Havis, Regina McCrary, Mona Lisa Young, Madelyn Quebec, 'Gonna Change My Way of Thinking' was a stalwart of the 1979 tour.

The song had the best possible start on the road: from the 1st November 1979, fourteen almost consecutive nights at the Fox Warfield in San Francisco where it was finely honed by Dylan and ensemble. The song would travel throughout the country with Dylan as his onstage evangelical rants became longer and somewhat distracting to the secular fan. On the following tours Dylan added a general mixture of 'Christian' era songs and 'Greatest Hits'. Throughout this time touring, the fine musicians with Dylan just got better, slicker, attaining a live musical sound that has rarely been bettered in the history of popular music. Whilst the increasingly longer onstage preaching may have garnered the headlines, the music and particularly the largely ever-present 'Gonna Change My Way of Thinking' hit very new musical heights.

Although over time and over live touring the song was slowed a little from its original barnstorming pace and the lyrics were changed (but never really watered down), 'Gonna Change My Way of Thinking' survived well beyond the three 'Christian' years. After the 1979 tour, the song popped up again on a US tour in 1988 to then be taken, and to open, in Tokyo, Vietnam, Hong Kong, London. Many years later in a setlist of largely greatest hits it was the opening number in China at the Beijing Workers Gymnasium. The song also kicked off a concert in Tel Aviv. 'Gonna Change My Way of Thinking', possibly one of the most directly evangelical songs from that era, was not only the only one to often survive on tour, played an impressive 85 times, but had surreptitiously made its way on to the 'Greatest Hits' setlist.

In 2003 Dylan was due to duet the song with Mavis Staples (as outlined in *Rolling Stone* magazine of 9th May 2016). Mavis Staples says that 'I remember in the song there's a line that says "I'm so hungry I could eat a horse" I said to Bobby, "I'm not singing this". He goes (gravelly voice) "OK, Mavis, I'll sing that, I don't think I've ever gotten so hungry I could eat a horse".' This is a song that is dear to the heart of Dylan, even if the lyrics are more blues than Bob.

'Gonna Change My Way of Thinking' is a Dylan song that has stood to the test of time and secular scrutiny very well. It is clear that, even now, it is a song that Dylan feels is important. If you're ever looking for a Dylan quiz question then you might not do better than this... What do the following Dylan songs have in common? 'Hurricane', 'Changing Of The Guards', 'Isis', 'Idiot Wind', 'Chimes of Freedom', 'Dignity', 'Mississippi', 'Queen Jane Approximately'? Not one of these songs has been played more times live by Dylan than 'Gonna Change My Way of Thinking'.

Bob Dylan at Massey Hall, Toronto, 18th April 1980 (Photograph by Jean-Luc Ourlin, licensed under the Creative Commons Attribution-Share Alike 2.0 Generic license CC-BY-SA 2.0).

Jean-Charles Khalifa

Have Times Changed?
A Corpus Comparison Between 20th- and 21st-Century Dylan

Words, words, words... (W. Shakespeare, *Hamlet*, II, 2)

The words fill my head / And fall to the floor. (Bob Dylan, 'With God on Our Side')[1]

This short essay picks up where Khalifa (2007) left off. Indeed, my purpose in the earlier study was 'to apply some of the tools of linguistics, especially corpus linguistics, to the songs recorded by Dylan... and... see if the findings can teach us something about his artistry' (Khalifa 2007, 1). The corpus of songs I used at the time covered the period 1962–2001. So, when Prof. Sandis did me the honour of inviting me to contribute to this volume, I took it as a golden opportunity to use the very same concordance and the very same methodology and find out what they might reveal on the 2001–2020 corpus of songs.[1]

---

[1]   For lack of space, we must refer the interested reader to Khalifa (2007) (available online) for details on methodology and earlier findings. In this paper, one-third the length of the 2007 one, we will not be able to get into such details as modal auxiliaries, latinate vs. Germanic vocabulary, and so on. Understandably, since we only include original Dylan lyrics in the database and only six original albums were released during this period, the 21st-century corpus (henceforth D-21) is more than four times smaller (25,000 words vs. 110,000) than the 20th-century corpus (henceforth D-20), which makes statistical conclusions somewhat more tentative.

The Bard of Hibbing turning 80 this year, the idea was to find out whether there had been any shifts or drifts in his underlying, unthought themes, as reflected in frequencies and patterns in his lexicon and syntax. As in the 2007 study, we will start with **nouns**, which typically refer to objects/entities of the world.

Dylan 21th-century Corpus			Dylan 20th-century Corpus			C.O.C.A.	
1. day	96	(3,840)	1. man	425	(3,825)	1. time	(1,799)
2. love	76	(3,040)	2. time	392	(3,528)	2. year	(1,810)
3. heart	75	(3,000)	3. baby	364	(3,276)	3. people	(1,626)
4. thing	65	(2,600)	4. love	254	(2,286)	4. way	(1,106)
5. night	61	(2,440)	5. night	232	(2,088)	5. day	(1,018)
6. way	54	(2,160)	6. day	210	(1,890)	6. man	(964)
7. town	51	(2,040)	7. heart	182	(1,638)	7. thing	(942)
8. baby	50	(2,000)	8. eye	172	(1,548)	8. woman	(803)
9. man	48	(1,920)	9. mind	149	(1,341)	9. life	(783)
10. time	46	(1,840)	10. lord	143	(1,287)	10. child	(785)

Table 1: Nouns

The most spectacular change in noun frequencies is undoubtedly that the #1 in D-20, i.e. MAN, is down to #9 in D-21, its relative frequency more than halved. What is more, in D-20 its distribution showed that its use was overwhelmingly **generic** (i.e. whether we have *a man, one man* or *men,* what Dylan is actually referring to is MANKIND). The best-known example of this being, obviously:

> [1] / How many roads must **a man** walk down / Before you call him **a man**? /
> // How many times must **a man** look up / Before he can see the sky? (Blowin' in the Wind)

In D-21, by contrast, a majority of *man/men* seem to be **specific**, i.e. referring to a single individual, with typical examples like:

> [2] Ain't talkin', just walkin' / Carrying **a dead man's shield** ('Ain't Talkin'')
> [3] I'm **a man** of contradictions and **a man** of many moods ('I Contain Multitudes')

Dylan thus seems to be drifting away from speaking in the name of others, in favour of increasingly introspective writing; this might appear contradictory with the official rationale for the Nobel Prize ('to those who, during the preceding year, shall have conferred the greatest benefit on mankind'), but it is worth remembering that the poet/songwriter was mainly distinguished in 2015 on the basis of his earlier work.

Just a few words of comment on other significant changes between D-21 and D-20. In the more recent corpus, item #1 is now DAY, which was only #6 in D-20. Its frequency has almost doubled, significantly to almost four times its frequency in our reference corpus[2] (see table). Given the fact that the frequency of NIGHT, even though its ranking is stable at #5, has nonetheless increased by about 20%, we may venture the assumption that the passing of time may have become a major obsession for the poet, as in:

[4] A good **day** to be living and a good **day** to die ('Murder Most Foul')

One major change we noticed is the way Dylan combines nouns to create novel images. Indeed, in D-20 we found that the bulk of his creativeness lay not in the 'Germanic-type' N Ø N combinations (e.g. *charcoal gipsy maidens* ('Blind Willie McTell'), *corpse evangelists / confusion boats* ('My Back Pages')), but in the 'Romance-type', N OF N combinations (e.g. *the pockets of chance / bordertowns of despair* ('Dignity'); *King of the streets, child of clay* ('Joey'); *the tombstones of damage* ('Ballad in Plain D'); *the crossroads of my doorstep* ('One Too Many Mornings')).

In D-21, however, we find comparatively even fewer N Ø N combinations, and all of them are highly conventionalised (e.g. *a union man* ('Cry a While'), *sharkskin suits / top hats* ('Early Roman Kings')); as for the N OF N type, even though they are also comparatively, albeit not significantly, less numerous, they are also mostly conventionalised (e.g. *I sing songs of love – I sing songs of betrayal* ('False Prophet') or *I'm a man of contradictions* ('I Contain Multitudes')); in comparison to D-20, we find significantly fewer flamboyant images, which we analysed as 'Dylan inventing and piling up layers upon layers of signification, for a genuine idiosyncratic effect'. Some examples are worth mentioning, however: *the*

---

2   Our 'reference corpus' is the one-billion-word C.O.C.A. (Corpus of Contemporary American English, available online). For each column, unbracketed figures are absolute, and bracketed figures are to be read as number of occurrences *per million words*, which is the standard metric in corpus linguistics. Of course, the two Dylan corpora being a lot smaller than one million words, figures had to be extrapolated, but they remain, in our view, significant enough for our analysis.

highway of regret ('Make You Feel My Love'), *the lonely graveyard of my mind* ('Can't Wait'), *In the courtyard of the golden sun* ('Narrow Way').

The same goes for similes & comparisons using *like*, which were very productive in D-20, and turn out to be less frequent and flamboyant, apart from only a few examples:

[5] Big white clouds **like chariots that swing down low** ('High-lands')

[6] My woman got a face **like a teddy bear** ('Honest with Me')

[7] **Like a walking shadow in my brain** ('Forgetful Heart')

Let us now take a quick look at lexical verbs:[3]

Dylan 21st-century Corpus			Dylan 20th-century Corpus			C.O.C.A.		
1. go	136	(5,440)	1. go	749	(6,741)	1. say		(4,506)
2. say	128	(5,120)	2. know	616	(5,544)	2. go		(2,708)
3. know	101	(4,040)	3. see	476	(4,284)	3. get		(2,335)
4. come	99	(3,960)	4. come	445	(4,005)	4. make		(2,016)
5. see	96	(3,840)	5. say	385	(3,465)	5. know		(2,100)
6. play	82	(3,280)	6. tell	298	(2,682)	6. think		(1,818)
7. make	71	(2,840)	7. make	259	(2,331)	7. take		(1,578)
8. tell	65	(2,600)	8. think	252	(2,268)	8. see		(1,561)
9. look	60	(2,400)	9. want	243	(2,187)	9. come		(1,478)
10. keep	55	(2,200)	10. look	233	(2,097)	10. want		(1,211)

Table 2: Lexical Verbs

As in the previous study, nothing really stands out here, most of the items being the same in both lists and the same as the top 10 in C.O.C.A. Two notable exceptions are to be found in D-21: PLAY (#6), but it is clearly an outlier here, 75% of the occurrences being in one song only, i.e. 2020's 'Murder Most Foul', where it is used as a rhetorical device. The second exception is KEEP, which is four times as frequent as in C.O.C.A. and more than twice as frequent as in D-20 (where the verb is far down the list); it is mainly used as a semi-auxiliary indicating ongoing action, as in:

[8] I look away, but I **keep** seeing it // I don't want to believe, but I **keep** believing it ('This Dream of You')

If we add that a verb like WANT, which featured prominently in D-20, is still, but hardly so, in the top 20 in D-21, but with a frequency that is

---

3   The verb GET has been ignored, as it is mostly used as an auxiliary.

almost halved, would it be far-fetched, or maybe over-simplistic, to link all of this to our previous remark about the inexorable passing of time?

Let us now turn to adjectives, which do look a lot more significant to analyse.

Dylan 21st-century Corpus			Dylan 20th-century Corpus			C.O.C.A.	
1. good	78	(3,120)	1. good	138	(1,242)	1. other	(1,288)
2. long	42	(1,680)	2. little	136	(1,224)	2. new	(1,025)
3. hard	31	(1,240)	3. old	118	(1,062)	3. good	(832)
4. black	29	(1,160)	4. hard	116	(1,044)	4. high	(602)
5. last	26	(1,040)	5. new	99	(891)	5. old	(556)
6. high	24	(960)	6. true	99	(891)	6. great	(529)
7. dark	23	(920)	7. last	97	(873)	7. big	(534)
8. other	22	(880)	8. dead	84	(756)	8. American	(505)
9. wrong	21	(840)	9. high	83	(747)	9. small	(436)
10. dead	17	(640)	10. far	79	(711)	10. large	(413)

Table 3: Adjectives

Even if the top 10 items (see Table 3 in appendix) have nothing rare or uncommon (almost all of them being in the top 25 adjectives in C.O.C.A.), what is striking is that almost all of them carry sombre, negative meanings or connotations; as it turns out, GOOD, which is #1 in D-21 as in D-20, is no exception. Indeed, in D-21, a good third of occurrences are accounted for by one song only,[4] and when we look closely at the rest of them, we do find quite a few associations such as:

[9] …from the mouth, he's as **good** as dead ('Tin Angel')

[10] …tell my heart that you're **no good** ('Honest with Me')

DEAD was already prominent in D-20 (frequencies are comparable in both corpora), and it would be hard to miss the fact that, together with the new ones which have made their way to the top of the list in D-21, i.e. BLACK, DARK and WRONG, the overall inner picture they paint is at least quite stark:

[11] The world has gone **black** before my eyes ('Nettie Moore')

[12] The **dead** bells are ringing / My train is overdue ('Can't Escape from You')

[13] What are these **dark** days I see in this world so badly bent ('Crossing the Rubicon')

[14] I think I must be travelin' **wrong** ('Rollin' and Tumblin')

---

4   i.e., unsurprisingly, 'It's All Good', where it is repeated all through the song.

And of course, the same goes for LONG,[5] overwhelmingly used in examples such as:

[15] Peace may he know / His **long** night is done ('Cross the Green Mountain')

[16] It's a **long** way down and I don't want to be forced / Into a life of continual crime ('Workingman's Blues #2')

Once, not too long ago, I received an email out of the clear blue from the (in)famous Alan J. Weberman, who, having read my 2007 paper, quite bluntly asked me what my conclusion was about Dylan's syntax and semantics. I just replied that 'Dylan' and 'conclusion' were mutually rather incompatible. And indeed, there are only two occurrences of 'conclusion' in the entire Dylan corpus, both of which date from the mid-60s (Dylan never mentioned the word again), and both being, in context, sneerful of the concept itself.[6]

In Khalifa (2007) I suggested that my corpus analysis was but a stepping stone. In this much shorter paper, there is all the more reason not to venture any definite judgments. What follows, therefore, is by no means to be taken as a conclusion, only as a humble opinion: to return to the title of this paper, of course times have changed, and changed dramatically. Years and decades have flown past, things have gone dark and the poet's mood has become a lot less sanguine and mercurial, to the point, paradoxically, of no longer desiring **change** itself. Indeed, one striking finding in the verb category, not to be found in Table 2 which only shows the top 10 items, is that the verb CHANGE itself, which was in the top 20 in D-20, is hardly to be found at all in D-21, only a handful of occurrences all together. And everything that emerges in the quantitative and qualitative analysis of the 21st-century Dylan corpus seems to converge naturally towards one song: the 17-minute 'Murder Most Foul', the last and longest of his recorded songs to date, and which, with its dirge-

---

[5] Note that, for LONG as well as HARD, adjectival and adverbial uses have been lumped together.

[6] 'In the dime stores and bus stations / People talk of situations / Read books, repeat quotations / Draw **conclusions** on the wall' ('Love Minus Zero/No Limit') and 'When all of your advisers heave their plastic / At your feet to convince you of your pain / Trying to prove that your **conclusions** should be more drastic' ('Queen Jane Approximately').

like delivery and conjuring up of classic and pop culture icons, I interpreted in a radio interview[7] as 'a Kaddish [the Jewish prayer for the dead] for America and perhaps for himself'.

Singing 'The Times They Are A-Changin'' during the In Performance *At The White House: A Celebration Of Music From The Civil Rights Movement* concert in the East Room of the White House, 9th February 2010 (Official White House Photo by Pete Souza, public domain).

---

7   Interview on *Radio France International* (*RFI*), 19th June 2020.

Lucas Hare

Turning Back the Clock
Bob Dylan's Modern Times

A quarter of a century ago, Bob Dylan emerged as if to announce the beginning of his astonishing second act. On 19th November 1995, at the Shrine Auditorium in Los Angeles, Dylan performed an old man's song that he'd written when he was barely at the legal drinking age. At 54, he'd been asked by Frank Sinatra to sing 'Restless Farewell' at a televised concert to celebrate Sinatra's 80th birthday. It had been six years since his latest 'return to form' and five since he'd written a song: Dylan's stock was low in the early 1990s. The era has its defenders — Supper Club lovers, feel free to stop reading now — but for me, it was a depressing time to be a fan. He seemed well past his best: the songwriting had dried up, and there seemed to be no chance of his staging another critical come-back, of which *Oh Mercy* had been the most recent. But here he was, delivering a kind of testament: a song written when he was 22 that suddenly, three decades later, sounded very timely indeed.

> Oh, a false clock tries to tick out my time
> To disgrace, distract and bother me;
> And the dirt of gossip blows into my face
> And the dust of rumour covers me.
> But if the arrow is straight
> And the point is slick,
> It can pierce through dust no matter how thick;
> So I'll make my stand
> And remain as I am
> And I'll bid farewell, and not give a damn.

As he'd done time and time again, Dylan was redefining something. Over a decade older than Elvis Presley or John Lennon ever were—and having arguably invented the concept in 1965—Dylan was refashioning what it meant to be a rock star. On the verge of recording an album that most critics would assume was an ending, a summing-up, a last gasp, he was in fact gearing himself up for a new beginning. It is apt that this period was announced with a song that seemed to say farewell, but also refused to be defined by simple notions of time (a false clock, indeed). Perhaps his reusing of the phrase 'no matter how thick' in 'Most of the Time' had sent him back to this song; perhaps the key was Frank. But, for the first time in a while, it seemed possible to imagine the arrow rather than the dust. For me, this performance—and particularly that final verse—seems like an announcement: a declaration.

Before that, the clearest signs of a new Dylan stirring could be found in the liner notes for *World Gone Wrong*: 'ABOUT THE SONGS (what they're about).' After the complete lack of care or songwriting information that had accompanied his previous covers album *Good as I Been to You*, these notes gave due credit and were, to quote Nick Hasted, 'electrifying evidence that Dylan's mind was still fiercely alive behind the senile, befuddled tramp's mask he now put on in public'. Post *Oh Mercy*, it is impossible to tell whether Dylan was completely at sea or if he simply wanted the world to think that. To see him in, say, 1991 was for me a deflating experience: he appeared a washed-up has-been, doomed never to be taken seriously again. But the liner notes to *World Gone Wrong* are something else: articulate, incisive, witty, prescient (it seems shocking now to see that the words 'Technology to wipe out truth is now available' were written by someone in 1993). They contain all sorts of phrases that are of huge significance: 'Not being pushed around by ordinary standards, it's about revival, getting a new lease on life', 'No man gains immortality thru public acclaim', 'Rebellion against routine seems to be (the) strong theme', and the big one: 'Learning to go forward by turning back the clock, stopping the mind from thinking in hours, firing a few random shots at the face of time'—a manifesto, if ever there was one, for Dylan's late period. From here onwards, his sense of progress was not only flecked with a remembrance of things past, but it also questioned conventions of modernity. Dylan seemed like a washed-up gunfighter shooting at a clock face, seeing if he could make the hands move differently: he looked half asleep, but he could still hit every target with alarming precision. More than ever before, he spent these years inspired by—and specifically referring to—old songs, building something new and yet old from whatever bits he could find. By the time he revealed *Rough and Rowdy Ways* to a planet caught off its guard in 2020, the notion had become explicit—a songwriting ethos hiding in plain sight:

All through the summers and into January
I've been visiting morgues and monasteries
Looking for the necessary body parts
Limbs and livers and brains and hearts
I want to bring someone to life—is what I want to do
I want to create my own version of you

From 1993 onwards (at the time of writing, roughly the second half of his career), time was not so much a jet plane as a magic trick. You could sense Dylan restarting both the stopwatch and the journey. On *Time Out of Mind* (1997), movement and time are inextricably linked: songs sound like metronomes. He's walking. He hears the clock tick. He's seen too much. He's got new eyes. He wishes someone would push back the clock for him (at the time, listeners and critics honed straight in on the fatalistic musings of 'Not Dark Yet': its key, resigned phrase seeming to be 'It's not dark yet, but it's getting there'. And yet, the further we travelled from 1997, the less I heard that 'it's getting there' and the more I noticed that 'it's not dark *yet*'). 'Love Sick' sets up the time/movement idea with 'I'm walkin'' set to a tick-tock beat that's straight out of Fats Domino's 'Walking To New Orleans', or Irma Thomas's 'It's Raining'. As David Hepworth has pointed out, American songs are about moving in ways that those of us who live in smaller countries might have difficulty understanding. Movement is central to the songs on *Time Out of Mind*. Dylan's walking in the first two songs, but then he's left standing in the doorway, crying. It's when he *stops* moving that the problems start: 'Shadows are fallin' and I been here all day', 'I'm twenty miles out of town, in cold irons bound' and, in a song that he would save for his next album, 'I've been in trouble ever since I set my suitcase down'. He's trying to get closer, he's walking that lonesome valley and through the middle of nowhere; he'd go crawling down the avenue, he'd go to the ends of the Earth, he's going down the road feelin' bad; and, in arguably the most important journey of all, he's tryin' to get to heaven before they close the door.

The album's final word, and its perfect punchline, saw Dylan turning a song that was to a degree about indolence—'Highlands'—into a suggestion of rebirth, with its final, understated shrug, 'And that's good enough for now'. At the time, these could have served perfectly well as the last words he ever wrote, but—against all odds—he still had a few years' worth of fuel left in the tank. Dylan had written endings before, but it was with *Time Out of Mind* that he most pointedly inverted the expected ending of the fifty-something rock star. This was the sound of him making a stand and not giving a damn.

Back in December 1965, a journalist in San Francisco asked Dylan what his role was. He responded, 'My role is to stay here as long as I can.' As with his comments that same day about selling out to 'ladies' garments' and being a 'song and dance man', it was impossible to tell how serious he was being. But, well over half a century later, there was a truth to all those remarks to which no one would have given a second thought.

If you were inventing the narrative arc of Bob Dylan, you'd be forgiven for ending the story here (as Martin Scorsese did in *No Direction Home*). As he edged closer and closer towards self-destruction in May 1966, it seemed inevitable that he might go the way of Hank Williams: his heart given out in the back of a car; or of Eddie Cochran or Buddy Holly: taken by the perils of touring; or even, according to Robbie Robertson, in the bath—prefiguring the mysterious death of Jim Morrison. But none of these rock star endings came to pass. It seems to us now that, at some point in 1966 or 1967, Dylan decided that enough was enough and, in order to play the long game, things would have to change. Much has been said about the idyllic Woodstock years, but it wouldn't be the last time that Dylan jumped off the carousel. This time, as the century ebbed away, he seemed to be reborn with a new persona fully formed. Even in the video for 'Things Have Changed' in 2000, his last song of the 20th century, that character was immediately there: the cynical sage with the cane who's seen it all, but he has time to tell you all the things that he's still going to do. We got so used to this new Dylan so quickly that it is easy to forget how impossible it would have been to imagine him a decade or two earlier, recording with Ralph Stanley or Mavis Staples. Almost every act of progression now came with an implicit or explicit reference to the past: his next album *"Love And Theft"* opened and closed with sound-alikes of, respectively, Johnnie and Jack's 'Uncle John's Bongo's' and Gene Austin's 'The Lonesome Road', breathing new life into ancient American song at every turn in between. He released an album in 2006 called *Modern Times* that pointedly sounded like no such thing. And yet, it was a new kind of modernity: he looked timeless, like your hip grandfather dressed up for a Western swing party. He advertised iPods with a new song called 'Someday Baby' that owed more than a little to Sleepy John Estes' 'Someday Baby Blues', not to mention Muddy Waters' 'Trouble No More'. Over the next few years he would gleefully skip through very specific blues tributes, epic ballads taking their cue from songs like William and Versey Smith's 'When That Great Ship Went Down', and a jaw-dropping five CDs' worth of American standards; many of which had been originally sung by—and this is where we came in—Frank Sinatra. When he casually released 'Murder Most Foul' from behind that locked door in the spring of 2020, and an album of new songs three months later, it was as surprising as it was fitting. Precisely as he had in the 1990s, he'd filled a long break from songwriting with a kind of self-education: by going right back to the songs that inspired him as a younger man. And when he emerged it was with new lessons learned, ready to begin again.

F. Scott Fitzgerald famously observed that there are no second acts in American lives. Of the many conventions that Bob Dylan has defied, this might be the most significant. The second half of his career started at the point that many people thought was the end, when expectations were zero and he had nothing more to live up to. He reset the false clock, learned a new way of going forward, and created a new version of himself. Again. And that's good enough for now.

References

Fitzgerald, F. Scott (1932) *My Lost City* and (1941) in notes on *The Last Tycoon*.

Hasted, N. (2003) *Uncut Magazine: Legends #1*.

Hepworth, D. (2011) notes from *David Hepworth's playlist of 100 American songs about moving*.

John F. Kennedy (public domain, PD-USGOV).

Mick Gold

A Voice Without Restraint
Singing Smooth and Rowdy Ways

I'd like to draw attention to the different voices I hear on *Rough and Rowdy Ways*, the album that 79-year-old Bob Dylan released in June 2020. I was first captivated by Dylan's voice in the 1960s and I wasn't alone. Philip Larkin listened to *Highway 61 Revisited* and described his singing as 'cawing, derisive' (Larkin 1985, 151). For Joyce Carol Oates, the effect of his early recordings was 'as if sandpaper could sing' (Oates 2004, 259). Dylan could sound epic and declamatory ('A Hard Rain'), accusatory ('Who Killed Davey Moore?'), lyrical ('To Ramona'), stoned and far away ('Visions of Johanna') and even mindlessly happy ('Oh me Oh my, Love that country pie').

As Dylan aged, so did his vocal timbre. In the 1980s, Christophe Lebold heard: 'Dylan's more recent broken voice enables him to present a world view at the sonic surface of the songs—this voice carries us across the landscape of a broken, fallen world' (Lebold 2007, 65). Dylan's creative trajectory reached a strange hiatus between *Tempest* in 2012 and *Rough and Rowdy Ways* in 2020. An eight-year absence of original material was filled by an exploration of the musical world of Frank Sinatra, a surprising detour for a singer whose origins were in folk, blues and early rock'n'roll. Michael Gray pointedly wrote that Sinatra's 'musical world was the one rock'n'roll was born to abolish—that of the jazz-tinged crooner who emerged from the era of the Big Band' (Gray 2006, 615). When Bill Flanagan interviewed Dylan about the making of *Triplicate*, his triple album drawn from the Great American Songbook, Dylan described how Sinatra's material had inflected his vocal style in new ways: 'You don't want to be spitting the words out in a crude way. That would be unthinkable. The emphasis is different and there is no reason to force the vernacular. "An airline ticket to romantic places" is a contrasting type of phraseology, than, say, "bury my body by the highway side". The intonation is different, more circumspectual, more internal' (Flanagan 2017).

The result is an extended sonic universe on *Rough and Rowdy Ways*. A place where Dylan is comfortable harnessing the lilting 6/8 rhythm of the barcarolle from Offenbach's *The Tales of Hoffman* to 'I've Made Up My Mind to Give Myself to You'. The opening lines lull you into joining Dylan in his reverie: 'Sitting on my terrace lost in the stars / Listenin' to the sounds of the sad guitars / Been thinking it over and I thought it all through / I've made up my mind to give myself to you.' Yet the sweep of the lyrics suggests to me the 3,064 concerts Dylan has played (thus far) on his Never Ending Tour. Commencing in June 1988 and pausing in December 2019, as the Covid-19 pandemic silenced the concert halls of live music, Dylan's determination to treat the whole world as his stage is evoked by lines like 'I'm giving myself to you, I am / From Salt Lake City to Birmingham / From East L.A. to San Antone / I don't think I could bear to live my life alone.' In concert Dylan seems to take minimal notice of his audience. Here we are all included.

As has been widely noted, the opener 'I Contain Multitudes' echoes Walt Whitman and talk of multiple personalities suggests many Dylans: 'the voice of his generation' (*The Times They Are A-Changin'*), the surreal rock'n'roller (*Highway 61 Revisited*), the picaresque storyteller (*Blood on the Tracks*), the born-again Christian (*Saved*), the fabricator of mordant parables about mortality (*Time Out of Mind*). 'My Own Version of You' takes the multiple personalities into ghoulish, Gothic realms as the singer assembles the creature of his dreams from spare parts purloined from 'visiting morgues and monasteries'. The insidious energy of the guitar is complemented by a gleeful, gloating pride in Dylan's vocal as he anticipates the triumph of his experiment: 'I'll bring someone to life—balance the scales / I'm not gonna get involved in any insignificant details.' The process described (the Frankenstein-like assemblage of a person from spare parts) also parallels Dylan's recent songwriting technique of hurling disparate ingredients into the mix. As we shall see.

The most complete immersion in the blues on this album is 'Goodbye Jimmy Reed'. It is almost a hinge. After the complexity of the opening songs which deal with multiple personalities, 'Goodbye Jimmy Reed' is a kick of energy before the final four songs, which address themes of murder, death and the classical world. Reed was born in 1925 near Dunleith, Mississippi. His light but catchy voice scored twenty Top 20 hits in the *Billboard* R&B chart in the 1950s and early 60s, but like many blues-men of his generation Reed's success ended in poverty and premature death at the age of 50—from epilepsy and alcohol. The influence of Reed's distinctive harmonica can be heard on Dylan's playing on *Blonde on Blonde* (Gray 2006, 568) and this is the only song on *Rough and Rowdy Ways* where Dylan reaches for his harp. 'Goodbye Jimmy Reed' is pro-claimed in a blues shouting voice and the strutting rhythm suits the urgency of the sexual language: 'Transparent woman in a transparent dress / It suits you well—I must confess / I'll break open your grapes I'll suck out the juice / I need you like my head needs a noose.'

But this doffing of the hat to a veteran blues singer is odd; it unexpectedly connects the listener to the sectarian landscape of Northern Ireland. 'I live on a street named after a Saint / Women in the churches wear powder and paint / Where the Jews and the Catholics and the Muslims all pray / I can tell a Proddy from a mile away.' Derek Barker has suggested that the language of this song is heavily indebted to a biography of Van Morrison by Johnny Rogan, *No Surrender*, published in 2006. Rogan's book contains many images and phrases which find their way into 'Goodbye Jimmy Reed': Catholics in Belfast went to schools named after saints whereas Protestants attended schools named after streets; chapter 21 of Rogan's book is titled 'Are you a Proddy?'; the Protestant version of the Lord's Prayer contains the line 'for thine is the kingdom, the power and the glory' which is absent from the Catholic version; Morrison's early band, The Monarchs, developed their show-manship when they began to play guitars behind their heads; 'thump on the Bible and proclaim a creed' leads to Barker pointing out that 'Rogan's book questions if Van Morrison's incantatory singing style is related to Ian Paisley's Bible thumping' (Barker 2021, 22-4). The shouted doxology of 'the power and the glory' fits surprisingly well with the bluesy exuberance of the song.

All this is a vivid example of intertextuality, Dylan's technique of dropping images and phrases from disparate sources into his own writing. Examples have included fragments of the novel *Confessions of a Yakuza* found in *"Love And Theft"*, the poetry of Henry Timrod in *Modern*

Times and the appearances of Ovid in *Modern Times* (Thomas 2017, 196–9, 234–6, 240–1).

On *Rough and Rowdy Ways* Dylan animates classical landscapes with the urgency of R&B, as if Orpheus's lyre had plugged into a Chicago blues club. 'Crossing the Rubicon' is an exploration of the moment when Julius Caesar transgressed the rule of the Roman republic and led his army across the fateful boundary. Dylan calls the Rubicon the 'Red River', which summons up associations with the Kingston Trio's 'she's the one I adore, she's the one I will marry on the Red River shore' and also the elusive girl from the Red River shore Dylan searches for on *Tell Tale Signs*, who seems to be a ghost, a vanished lover he can never find again unless he has the help of 'a guy who lived a long time ago / A man full of sorrow and strife' who knew how to bring the dead back to life.

John Lee Hooker guitar lines underscore the dogged conviction of Dylan's voice. At the end of each verse he piles up details to suggest both honouring old customs and breaking away. As R.F. Thomas has noted, these images are worth isolating: 'I painted my wagon, abandoned all hope'; 'I prayed to the cross, I kissed the girls'; 'I embraced my love, put down my hair'; 'I pawned my watch, I paid my debts'; 'I poured the cup, I passed it along'; 'I stood between heaven and earth'; 'I'll strap my belt, I'll button my coat'; 'I turned the key and broke it off'; 'I lit the torch, I looked to the east.' Each suggests a decisive break, its drama only heightened by the final 'And I crossed the Rubicon' (Thomas 2020, 55). To which I will add there's a marvellous moment (after 'it's darkest 'fore the dawn' at 5:24) where Dylan sobs 'Oh Lord' as if overwhelmed by awe or terror.

'Key West' could be described as Dylan's version of 'Over the Rainbow', an evocation of other-worldly transcendence, sustained by a lovely melody on Donnie Herron's accordion. The song begins with a quote from 'White House Blues', recorded by Charlie Poole (1926) about the assassination of President McKinley. Poole's version is urgent, violent: 'McKinley hollered—McKinley squalled / Doc said to McKinley, I can't find that ball.' Dylan slows it down to a death-bed reverie: 'McKinley hollered—McKinley squalled / Doctor said McKinley—death is on the wall / Say it to me if you got something to confess'[1] as he departs for some enchanted land, perhaps borne aloft on pirate radio waves broadcasting from Luxemburg and Budapest.

The landscape of *Rough and Rowdy Ways* is vast, looking back more than 2,000 years to the cradle of western culture. 'Mother of Muses sing for me' is an invocation of the goddess of memory Mnemosyne who slept with Zeus in order to give birth to the nine muses. Appropriately, Dylan has his eye on Calliope, the muse of epic poetry, and this double album ends with a 17-minute journey through the traumatic events of 22nd November 1963.

I find it hard to banish thoughts of William McGonagall when I hear 'Twas a dark day in Dallas—November '63' and yet the imagery of 'Murder Most Foul' emphasises the grisly details of that day: 'they blew off his head', 'shot down like a dog', 'they blew out the brains of the king', 'they mutilated his body and they took out his brain'. Zapruder's film is described as the 'ugliest thing that you ever have seen'. The voice that sings/recites this strange catalogue of traumas and musical aftershocks is hypnotic, maybe hypnotised or shocked by the tale he tells. Almost devoid of melody, a bowed bass, three keyboards and a drummer swirl in eddies around the vocal. Dylan acknowledges that The Beatles' arrival in February 1964 helped to ease the pain of Kennedy's assassination and also prepared the way for subsequent 1960s convulsions: 'The Beatles are comin', they're gonna hold your hand / Slide down the banister, go get your coat / Ferry across the Mersey and go for the throat.' As the musical memories mount up, they feel disparate, almost arbitrary. 'Play John Lee Hooker play Scratch My Back / Play it for that strip club owner named Jack / Guitar Slim—Goin' Down Slow / Play it for me and for Marilyn Monroe / And please, Don't Let Me Be Misunderstood / Play it for the First Lady, she ain't feeling that good.' Our pop memories have become bandages over all this hurt. The flag fluttering over this republic is the Blood Stained Banner. The song becomes the nightmare of American history from which we cannot awake—with only one exit available. 'Hate to tell you, Mister, but only dead men are free.' There's something

---

[1] 'White House Blues', folk tune, revised and arranged by Charlie Poole and the North Carolina Ramblers (1926).

sepulchral about the way Dylan intones the last line which adds his new song to this long lineage of musical history: 'play Murder Most Foul.'

References

Barker, D. (2021) Jimmy Reed indeed, *Isis*, issue 211.

Flanagan, B. (2017) Q&A with Bill Flanagan, *BobDylan.com*, [Online], https://bobdylan.com/news/qa-with-bill-flanagan/

Gray, M. (2006) *The Bob Dylan Encyclopedia*, London: Continuum.

Larkin, P. (1985) *All What Jazz: A Record Diary*, London: Faber and Faber.

Lebold, C. (2007) A face like a mask and a voice that croaks: An integrated poetics of Bob Dylan's voice personae, and lyrics, *Oral Tradition*, 22 (1).

Oates, J.C. (2004) Joyce Carol Oates, in Hedin B. (ed.) *Studio A: The Bob Dylan Reader*, New York: W.W. Norton.

Thomas, R. (2017) *Why Dylan Matters*, London: William Collins.

Thomas, R. (2020) And I Crossed the Rubicon: Another classical Dylan, *Dylan Review 2.1*.

Bob Dylan and his band, Oslo Spectrum 30th March 2007 (photograph by Tore Utheim, licensed under the Creative Commons Attribution-Share Alike 3.0 Unported license. CC-BY-SA 2.0).

Laura Tenschert

A Love So True
Bob Dylan is Giving Himself to the Muse

The heart of Bob Dylan's latest album *Rough and Rowdy Ways* is the song 'I've Made Up My Mind to Give Myself to You', which is the closest the album comes to having a straightforward love song, something akin in emotional intensity to *Time Out of Mind*'s 'Make You Feel My Love'. But compared to Dylan's earlier ballad, 'I've Made Up My Mind' is firmly anchored in certainty; there is no mention of a time when the singer '[hadn't] made [his] mind up yet'. Instead, the song begins with the moment of reflection and contemplation that leads to his decision ('I'm sittin' on my terrace, lost in the stars / Been thinking it over and I thought it all through / I've made up my mind to give myself to you'). The choice is intuitive; there's no reason or justification given ('I don't think that anyone else ever knew' and 'No one ever told me, it's just something I knew'). Unlike in yet another Dylan song with a similar theme, 'Got My Mind Made Up' from *Knocked Out Loaded*, where the singer is offering actual and social currency ('I gave you all my money, All my connections too / There ain't nothin' in this world, girl / You can say I didn't give to you'), the singer in 'I've Made Up My Mind' is freely giving no more, no less than himself.

So who is Dylan devoting himself to? The passive 'you' is no further defined, we don't find out what they look like, or how the singer feels about them, which suggests that this is a different kind of love song than 'Make You Feel My Love'. One important theme in this song is travel ('From Salt Lake City to Birmingham / From East L.A. to San Antone', 'From the plains to the prairies / From the mountains to the sea' [on the album he sings: 'I've travelled from the mountains to the sea']), which is described sometimes as a conscious venturing out in the company of others ('Take me out traveling you're a traveling man',[1] 'I'll go far away from home with her'), other times as a solitary venture ('I traveled the long road of despair, I met no other traveler there'). But either way, the travel theme is continuously punctuated by the refrain, suggesting that it is the act of devotion that either motivates or necessitates the travel. Considering Bob Dylan has literally dedicated more than three decades to being a travelling performer on the Never Ending Tour, playing for fans all over the world, could Dylan be declaring that he's giving himself – to his audience?

Rough and Rowdy Ways is a remarkably personal album, in which we see Bob Dylan reflecting on his own persona, his career and his work, so in that context, it's not too abstruse that Dylan might dedicate a love song to his fans. But what if the song was addressed to a certain figure who has played an important role in the genesis of these songs, going back to before the album's inception? Please allow me to make my case for why I think Bob Dylan is using this song to proclaim that he is giving himself to the Muse!

In 2016, Bob Dylan became the first ever popular songwriter to receive the Nobel Prize in Literature. I believe that this extraordinary honour inspired the new album, which grapples with themes related to Dylan's identity as an artist and as a public figure, and explores the importance of songs in our personal and cultural histories (a topic Dylan first took up in his Nobel lecture).[2] This connection between Dylan's Nobel win and *Rough and Rowdy Ways* is nowhere more palpable than in the recurring figure of the Muse: when Bob Dylan received his Nobel medal and diploma in a secret ceremony in April 2017, Sara Danius, then the secretary of the Swedish Academy, reported that Dylan spent 'quite a bit of time... looking closely at the gold medal', which depicts the poet and the Muse. Clearly, this image stayed on Dylan's mind, since two months

---

[1]   I'm assuming this is not the same 'you' addressed in the refrain, although it wouldn't be the first time Dylan addresses a man (that isn't Jesus) in a love song: back in 2018, he recorded a version of 'He's Funny That Way' for the LGBTQ+ themed compilation *Universal Love*.

[2]   This is of course assuming these songs don't date back further than 2016 or 2017.

later he closed his Nobel lecture with the beginning lines of the Odyssey: 'I return once again to Homer, who says, "Sing in me, oh Muse, and through me tell the story"'. *Rough and Rowdy Ways*, an album that is a standout even among Bob Dylan's back catalogue, is evidence that the Muse answered his call, and, in these songs, Dylan's infatuation with the idea of the Muse has been translated into a reciprocal relationship.

In order to understand the role the song 'I've Made Up My Mind to Give Myself to You' plays in this relationship, it is important to note that love appears mostly as an abstract concept on *Rough and Rowdy Ways*, something the singer is either striving for or singing about ('I sing songs of love, I sing songs of betrayal', 'I'd preach the gospel, the gospel of love', 'If I survive then let me love'). Significantly, the only explicit love interest that we encounter on the entire album is the Muse. And not just any of the nine Muses: on 'Mother of Muses', the singer confesses, 'I'm falling in love with Calliope.' As the Muse of epic poetry, it was Calliope whom Dylan was addressing via Homer at the end of his Nobel lecture, and it is possibly also her who is pictured holding her attribute the lyre on the Nobel medal. The singer is falling in love with inspiration personified, which is a theme that reappears two songs later on 'Key West (Philosopher Pirate)', where the singer is 'searching for love, for inspiration on that pirate radio station'.

Let's stay with 'Mother of Muses' for a moment, a key song in which several of the record's thematic strands run together, and which also contains several lyrical echoes of 'I've Made Up My Mind' ('I've traveled from the mountains to the sea' is echoed in 'sing of the mountains and the deep dark sea'; likewise 'I lay down beside you when everyone's gone' echoed in 'Let me lay down in your sweet, loving arms'). 'Mother of Muses' revolves around an invocation that recalls the end of Dylan's Nobel lecture, but here it is modified to address the Titaness Mnemosyne, goddess of memory and mother of the nine Muses. While the traditional invocation of the Muse is asking for inspiration, the singer here is instead asking Mnemosyne to help him recall and remember, a process crucial for an artist like Dylan, whose creativity is so deeply rooted in traditional songs.[3] Through this act of remembering, the singer hopes to gain access to inspiration, pleading with Calliope's mother, 'she don't belong to anyone, why not give her to me?' It might not be the most romantic of gestures, the wish to possess the object of your affection, but this line takes on a different tone if we see it in connection with, and as counterpart to, the act of devotion that occurs on 'I've Made Up My Mind'. Inspiration 'don't belong to anyone', and can therefore only be found through a reciprocal act—it is given to those that are willing to give themselves.

However, the most intriguing argument for why I believe that Dylan is declaring his devotion to the Muse in 'I've Made Up My Mind' is beautifully subtle, subliminal, yet hidden in plain sight. Out of the numerous borrowings Bob Dylan has included on *Rough and Rowdy Ways*, the music for 'I've Made Up My Mind' was very quickly identified as being based on the *Barcarolle*, or *Belle nuit, ô nuit d'amour* ('Beautiful night, oh night of love'), the gondolier's song from the late 19th-century *opéra fantastique The Tales of Hoffmann* by German-born Jewish French composer Jacques Offenbach. Dylan leaves this sweeping melody to the musicians and the humming choir, while his own melody and lyrics freely float above it. The opera *Tales of Hoffmann* is based on three short stories by the German Romantic writer E.T.A. Hoffmann, which are placed within a frame narrative, in which the character of Hoffmann himself is telling his audience at a tavern in Nuremberg the stories of the three loves of his life, which are eventually exposed to be representations of different sides to one woman: his real-life love, Stella. At the beginning of the opera, we meet the Muse of poetry, who addresses the audience to reveal that it is her purpose to make Hoffmann abjure all earthly loves so he can be devoted only to her, and therefore to his art. So in a sense, the opera opens with an inverted invocation of the Muse, by having the Muse herself speak. She then takes the form of Hoffmann's best friend for most of the opera, and only reveals her true identity at the end of the three narrations, when the writer decides to swear off all earthly love. The Muse urges Hoffmann to instead dedicate himself only to her, exclaiming: 'Be reborn

---

3   For more on this, listen to chapter 2 of my *Definitely Dylan* podcast on *Rough and Rowdy Ways*, in which I discuss the themes of creation and creativity in 'My Own Version of You' and 'Mother of Muses'.

a poet! I love you, Hoffmann! Be mine!'[4] As they sing together, Hoffmann, enchanted, ends up rejecting Stella, the love of his life, in favour of the Muse, singing: 'Muse, whom I love, I am yours!'[5] In other words, the opera ends with the poet having made up his mind to give himself to the Muse.[6]

Bob Dylan and the Muse go way back. As a young man he became fascinated with *The White Goddess* (1948), Robert Graves' book on 'the psychological and mythological sources of poetry', as it is described on the official Dylan website, where it is still listed as a 'book of interest'. Back then, as Dylan writes in *Chronicles Vol. 1,* 'invoking the poetic muse was something I didn't know about yet. Didn't know enough to start trouble with it anyway' (Dylan 2004). Graves' influence can be traced in many of Dylan's songs in which inspiration is drawn from the deification of a woman ('Love Minus Zero/No Limit', 'Visions of Johanna', 'Isis'), but on *Rough and Rowdy Ways,* Dylan's love for the ancient world has culminated in a new kind of relationship with the Muse, in which she takes on the role of an earthly love interest, like at the end of Offenbach's *Tales of Hoffmann.*

As in the opera, what a dedication to the Muse really symbolises is a dedication to one's art, and *Rough and Rowdy Ways,* Bob Dylan's first album of original songs in eight years, certainly comes across as a reaffirmation, a reminder that he is still capable of creating the kind of art that gained him the Nobel Prize. But did we really need a reminder that Bob Dylan has fully devoted himself to his art? The Never Ending Tour, which has thus far spanned more than a third of his life, sees Dylan spending the majority of his time on the road (at least when there isn't a

---

4   *'Renais poète! Je t'aime, Hoffmann! Appartiens-moi!'* in the original French libretto by Jules Barbier.
5   It's worth noting that this detail does not appear in the original French libretto, but is described on the *Tales of Hoffmann* Wikipedia page, a source that might not be acceptable in academic circles, but is one that Bob Dylan himself, who is not above quoting study guides, might have come across.
6   If this hidden layer of meaning strikes you as too obscure to possibly be a conscious decision on Dylan's part, then I'd like to remind you that *Rough and Rowdy Ways* is littered with Easter eggs like this (such as Dylan's use of the *CliffsNotes* summary for *Frankenstein* in 'My Own Version of You'), as if Bob Dylan was anticipating that fans and scholars would be pouring over every minute detail.

pandemic going on), travelling from performance to performance, with the certainty and discipline of someone who made up his mind a long time ago. Luckily for us, Dylan's commitment to the Muse feels a lot like a commitment to his audience.

References

Dylan, B. (2004) *Chronicles: Volume One*, London: Simon & Schuster.
Graves, R. (1948) *The White Goddess*, London: Faber and Faber.

Laura Tenschert (photograph by Steve Paul).

Constantine Sandis

Dylan's Own Version of Us
('n Our Own Version of Dylan)

I don't see myself as covering these songs in any way. They've been covered enough. Buried, as a matter a fact. What me and my band are basically doing is uncovering them. Lifting them out of the grave and bringing them into the light of day. (Bob Dylan, 13th May 2014)

All through the summers and into January
I've been visiting morgues and monasteries
Looking for the necessary body parts
Limbs and livers and brains and hearts
I want to bring someone to life—is what I want to do
I want to create my own version of you.

—'My Own Version of You' (2020)

Making Monsters

Dig this: the third cut of Dylan's *Rough & Rowdy Ways* sees the narrator as a kind of Victor Frankenstein, creating new life out of human remains. Could it be that the Bard of our time is here describing the curation and production of his recent collections of 'uncovers' from the so-called Great American Songbook? Or is he perhaps referring to the process of creating his own songs, sourced from the 'body parts' of underground literature, cinema and music? Or, again, might it be the body of work left behind by his earlier selves that is being pillaged for resurrection by Dylan-gone-electric?

The answers lie buried in the text, waiting to be dug out. Except the death of the author has *itself* come into question and the question is being raised by none other than the author as raiser of his own dead:

> One strike of lightning is all that I need
> And a blast of electricity that runs at top speed
> Shimmy your ribs, I'll stick in the knife
> Gonna jumpstart my creation to life

In fact, the three possibilities are not as distinct as they might first appear. Dylan is labouring within a tradition in which the line between cover versions and new songs is pretty vague. At times, he blurs it further, as when he allows the melody of his rendition of Price, King and Stewart's 'You Belong to Me' to influence the writing of 'Make You Feel My Love', in turn first released in a version by Billy Joel and subsequently covered more than any other post-sixties Dylan:

> I'm working within my art form… I work within the rules and limita-
> tions of it… It has to do with melody and rhythm, and then after that,
> anything goes. You make everything yours. (in Gilmore 2012)

From the very outset of 'My Own Version of You', the narrator (call him 'Dylanstein') crosses the Rubicon that separates buried material from new compositions. As Laura Tenschert (2021) observes, the song's opening lines are adapted from the *CliffsNotes* summary for Chapter 4 of Mary Shelley's *Frankenstein* (which he expects the internet sleuths to uncover, just as they did for his Nobel lecture):

> Visiting morgues and cemeteries for the necessary body parts, Victor
> fails several times before successfully bringing his creation to life…
> This gruesome work carries on through the spring, summer, and fall
> of that year. (Coghill 2001)[1]

---

[1]   Mary Shelley's original sentence reads: 'winter, spring, and summer passed away during my labours' (Shelley 1818, 76). Dylan's line 'I study Sanskrit and Arabic to improve my mind / I want to do things for the benefit of all man-kind' also owes more to *CliffsNotes* than it does to Shelley's novel, though it

In a final twist to this first line, Dylanstein's appropriation of it also echoes the beginning of the Mississippi Sheiks' 1930 song 'Sitting on Top of the World', as played by him in 1992's *Good as I Been to You*: 'Was all the summer, and all the fall's.' Other borrowed lines include 'gunpowder from ice' from Jonathan Swift's *Gulliver's Travels* via *CliffsNotes* (once more), 'It must be the winter of my discontent' and 'to be or not to be' (that are hardly buried within Shakespeare), 'you can feel it you can hear it' from his own song 'Solid Rock', and the title track of Frank Sinatra's own uncovers album *In the wee small hours.*

With each new refrain, Dylanstein exclaims that his labour is (i) painstaking, (ii) impervious to trivialities (such as which lines owe what to whom), yet also (iii) undertaken within the accepted limits of his artform:

I'll bring someone to life—in more ways than one
Don't matter how long it takes—it'll be done when it's done

I'll bring someone to life—balance the scales
I'm not gonna get involved in any insignificant details

I'll bring someone to life—spare no expense
Do it with decency and common sense

Frankenstein's monster is a motherless child. But the mother of invention is the strike of creative inspiration. You might call it lightning, you might call it Muse. Robert Graves called it *The White Goddess,* but Laura Riding complained that his creation of this Triple Muse of birth, love and death involved the assassination of her true self and its replacement with what her biographer describes as 'a Frankenstein pieced together from the shards of her appropriated life and thought'.[2]

Cut-Ups

During his 'classic period', Dylan's songs would piece together real and fictional figures, often in pairs, and then place them in situations (the

---

perhaps also doubles (alongside his descent into the underworld in the final verse) as a nod to the inscription on his Nobel Prize medal (see Tanschert 2021).

[2]   See Baker (1993, 402).

penny arcade, prison, the jungle, the top of the hill...) in which they perform all sorts of actions, as a child might do with toy figurines. Within 'Tombstone Blues' alone we have:

The reincarnation of Paul Revere's Horse
The Ghost of Belle Star, Jezebel the Nun, and Jack the Ripper
The hysterical bride and the medicine man
John the Baptist and the Commander-in-Chief
The king of the Philistines and the pied
Gypsy Davey with his faithful slave Pedro
Galileo and Delilah
Brother Bill[3] and Cecil B. DeMille
Ma Rainey and Beethoven

And in 'Desolation Row':

The blind commissioner and the tight-rope walker
Cinderella and Romeo
Cain and Abel
The hunchback of Notre Dame and the Good Samaritan
Ophelia and Noah
Einstein disguised as Robin Hood
Dr. Filth and his nurse
Phantom of the Opera and Casanova
The superhuman crew and insurance men
Nero's Neptune and the Titanic[4]

Fifty-five years later Dylan seems to be writing a song about the alchemy of writing such songs:

I'll take Scarface Pacino and the Godfather Brando
Mix 'em up in a tank and get a robot commando

---

[3]   William S. Burroughs, whose cut-up technique is at work in this very song that's mentioning him.

[4]   Others he'd make up, if not quite out of thin air: Cream Judge & the Clown, Savage Rose & Fixable, Judas Priest & Frankie Lee... By the time of *The Basement Tapes*, the number of characters and situations that make up Dylan's invisible republic is Legion.

If I do it upright and put the head on straight
I'll be saved by the creature that I create

Yet even as we are guided through this Frankensteinian plan for salvation
via one's works rather than 'by faith in Him who called' ('Saved'), Dylan
is nodding to Tom Waits' storytelling about songwriting:

> You know some songs come out of the ground just like a potato.
> Others you have to make them out things you've found: like your
> mother's pool cue, and your dad's army buddy, your sister's wrist-
> watch, and that type of thing. You'd be surprised what you can find if
> you are… resourceful. (Waits 1999)

As 'My Own Version of You' progresses it becomes populated by Julius
Caesar, Leon Russell, Liberace, St. John the Apostle, St. Peter, Jerome, the
Trojan women and children, Freud, Marx,[5] in fact 'the history of the
whole human race'. Conspicuous by their absence are Mary Shelley,
Frankenstein and his monster.[6]

Love and Theft: Ex Nihilo Nihil Fit

Critics complain that his muse is waning, but he's been engaged in this
kind of thing before. Dylan has lifted melodies and lyrics to bring his own
songs to life from day one, e.g. Dominic Behan's 'The Patriot Game' for
'With God on Our Side', 'Sent For You Yesterday' for 'It Takes a Lot to
Laugh, It Takes a Train to Cry', 'Scarborough Fair' for 'Girl from the
North Country', 'Joe Hill' for 'I Dreamed I Saw St Augustine', 'Pony
Blues' for 'New Pony', etcetera, etcetera, etcetera; *Empire Burlesque*'s 'Tight

---

[5]   'Mister Freud with his dreams and Mister Marx with his axe' is the strange re-
       incarnation of 'Karl Marx has got ya by the throat, Henry Kissinger's got you
       tied up in knots' ('When You Gonna Wake Up').

[6]   The album's closing track, 'Murder Most Foul', ends with a litany of names,
       including Tom Dooley King James, Etta James, John Lee Hooker, the First
       Lady, Marilyn Monroe, Don Henley, Thelonious Monk, Charlie Parker, the
       Birman of Alcatraz, Buster Keaton, Pretty Boy Floyd, Lindsay Buckingham,
       Stevie Nicks, Nat King Cole, the Merchant of Venice, Lady Macbeth, Bud
       Powell and Houdini. These are paired with song requests for DJ Wolfman Jack,
       the last of which brings to life the very song that Dylan is singing as the
       necessary body part.

Connection to My Heart' appears to be primarily made up of Humphrey Bogart lines (see Gray 2008, 226–7); and the entirety of *"Love And Theft"* (were it not for the capitalized 'And', the album's name would quite literally be quoting the title of Eric Lott's book on blackface minstrelsy and the American working class),[7] is a confessional journey through cultural and emotional appropriation which unfolds through the "thefting" of phrases from 'The Cuckoo' to Henry Rollins.[8]

While the younger Dylan chiefly populated his songs with famous characters and lifted lines and melodies from older songs, his more recent incarnations have involved a broader range of inspiration. Dylan has now himself most probably read all of F. Scott Fitzgerald's books (the joke was always that there aren't that many of them) and affirms that you *can* repeat the past, even if you can't come back all the way (and looking back will get you stoned). Asked by Mikal Gilmore about his use of material in *Tempest*, such as Junichi Saga's *Confessions of a Yakuza* and Henry Timrod's Civil War poetry, Dylan protests:

> And as far as Henry Timrod is concerned, have you even heard of him? Who's been reading him lately? And who's pushed him to the forefront? Who's been making you read him? And ask his descend-ants what they think of the hoopla. And if you think it's so easy to quote him and it can help your work, do it yourself and see how far you can get... Newsweek printed that some kid from New Jersey wrote 'Blowin' in the Wind'... People accused me of stealing the melody from a 16th-century Protestant hymn. And when that didn't work, they said they made a mistake and it was really an old Negro spiritual. So what's so different? It's gone on for so long I might not be able to live without it now... I'll see them all in their graves. (in Gilmore 2012)

Dylan sees himself bringing Timrod and his poetry back to life while also creating his own work in the same process. The monster is his, whatever the parts that make up the song. Having created so many versions of his

---

7   Consciously or otherwise, Lott's own title echoes Robert Graves' poem 'The Thieves'.

8   See Browning (2013, 2014) for how Dylan walks the line of creativity between influence and plagiarism.

own self, through these refrains Dylan can be heard as telling his listeners that he is creating his own version of *us*:

> I'll bring someone to life — someone for real
> Someone who feels the way that I feel
>
> I want to bring someone to life — someone I've never seen
> You know what I mean — you know exactly what I mean

Perhaps this is revenge for his fans and critics creating so many versions of him, onto which they project themselves:

> Everything people say about you or me, they are saying about them-selves… In my case, there's a whole world of scholars, professors and Dylanologists, and everything I do affects them in some way. And, you know, in some ways, I've given them life. (in Gilmore 2012)

But then again (but then again, but then again, but then again), in other ways, we've given Dylan life too. It's alright, Bob (it's life and life only).

References

Baker, D. (1993) *In Extremis: The Life of Laura Riding*, New York: Grove Press.

Browning, G. (2013) Bob Dylan: The politics of influence, *Popular Music History*, 8 (2), pp. 222–239.

Browning, G. (2014) Creativity and plagiarism, *P.org*, [Online], https://www.plagiarism.org/paper/bob-dylan-creativity-and-plagiarism

Coghill, J. (2001) *CliffsNotes On Shelley's Frankenstein*, Hoboken, NJ: Wiley Publishing.

Gilmore, M. (2012) Bob Dylan unleashed, *Rolling Stone*, 27th September, [Online], https://www.rollingstone.com/music/music-news/bob-dylan-unleashed-189723/

Gray, M. (2008) *The Bob Dylan Encyclopedia*, revised and updated ed., London: Continuum.

Greene, A. (2014) Bob Dylan releases Frank Sinatra cover, plans new album, *Rolling Stone*, 13th May, [Online], https://www.rollingstone.com/music/music-news/bob-dylan-releases-frank-sinatra-cover-plans-new-album-247736/

Shelley, M. (1818) *Frankenstein; or, The Modern Prometheus*, Vol. I, London: Lackington, Hughes, Harding, Mavor, & Jones.

Tenschert, L. (2020) Chapter 1: 'Sing In Me, Oh Muse': *Rough and Rowdy Ways*, the Nobel Prize & the shaping of Bob Dylan's legacy, 11th October, *Definitely Dylan*, [Online], https://www.definitelydylan.com/ podcasts/2020/10/11/chapter-1-sing-in-me-oh-muse-rough-and-rowdy-ways-the-nobel-prize-amp-the-shaping-of-bob-dylans-legacy

Tenschert, L. (2021) Chapter 2: The other side of the coin—The myth and mystery of creation on *Rough and Rowdy Ways*, 19th February, *Definitely Dylan*, [Online], https://www.definitelydylan.com/ transcripts/2021/2/19/transcript-for-chapter-2-the-other-side-of-the-coin-the-myth-and-mystery-of-creation-on-rough-and-rowdy-ways

Waits, T. (1999) *VH1 Story Tellers*.

Plate from page 7 of the 1922 edition of Mary Shelley's *Frankenstein* (Cornhill Publishing Company edition), captioned 'FRANKENSTEIN AT WORK IN HIS LABORATORY' (public domain).

Anne Margaret Daniel

A Pirate Looks At Eighty

I'm in Key West: to date it's the best thing I've found in America. It's hot and falling to pieces and people seem happy. Nothing much goes on, languidly a sponge or a turtle gets fished, people live on relief cosily, steal coconuts off the municipal streets, amble out and catch a foul local fish called the grunt, gossip, maunder, sunburn and wait for the lazy easy years to pass. (Martha Gellhorn to Eleanor Roosevelt, January 1937)[1]

Once when I was lying on the beach in Coney Island, I saw a portable radio in the sand… a beautiful General Electric, self charging — built like a battleship — and it was broken. (Dylan 2004, 173)

Key West was not named for being the westernmost of the Florida Keys, that broken necklace of coral and sand that stretches a hundred and twenty miles or so from the tip of Florida into the Gulf of Mexico. 'Key West' is a corruption of the Spanish name given it after 1513, when Ponce de Leon laid claim to it, which is Cayo Hueso, islet of bones. Some say the coral reef underlying the four miles of Key West is its bones; others say that the bones in its name came because the native tribes living there when the Spanish sailed in had used this farthest land as a graveyard. The isle changed hands repeatedly in its known history; once it was traded away for a sailboat. Its strategic location for pirates sailing southern seas and later shipping lanes, and its proximity to Cuba — '90 miles from Cuba', as President John F. Kennedy said more than once during the

---

[1] In Moorehead (2007, 44).

Cuban Missile Crisis of 1962[2] —once made Key West invaluable to the United States of America. Now, its tropical mystique, legendary assertions of independence, and the artists, writers and freethinking folk it attracted during the last century have made 'the Conch Republic' a beloved and expensive vacation destination.

Bob Dylan seems to love oceans and lakes, seas and wide rivers. He knows a lot about them, too. In his autobiography, *Chronicles Vol. 1*, he speaks of the Black Sea, from whose shores his grandmother came —and the fact that Lord Byron calls it the Euxine (he doesn't mention, but perhaps expects a reader to know, that Byron rhymes the rough sea's name with 'pukes in'). His glimpse of his 'old-fashion garden' (Dylan 2004, 162) in Malibu, where gulls' cries come 'whipping through the wind' and he can see the Pacific through the trees, and 'feel the power beneath its colors', is one of the loveliest moments in the book. It's followed directly with the account of his own sailboat foundering on a reef and sinking in Panama, which is 'an unwelcome shock': 'In the ten years that I had her my family and I had sailed the entire Caribbean and spent time on every island from Martinique to Barbados.' Terry Gans' account of Dylan writing the songs on *Infidels* while sailing the Caribbean on this boat, a 68-foot wooden schooner named *Water Pearl*, is both detailed and persuasive (Gans 2020, 21ff.). Truly, though, little testimony that Dylan loves the sea, sailing and sailors' chanteys is needed —just listen to his covers of ballads like 'The Golden Vanity' and 'Handsome Molly', and consider all his songs from 'When The Ship Comes In' to 'Mr. Tambourine Man', 'Caribbean Wind' to 'Sad-Eyed Lady of the Lowlands' to the several tracks on *Rough and Rowdy Ways* in which the sea figures. In one track, 'Key West (Philosopher Pirate)', it commands.

When I received a review copy of *Rough and Rowdy Ways* in spring 2020, I listened to the songs straight through and in order. The first and last, 'I Contain Multitudes' and 'Murder Most Foul', had already been released, with 'Murder Most Foul', an almost seventeen-minute song circling around President Kennedy's assassination, having a whole side to itself. This essentially rendered a song named in my download as 'Key West: Philosopher Pilot' as the closing track of the album. Its similarity to

---

2   John F. Kennedy speech, 163rd Street Shopping Center, Miami Beach, Florida, 18th October 1960, *et seq.*

'Highlands', both in its yearning, playing-both-sides homage to wherever home is, and its situation at the end of the album on which it appears, hit me keenly from the first. But I was most floored by the beauty and mystery of 'Key West (Philosopher Pirate)' from the simple tune propelled by Donnie Herron's accordion, and then by its lazy but watchful energy, its sense of time and refusal to be timebound, and its ability to take me back to trips to Key West when the East Coast was locked in ice and snow, to Fantasy Fests of Octobers long ago and the wonderful painted people we met then. The sweep of the long song hits in a surprisingly personal way: Dylan's best songs, like William Shakespeare's finest lines, make the universal particular, and *vice versa*.

An assassinated President, William McKinley, begins this song — whose proper title is 'Key West (Philosopher Pirate)' — as a filtered, strange introduction. I say filtered, through Charlie Poole's 'White House Blues', which begins 'McKinley hollered, McKinley squalled / Doc said to McKinley, "I can't find that ball"' and strange, because the first verse comes as something heard on the radio by the narrator/singer, listening in from Key West. McKinley was killed in 1901, critics cried, and the radio not publicly sold until the 1920s. Open up your ears and minds, and hearts: have sixty years of listening to Bob Dylan's original songs taught you nothing about his refusal to be nailed down with facts, and about the power of the artist's imagination? Allen Ginsberg's 'Walking at Night in Key West' is not about walking at night in Key West. Think instead of what the radio symbolises, connects and provides to someone singing a song of an island both in reality, and in the mind.

When you are on an island connected only tenuously to any mainland, and that by manmade rails and roads, how does the news get through? How does music and information come to you? By sea, of course, and by air — in this song, through the airwaves of that wireless radio, that pirate radio station. Radio Luxembourg was one of the original "pirates" in the United Kingdom, its signal powerful enough to reach across the Channel since 1933 and circumvent the British Broadcasting Corporation's monopoly. However, when in 1964 Luxembourg refused to play pop music not associated with major labels, Ronan O'Rahilly founded Radio Caroline. Named for President Kennedy's daughter, Radio Caroline's series of intrepid little ships brought music from smaller record labels, and eventually television, to England's tight little island from the relative safety, despite occasional raids, of international waters. Dylan doesn't specify exactly what 'pirate radio station' it is, of course. I hear the one named for Cuban poet José Martí, which first began its radio, and later television, broadcasts to Cuba from the Keys. The radio is how most people first heard Bob Dylan and his songs: don't forget that, either.

One does not often think of a pirate as being a philosopher, no matter how eloquent a character like Long John Silver or Captain Jack Sparrow, or Jimmy Buffett's 'A Pirate Looks At 40', might be. Buffett, Tennessee Williams and Ernest Hemingway, a literary pirate of sorts, or at least a man who styled himself as a brawling buccaneer during his days on the island, are the artists most popularly associated with Key West. This is probably why none of them appear in Dylan's song, though a 'Jimmy' is name-checked in the third verse, but Buffett's 'A Pirate Looks at Forty' and Warren Zevon's 'Mutineer' are definitely two of the unsung songs of influence—and of experience—here. A well-known story about Heming-way and his son might be a background, if any factual one is needed, for Dylan's verse about a child marrying a prostitute. Once when Heming-way's firstborn son, Jack, sailed from Key West to Cuba with his father as a teenager, Hem purchased a prostitute for Jack as his sexual initiation, without knowing that Jack (according to his own account) had already spent a night with the woman. The story was ribald legend in Key West, enough so that it featured in Jack's *New York Times* obituary (Martin 2000, §1, 61).

The image of the "I", the singer of this song, shares some things with Odysseus, to me: that most celebrated and doomed of travellers by water, struggling not so hard to get home after the Trojan War ended. Odysseus could only reach the island of Ithaca by travelling through three seas; do not ever enrage Poseidon, the god of the sea, if your kingdom is an island. Washed up repeatedly on islands not his own—Aiaía, Ogygia, Aeolia—Odysseus walks the sands, on the margin of land and water, retelling old tales and thinking of home. Yet the voyages being taken in 'Key West' are more grounded and mental, like the tale told by the rather similar narrator of Byron's *Don Juan*. He has fetched up on the 'horizon line' after chasing it for ages. The sand may be shifting but the singer's feet are 'planted square on the ground'. Amelia Street and Bayview Park are where he walks in the shadows after dark; even when he does travel, he's 'not that far from the convent home' — not named, but, if in Key West, the Convent of St. Mary Immaculate, Star of the Sea.

Dylan loves horizons, borders, those spaces in between. He loves to be on the line. The album *Highway 61 Revisited* is packed full of songs about, and set in, mysterious marginal places. 'Key West (Philosopher Pirate)' is closer to the feeling of those songs than anything Dylan has written for years, and the repeated 'horizon line' in the first and last refrain keep you on the road, trying to get there. Dylan is also fond of heading south, in the United States, in his songs; for every early trip back to the Minnesota snows, like 'Girl from the North Country' or 'Something There Is About You', there are the sunshine and southbound seductions of 'California' and 'As I Went Out One Morning', the political songs dealing with lynchings, murders and cruelty in the South, and songs set — as Dylan once said of 'Desolation Row' — somewhere in Mexico. Key West is as far south as you can go in the mainland United States, down on the bottom, way down. Dylan calls it 'the gateway key / To innocence and purity', but which way are we going through the gate?

Walking through the verses, past the buildings and squares of the little town, the singer is more concerned with its lush fauna: tropical plants that can kiss or kill, and you'd better know which is which. Hibiscus flowers go behind the ear, a link to other warm islands from Hawaii to Tahiti. But an unnamed plant is toxic and dizzying, while orchid trees 'can give you the bleedin' heart disease' — the beauty that produces compassion can be an illness. This may seem like an enchanted land, but nobody actually lives in the land of Oz. Remember, Oz was just Kansas, all along. However, the dangers and exotic toxicities fade in Key West, once you've been there awhile and gotten to know the place. Gumbo-limbo spirituals, constantly blooming bougainvillea (banks of which grace Dylan's home in Malibu) and the feel of 'sunlight on your skin / And the healing virtues of the wind' rise to the fore in this 'land of light'. What brightens the place, and makes this song turn increasingly toward the beautiful? Can it be love?

Between songs in Bristow, Virginia, while on his 1999 tour with Paul Simon, Dylan joked about love meaning nothing to his ex-wife, who was a tennis player. 'Love, awwwww. Love', he said, shaking his head.[3] Yet

---

3   Bob Dylan in concert, Nissan Pavilion, Bristow, Virginia (16th July 1999).

he uses the word in hundreds of his own songs, more memorably as a noun than as a verb ('my own true love'; 'My love she speaks like silence'), and has recorded and performed hundreds more covers of songs about love. Since *Blood on The Tracks*, Dylan has tended to shy away from love as something to be confessed or proclaimed, or even sought—until *Rough and Rowdy Ways*. 'Mother of Muses', 'I've Made Up My Mind to Give Myself to You' and 'Key West' stand out together in their manifestation of love. Dylan is not given to penning lines like 'I'm so deep in love I can hardly see' and 'I'm stickin' with you through and through', and though they are offset by the marriage to a prostitute (which is itself qualified with 'She's still cute and we're still friends') and the statement 'I don't love nobody' (which yields to 'gimme a kiss') it's clear to me that 'Key West' is a love song. I'm not saying a love song to anyone in particular, mind, or even to a person, but a love song all the same. Dylan doesn't limit himself that way. Much ink has been spilled over which of his love songs, or 'breakup songs', are for which woman, or women. He doesn't usually say.

Surely, though, this is an ode to all the golden isles of the blessed from Ogygia to Tír na nÓg, from Avalon to Key West—Key West, America's very own Bali Ha'i, the enchanted tropical place where liberty and *laissez faire* define the locals, drawn from over the world to make their homes there. No man is an island, John Donne said, but every person wants one, or has one, in their mind's eye, to give them the isolation and peace they need. That's the essence of W.B. Yeats's 'Lake Isle of Innisfree', which shares much with Dylan's Key West. 'Key West (Philosopher Pirate)' is also a song about the singer's ongoing love for the search, following the sunset, and travelling on... in a place that can also be home. Dylan doesn't say that this island is a place where you can be immortal, but that it's 'the place to be / If you're lookin' for immortality'; he doesn't say he has lost his mind, but that 'If you lost your mind you'll find it there.' That "if" is a powerful Modernist conditional. Key West is, itself, conditional. What's the key to it all? That is up to you. To me, my favourite Key West writer best understood the point of how much a Dylan song like this one can matter long ago:

> There is such a lovely yearning in Dylan's songs, in his voice, in the construction of his lyrics. For me—for this writer—yearning is walking, crawling, perhaps, towards some understanding, and I can

listen to him, and I can lose myself in the journey he has constructed, and I can be saved. (Tennessee Williams, 1982)[4]

References

Dylan, B. (2004) *Chronicles: Volume One*, London: Simon & Schuster.

Gans, T. (2020) *Surviving in a Ruthless World: Bob Dylan's Journey to Infidels*, Falmouth: Red Planet Books.

Moorehead, C. (ed.) (2007) *Selected Letters of Martha Gellhorn*, London: St. Martin's Press.

Martin, D. (2000) Jack Hemingway dies at 77; Embraced father's legacy, *The New York Times*, Obituary, 3rd December.

Grissom, J. (2015) The salvation of Bob Dylan, 21st April, [Online], https://jamesgrissom.blogspot.com/2015/04/the-salvation-of-bob-dylan.html?view=flipcard

---

[4]   Tennessee Williams in conversation with James Grissom, New Orleans, Louisiana, 1982; as published in Grissom (2015).

28th April 2006, New Orleans Jazz and Heritage Festival (photograph published under a Creative Commons Attribution-Share Alike 3.0 Unported license CC-BY-SA 2.0).

Tim Shorrock

The Troubadour as Teacher

As I look back on Bob Dylan at 80 years old, I'm most struck by his role as a teacher. That phase began for me in 1964, when I first knowingly heard a Dylan song. It was the visionary 'A Hard Rain's A-Gonna Fall', as performed by Pete Seeger in Tokyo, Japan, where I grew up. I was mesmerised, hooked for life: as Bob would write years later about the Italian poets he loved, 'every one of them words rang true, and glowed like burnin' coal.'

Since the days of my youth, Bob Dylan has taught me a great deal about love, politics, war, culture, music, history, religion and the full scope of the human condition, from kindness and nobility to treachery and plunder. His work will last for generations as a guidepost to our forgotten past and our uncertain future on this earth. 'Wasn't that a time?' the Weavers sang during the Cold War years when Dylan got his start. It was indeed.

The first insights Dylan passed to me were about America itself. Like many of my fellow contributors, I was raised outside of the United States, and into my early teens knew very little about the political and social realities of the USA. But my eyes were soon opened wide. Not long after Seeger introduced me to Dylan in Japan, a friend just back from living in New York City lent me all of his records up to then, starting with his debut folk album and ending with *Bringing It All Back Home.* I taped them all onto a Sony reel-to-reel and sat in my room and listened intently, not really knowing which record was which.

As my tapes rolled, visions of America's dark side of racism, militarism and inequality flew by, juxtaposed against deeply moving songs of love and passion, all of them fuelled by fierce guitar strumming and wild harmonica blowing. What I heard was markedly different from the R&B, folk and rock music on the radio back then, and seemed almost from another world. His songs were gritty, soul-crushing and eye-opening. Some were angry, others were mournful. But they were all a direct line into the truth. 'I don't need *Time*, I don't need *Newsweek*', Dylan mockingly told a London reporter in 1966, in D.A. Pennebaker's bio-epic *Dont Look Back*. Well, I didn't either; I had Bob. And from him, I heard the news, oh boy.

On 'The Lonesome Death of Hattie Carroll', one of his greatest songs, he offered the horrifying tale of the racist William Zanzinger, a spoiled child of 'rich wealthy parents from the politics of Maryland', carelessly throwing his cane across a barroom floor and killing 'the maid in the kitchen' who 'never sat once at the head of the table'. For that, he only got only a six-month sentence, so you'd damn well weep now, Dylan told me.

I can still remember the shock I felt upon hearing 'Ballad of Hollis Brown', Dylan's story of a broken man on a South Dakota farm who shoots his entire family and himself with a shotgun. It was a deep lesson in poverty and hopelessness in rural America, told through the eyes of the killer himself. Words like these brought shivers:

> Your baby's eyes look crazy
> They're a-tuggin' at your sleeve
> Your baby's eyes look crazy
> They're a-tuggin' at your sleeve
> You walk the floor and wonder why
> With every breath you breathe.

Dylan's use of 'you' and 'your' gave this song its power. He made me look at the awful situation through the dirt farmer's own eyes. I felt the terror that must have engulfed him as he realised he was holding a shotgun in his hand and was pulling the trigger, again and again, as 'seven shots ring out like the ocean's pounding roar.' The visceral images helped me understand why he may have done this terrible deed.

'Only a Pawn in Their Game' had a similar effect. It was all about how beaten-down white men like Hollis Brown were manipulated by the powerful into turning their smouldering anger about the condition of their lives into raging hatred for black men like Medgar Evers; Dylan bravely played that song at the great Civil Rights March of 1963. The torrent of music that flowed from his brain informed both the past and our painful present.

In 'North Country Blues', he sang of the poverty and instability caused by capitalists shutting down mines in Minnesota and buying from abroad; you can hear similar words today in the laments of laid-off miners on the Iron Range: 'They complained in the East / They are paying too high / They say that your ore ain't worth digging / That it's much cheaper down / In the South American towns / Where the miners work almost for nothing.' There were lots of tunes about coal mining and work back then. But nobody was writing songs like this, linking poverty and joblessness with globalisation and the corporate search for cheap labour.

In 'Masters of War' on *Freewheelin'*, he even took on the military industrial complex. His bitter lyrics still resonate as I seethe inwardly at the cruelty of America's militarist mindset: 'You fasten the triggers / For the others to fire / Then you sit back and watch / When the death count gets higher / You hide in your mansion / As young people's blood / Flows out of their bodies / And is buried in the mud.' These weren't "protest" songs, like journalists liked to call them; they were *empathy* songs. They helped us see the racism and injustice amidst the American dream as something real, something tangible that maybe we could do something about.

Yet, even with this achievement, I think Dylan's greatest contribution as teacher is what he's taught us about music. I first became conscious of this role in 1993, on *World Gone Wrong*. It was his second acoustic collection of the old blues and folk classics that he learned in the coffee shops and clubs of Minneapolis, New York, Boston and London, and an education unto itself. I'd heard a lot of the songs before, but not the title song and 'Blood in My Eyes', two haunting ballads about trying to survive and find love in a twisted world of pain and sorrow. I was enthralled and curious about their origins. Luckily, Dylan had included extensive liner notes, a practice from his first few albums on Columbia. He laid it all out for me.

These tunes were 'done by the Mississippi Sheiks', he wrote, 'a little known de facto group whom in their former glory must've been something to behold. rebellion against routine seems to be their strong theme.

all their songs are raw to the bone & are faultlessly made for these modern times (the New Dark Ages) nothing effete about the Mississippi Sheiks.' *World Gone Wrong*, he added, 'goes against cultural policy', by which he meant 'strange things like courage becoming befuddled & nonfundamental. evil charlatans masquerading in pullover vests & tuxedos talking gobbledygook, monstrous pompous superficial pageantry parading down lonely streets on limited access highways. strange things indeed.'

To me, this was truth in a most uncertain time. In 1993, we were two years into the first Gulf War, the start of the 'forever wars' of today, and the airwaves were full of images of a new, troubled America — right-wing preachers and dot-com hucksters screaming against the background of smoke and flame billowing from the first bombing of the World Trade Center in Manhattan or the horrific federal attack on the Branch Davidian compound in Waco, Texas. Dylan had denounced the madness in 1991 at the Grammys, when he was presented with a Lifetime Achievement Award; he sang a dark, almost taunting version of 'Masters of War' that stunned and baffled the audience. But amidst the calamities of the day, he was telling me to find some old vinyl and listen to the Mississippi Sheiks. I was all ears.

Those liner notes set me on a course in American musicology that's never ended. The Sheiks, it turned out, were a black string band from the 1930s, founded by a fiddler who was once a slave. I loved their unique, early jug-band style of music, and realised that I'd been hearing their stuff for years; they were the originators of 'Sittin' on Top of the World', one of the best-known songs in the folk and country vein that was popularised early by the Grateful Dead and recorded by Dylan on his *Good as I Been to You* in 1992.

As I delved into these musicians of old, I realised that Dylan has been teaching us about American music since he recorded 'Song to Woody' ('here's to Cisco and Sonny and Leadbelly too') on his first album, way back in 1962. His deep interest in American roots music became evident in 1972, when he played on the fabulous *Doug Sahm and Friends* with the New Orleans gris-gris man Dr. John (Mac Rebennack), the San Antonio organ player Augie Myers and many others. He'd hook with these musicians again and again, particularly Myers, who played on Dylan's *Time Out of Mind* decades later.

The TOOM sessions also included on keyboards the legendary Memphis producer and raconteur Jim Dickinson. Although this was their first recorded collaboration, Dickinson and Dylan were already good friends, going way back to the early '70s, when the late Dickinson (who appears briefly in the autobiographical *Chronicles*) won the bard's respect by recording 'John Brown', perhaps Dylan's most searing anti-war song. I spent a lot of time in Memphis from 2005 to 2008, and my experiences there taught me another great lesson about Dylan: the pains he takes to learn.

According to Dickinson, Dylan came to see him once at his Zebra Ranch, just south of Memphis, to talk through his experience with producer Daniel Lanois during the recording sessions for *Oh Mercy* in New Orleans. He really liked Memphis and knew all the bands, even the obscure ones. Around 1999, he recorded a video at the New Daisy Theater on Beale Street and invited a select group to listen in. One of them was Robert Gordon, the local music journalist and the author of *It Came From Memphis*, a deeply researched book on the city's lively blues and rock scene. Dylan asked to meet Gordon; after shaking hands, the writer says, the famous songwriter told him: 'your book's a *classic*, man.' That's how much he knew the music.

But he also understood the history of Memphis as a crossroads, the place where black and white musicians came together even during the darkest days of segregation to create the culture that became rock & roll. He explains that riddle in the haunting 'Mother of Muses' on *Rough and Rowdy Ways*, his last LP, when he sings the praises of Zhukov and Patton, the Soviet and American generals most responsible for defeating fascism, 'who cleared the path for Presley to sing / Who carved the path for Martin Luther King'. It was a profound thought, and again I was reminded of Dylan's deep knowledge of my country, from the Civil War to today.

That knowledge, of course, has been part of his public persona since 2006, when Dylan displayed his intricate knowledge of America with his *Theme Time Radio Hour*, every minute of which was a virtual encyclopaedia of our musical heritage. His truth-telling is even more evident a few songs later on *RARW*, which he closes with his 17-minute elegy, 'Murder Most Foul'. With great emotion, Dylan presents JFK's murder and its meaning as breaking news, almost exactly as I remember it from

1963. Then, with the help of Wolfman Jack, the great DJ in the sky, he winds up his tribute by ticking off the names of dozens of musicians and artists who influenced him, and all of us, along the way.

At age 80, we must now add Dylan to that list, so he stands before us as a living link to all the greats who came before. Our troubadour, it turns out, was our teacher all along. Bob Dylan, Presente!

Theatrical release poster for the 1967 documentary film Dont Look Back (public domain).

Amy Rigby

I Believe in You

'So, you're a Dylanologist now?', said a friend when I told her I was writing something for *Dylan at 80*.

'No, just a fan', I said.

I didn't want to admit the truth. When it comes to Bob Dylan, I'm a quivering acolyte.

I was never a good Catholic, and with Dylan—concert tours and albums ticked off the discography—I've been a patchy devotee. But I turn to him often as organising principle and source of strength.

When I was a six-year-old student at St. Winifred's elementary school, they rolled out an old projector and showed a film called *Our Lady of Fatima* where three peasant children in Portugal are visited by an apparition, a mysterious lady who bids the kids to gather the locals and promises to perform a miracle. There was a scary part where the sun started spinning in the sky and moving closer and closer to earth. Everyone acknowledged God, dropped to their knees and were rewarded by not being roasted alive. It was a vivid illustration of the effectiveness of faith.

The story made a big impression on me. But the part about the sun hurtling towards earth went against everything they taught us in science class, so I was sceptical. I needed something to believe in, and that thing was music.

I heard Bob Dylan for the first time at my Girl Scout troop spring picnic. I left the other girls under a sedate park shelter to go spy on a couple lounging in the grass. Can you do that? I wondered. Stray from the designated area and find your own spot?

A voice barked out of a transistor radio about being stuck in Mobile with the Memphis blues again. I had to ask: 'What's that music?' A boy drank beer out of a bottle hidden by a paper bag. His girlfriend in a bright patterned shift dress leaned against him, already-brown knees bent at an angle that made me wonder what kind of underpants she had on. 'That's Dylan', the boy said.

I'd seen Dylan's picture in *Time* magazine, but photos couldn't convey the urgency in his voice. It made no attempt to please and that pleased me: this was not music my parents would like. Probably the opposite. I didn't know what he was talking about, but I felt certain my parents wouldn't understand it either and somehow that felt like it gave me an advantage.

Later I rode my bike down the tallest hill near our house. I wore a loose shirt, my hair nearly grown out from a short-lived Susan Cowsill pixie cut.

'Are you a boy or a girl?', a carload of teenagers shouted. 'Stuck Inside Of Mobile' blared from a radio in the neighbours' garage. 'That's Dylan', I said out loud, standing up on the pedals. That's what music could do. It gave me authority and a path to follow.

Moving into adolescence, I felt safer with Elton John. I didn't want to be pulled all the way down into a life of creativity when there was still hope I could be a Catholic wife and mother. In the seventies, Bob smeared makeup on his face and Elton's cartoon shoes and feathered glasses were a friendlier licence to question everything.

Punk gave me an outlet for my angst and the impression I could make something of my imperfect self. Old country records told me songwriting was the way to do it. I followed the stories in Loretta Lynn songs, linear tales that started one place and ended up somewhere else. But in a studio apartment in the East Village of New York City I turned to Bob Dylan— for real this time. Loretta showed it was important to be honest, but Bob said the opposite was also correct; that to find the truth you had to make shit up. I stood and strummed an acoustic guitar, tethered by headphones to a cassette player so I wouldn't disturb the neighbours. 'Lily, Rosemary and the Jack of Hearts' took me through my paces and brought me back around to the beginning again and again. Who did what to whom? Does the G chord go here or *here*? His musical, lyrical knowledge beamed down from a star too far away to fully translate, so I grabbed what I could and freestyled the rest.

My first husband wooed me with a handmade multi-cassette Dylan collection that pre-dated *Biograph* by about a year. I learned it by heart, partly for myself and partly to turn myself into a woman a man who loved Bob would want to be married to. I remember him leaping out of bed in disbelief when Dylan played 'Jokerman' on the Letterman show in 1984, his curly head silhouetted in front of Bob's curly head on the TV set as he stood, rapt. I knew — even so early in our lives together — this guy would never jump like that for me.

I became a mother and we sealed the deal with a family trip to see Dylan at Jones Beach. How selfish were we to sacrifice our ten-month-old in the heat of summer? G.E. Smith came across a little too broad-shouldered on guitar, and the sound in Robert Moses' custom shed wasn't all that sympathetic. But I took my restless daughter to the concession stand midway through the show, then held her facing away from me towards the stage. She was transfixed by Bob acoustic and illuminated beneath the cement stands above. It was just us and him. Sweating through 'Song to Woody' was the closest thing to a baptism I'd give my only child.

Writing songs for an early band I shared with a younger brother, my Irish twin, highlighted how not everyone got this kind of religion. 'Explain to me why you like Bob Dylan', he said one day. 'Why do I... breathe oxygen?' was all I could formulate. We made an album together but I had to move on.

When I left bands behind and became a solo artist, Dylan catechism answered more questions than I'd asked and upped my performing abilities. Assuming his words, chords and melodies as my own gave me powers I hadn't imagined I possessed. 'Tom Thumb's Blues', 'It's All Over Now, Baby Blue', 'Hurricane' — always without a lyric sheet. The better I could remember, the deeper his ease lodged in my psyche. I moved like he moved without knowing exactly how he moved, just feeling it.

Temping at Sony Music in the early to mid-nineties, I faxed song licence requests to Jeff Rosen, Dylan's manager. If you say it's alright, Bob, it's alright. Go Hollywood. Have a laugh, make some money so I know it's okay to want that too. It's not all art.

Does every newly-divorced woman get the hots for/from *Street Legal* Bob? My marriage broke up (goodbye *Basement Tape* bootlegs). 'New Pony' on cassette was like the first humid spring day after a bitter five-year winter.

There was a man I fell in love with who'd played on a Dylan album, in particular one epic track I climbed inside like we were a threesome.

From a balcony pew in Nashville's Ryman Auditorium, the first church of country music, I watched Bob and his four musicians. I'd gone to the concert alone to convince myself I could do that and anyway, in my mind I was up onstage in the band.

I sat in a songwriters' round in the centre of the Bluebird Café in Nashville. To my right was Bob Neuwirth whose albums I'd just discovered but mostly knew as Bob Dylan's friend, the scary consigliere from *Dont Look Back* always quick with a withering remark.

My turn came and I played a song I'd written a few months before. I'd felt as the words and melody spun out of me that I was making a break-through as a writer; being honest and real in a deeper way than I had before. That feeling doesn't happen all the time. But every now and then you're solving the unsolvable, spouting wisdom you never knew you possessed.

'Man', Neuwirth said when I'd finished. 'You've got it with that song. If you're ever playing somewhere and you don't know what you're doing there, just play that song. You'll be alright.' I took it as a de facto nod from the other Bob. Later, Neuwirth and I hung out. He gave me dating advice.

Living in Nashville I tried every acoustic guitar in every store in town before settling on a sweet Gibson J-45 sunburst. 'You mean like Dylan plays?', said a friend. Oh, yeah.

Never go to a Dylan show with someone you don't trust. At Chicago's Auditorium Theatre, Merle Haggard opened. Hard to disagree about a piece of granite. But when Bob took the stage, his grace and presence fuelled my resolve to leave. 'He shouldn't play the piano. Why can't he just stand there and play his songs, all the ones we want to hear?' No, never go to a Dylan show with a guy you don't trust. Or maybe do, if you want the end to come sooner.

In a bid for freedom, I popped the new album *Modern Times* into the minivan disc player and drove away from Nashville. I'd lasted almost five years in that five-year town, but it was a man I was running from, not Music City. Make me brave and fearless, I would've prayed, if I still prayed. Instead I inched the accelerator up to eighty, punched cruise control and bounced in my seat to 'Thunder On The Mountain'.

When I found real love — a partner, together through life — Bob sealed the deal, blessing our union from the stage. Eric had never seen Bob Dylan before and for me it had been at least a decade. As we waited for the show at Kingston, New York's Hutton Brickyards to begin, I had a brief vision of somebody helping him onto the stage but I shook that thought out of my head. No. He was in his seventies, not his nineties.

And then: the rhythm guitar player, stage left in a sharp silvery suit and low fedora and the rest of the band and among them, Bob. Looking the same. Impossible. Rangy, roguish, the stage light illuminating that head of hair. He stood behind the piano. Launched into 'Things Have Changed'. I was in my own Bob Dylan dream and he was singing this one for me.

Then Bob ambled over to the straight mic stand to croon one for *us*. The golden backlights and footlights, the lyrics and melody: 'Why Try To Change Me Now'? He posed with the straight mic stand so naturally and when he sang 'I always was your clown' the song touched me in a way it never did by Sinatra because I hear Frank through a glaze of sepia as forever our parents' era and music, but Bob's been where we want to go and done what we want to do.

Another decade, another thirty or forty songs. Him, the Nobel Prize. I wrote with borrowed hubris in the voice of a man he beat to the honour. I rose to the occasion and pulled a word out of the air that felt worthy of him: Spartacus.

I saw a billboard in Pennsylvania — my home state — ANGRYCATHOLIC. COM it said. I'm not Catholic anymore but the hard-to-shake belief that there's a force strong enough to spin the sun around in the sky is worth the accompanying guilt. Meaning-seeking openness — sure, I can let a man's body dissolve on my tongue — brought me closer to Bob. He became a part of me, a part that has helped me transcend; to create a self I couldn't get to on my own.

'Not Dark Yet' or 'Emotionally Yours' — I believe, and swallow it all.

Amy with Telecaster (photograph by Ted Barron).

Galen Strawson

The Bridge at Midnight
– Liner Notes

When I was a boy of 10 11 12 and bought my first 45s for 6/8d (six shillings and eightpence) they were sentimental songs of loss (Brenda Lee, Skeeter Davis, Edith Piaf), nb 'sentimental' is not necessarily a criticism; although some of the songs were criticisable. I think this explains why 'Positively 4th Street' took over my life for a while after somebody – wish I could remember who – gave me the single on New Year's Eve 1965 when I was 13.

I saw a peeling bumper sticker LIVE A GREAT STORY on a 6.7-litre pickup truck thrumming in a traffic jam on 38th Street in Austin, TX (this was 55 years later). It seemed a perfectly mistaken instruction. It went on three words too long. It revived in my mind the feud I have with the NARRATIVISTS, the people who say you should think of your own life as a story. In reply I quote BOB DYLAN saying, 'I don't think I'm tangible to myself. I mean, I think one thing today and I think another thing tomorrow. I change during the course of a day. I wake and I'm one person, and when I go to sleep I know for certain I'm somebody else. I don't know who I am most of the time. It doesn't even matter to me [laughs]' (*Newsweek* 1997). The NARRATIVISTS say 'Yeah that's just his narrative, his self-narrative.' And D says 'I cannot say the word eye any-more… when I speak this word eye, it is as if I am speaking of some-body's eye that I faintly remember… there is no eye – there is only a series of mouths – long live the mouths' (*Highway 61 Revisited* liner notes 1965). Up comes Rimbaud and says 'it's false to say *I think* [as in *cogito ergo sum*]:

I is an other. Too bad for the wood that finds itself to be a violin... If a lump of copper wakes up as a bugle, it isn't its fault... It's obvious to me: I'm just a spectator at the unfolding of my thought—I watch it, I listen to it.' And D says 'I'd become a different person since I'd written [my early songs], and, frankly, they mystified me' (*Time* magazine 17th September 2001).

Long live the mouths. Nevertheless the songs on *"Love And Theft"* are autobiographical. 'Yeah, all of 'em. Every single one, every line. It's completely autobiographical, as most of my stuff usually is on one level or another' (*Time* 2001) → the best way for most of us to write about D is to write about ourselves. In March 1967 when I was just 15 my friend Darrell Nightingale was expelled from our boarding school. When he left he gave me five LPs: *Bringing It All Back Home*, *Highway 61 Revisited* (hadn't heard of *Blonde on Blonde*), Joan Baez's *Farewell Angelina* and two other Baez albums. I jumped right in with 115 million others. D was like W.H. Auden's Freud, 'no more a person... but a whole climate of opinion.' Very difficult for him—but it's not hard to understand why it happened. He evinced the epic in the everyday, the glamour of existence —some would say glory, although there is no universal glory. In any case we mislay it. We forget with Ralph Waldo Emerson: 'the days come and go like muffled & veiled figures from a distant friendly party, but they say nothing, & if we do not use the gifts they bring, they carry them as silently away.' D intervenes, not with a palliative but with a refutation. 'It's life and life only.' But it's not 'the long littleness of life' (Frances Cornford). Right. Even though there are too many suffering, too much injustice, too many who have to work too hard just to stay alive. No universal glory. Don't say how could The Beatles sing 'Oh that magic feeling, nowhere to go'? Just say it doesn't always apply.

First love, red light bulb, January, another 45, 'Don't think Twice, It's All right' and 'Corinna, Corinna' over and over. Walk home five miles late under sodium orange lights. Paul Valéry: 'God made the world out of nothing. But the nothingness shows through.'

Stuck here in Austin in 2021 thinking of my browning paperback copy of *Tarantula* back in the UK on acid-rich paper. Bought as a totem you had to have it. Will I ever open it again, did I ever read it right through? I think I read *Chronicles One*, I can't remember, I know I gave it to my brother. Also bought a big Beethoven biography, never read it. Need not to know about musicians except for a few stories like 'Es muss sein!' (Beethoven op. 135) and 'Play fucking loud!' (D shouts back at his band when someone in the audience yells 'Judas' at him in the Free Trade Hall Manchester on 17th May 1966; we couldn't hear it on the original bootleg.) Right now I'm a mouth for other mouths. I collect quotations. They conquer my mind. This doesn't mean it isn't me. On the contrary. And I'm exaggerating.

The words you mishear when you're 15 years old and English (or Egyptian or Estonian or Ethiopian) and you've never heard of Juarez and you're lost in the rain and worried (*wahrredd*) and it's Eastertime (and the internet doesn't exist—different universe). I still hear 'She's an artist, she don't look bad' long after seeing Pennebaker's 1967 film *Dont Look Back*. These things root in your life, I'd say it's pretty nice. You're 15, smoking surreptitiously and incompetently, emotional because she's delicate and seems like veneer or Vermeer. You're Robyn Hitchcock, mystified by a bibantress on a bottle of wine. You go to Woodstock in Oxfordshire in 1969 with your best friend, Simon Halliday, because you heard that Dylan might be there and sit above the lake in Blenheim Park smoking and feeling beautiful in the '60s sense and yearning most imprecisely.

Mouth: More seriously now. Sometimes you come out mean—with everyone wanting to canonise you. Emily Dickinson says, 'They talk of hallowed things aloud—and embarrass my dog.' D agrees.

Mouth: Nietzsche says, 'There are occurrences of such a delicate nature that one does well to cover them up with some rudeness to conceal them; there are actions of love and extravagant generosity after which nothing is more advisable than to take a stick and give any witness a sound thrashing: that would muddle his memory.'

Mouth: D would have to thrash himself too. 'God rest his soul & his rudeness' (*Tarantula*). Self-defence, not defining or confining. When you're not a fraud you have to defend your ordinariness against fame.

Mouth: What about the past? There's plenty when you're 80.

Mouth: Speak for yourself. Some of us are more like Samuel Hanagid, 977 years ago in Granada: 'She said [to me] "Rejoice, for God has brought you to your fiftieth year in the world!" But she had no inkling that, for my part, there is no difference at all between my own days which have gone by and the distant days of Noah about which I have heard. I have nothing in the world but the hour in which I am: it pauses for a moment, and then, like a cloud, moves on.'

Mouth: 'The past is never dead. It's not even past.'

Mouth: Sleeve notes, it's Faulkner's most quoted line, that doesn't make it true. It could be true for the Queen and flat false for the Jack.

Mouth: Yes but 'She says, "You can't repeat the past." I say, "You can't? What do you mean, you can't? Of course you can!"' (D, 'Summer Days', 1969). D is quoting F. Scott Fitzgerald. That's what Jay Gatsby replies to Nick Carraway.

Mouth: Yes but who's who? Summer days, summer nights are gone. Memory doesn't have to be personal. You can remember ten thousand singers and ten thousand songs and the view from Popocatépetl and yourself not at all.

Mouth: *Si, pero* this doesn't apply to a person who says that 'we try and we try and we try to be who we were… Sooner or later you come to the realization that we're not who we were. So then what do we do?' (D, *Newsweek* 1997).

Mouth: We stay in our footsteps, New York, East Orange, Harlem, Staten Island, Cal-i-for-ne-ay, Oklahoma, New Orleans, Cripple Creek, Utah, Mississippi, Chicago, Nevada, New Mexico, Arizona, Idaho, Cheyenne, Denver, Wichita, Arkansas, Arlington, Washington, Oregon, Memphis, Texas, Kansas, Seattle, WA, New Orleans, Louisiana, Mexico, Oxford, MS, 42nd St., Red Wing, Florida, Michigan, Wisconsin, Minnesota, Fargo, Aberdeen, Black Hills, Montana, St. Petersburg, FL, South Dakota to begin with.

Galen Strawson and Simon Halliday, King's Bar, Cambridge, 1971.

Robyn Hitchcock

Measuring Out My Life in Bob Dylan

It's 5am London time on 20th February 20th 2021. Fifty-five years, one month and two days ago I entered a medieval Victorian boot camp for the clever sons of the British establishment. I was 12 years old, sent to live away from my family for the first time, in a chilly academic penitentiary where they had only that term put doors on the cubicles in the communal toilets. It was a very communal place, rich in cubicles — our beds and our desks were also enshrined in ancient wooden open-ended boxes in vast, cold rooms.

I surrendered to my fate as all inmates must. There was no mum, no dad, no sisters, no television: just a horde of alien teenage boys. However, in the central hive of our gothic module, ringed with the cubicles where our few permitted possessions were stashed, was embedded a powerful mono gramophone. When every study period ended, a horde of young gentlemen would stampede this record player brandishing their vinyl.

It being January 1966, the Beatles, the Stones and the Kinks were in sonic bloom on that turntable, reminding us kids of Life Outside and watering our young lust for life. But a voice new to me began to cut through them all: a voice from an orange label on a little black disc. 'How does it feel?', the voice would wail, in a tone that demanded a response: 'How does it feel to be on your own? With no direction home?' Where the Beatles sang to you, caressing your ears with romance; Bob Dylan sang at you, piercing your reverie like an alarm clock: wake up, kid — what the fuck is happening to you?

I'm a compulsive person. There's a thin barrier between 'What's that noise?' and 'I've gotta hear it.' Bob Dylan is a compelling artist, as this collection of essays shows, yet again. Three weeks of 'Like A Rolling Stone' three shots a day and I was beginning to crave it. I located the boys who owned copies (and one holy dude owned *Highway 61 Revisited*, the mothership in which that song was housed) and I began to request it. 'Relax, Hitchcock—it's coming on after Donovan...'

Then one day, maybe by mistake, somebody dropped the needle on the B-side, 'Gates of Eden'. Dylan's visionary incantation droning over his acoustic guitar came on like a grail in a castle window. Listening at rock'n'roll volume to him singing about a lamppost with folded arms and iron claws, an alchemical transformation was happing inside me. That angry, resigned, soulful, cynical, all-knowing voice had saturated me to a crucial point. By the time I turned 13, seven weeks into my time in the college, my compass no longer pointed back to my family in Surrey—it pointed to Bob Dylan. Like a child lost in the woods who thinks the first creature it sees must be its parents, I had blundered across Dylan, the Jewish sage from across the Atlantic—and he'd became the older brother I'd never had. He must have fulfilled that role for millions of us by now.

One evening as the dusk glowed blue through the barred windows of our great hall, I was sweeping up when the holy dude with a copy of *Highway 61 Revisited* decided to play Side 2 before evening study. Nobody stopped him. Boys came and went, coasting on their hormones, carrying their books and their coffee mugs. My broom pushed itself around the floorboards as Dylan and his wailing harmonica serenaded Queen Jane, told the stories of God & Abraham & Mack The Finger, of Saint Annie & The Sergeant-at-Arms. Then came a relentless hypnotic dirge that I first heard as 'Destination Roll'; along with Einstein, TS Eliot and Ophelia in this 11-minute song was Cinderella, who, like me, was sweeping up. A peek at the album cover afterwards revealed this song's true title— 'Desolation Row'. The exquisite futility of human existence engulfed me in a way that has never left. From now on, all my letters would be mailed from that address.

Thereafter, I measured out my life in Bob Dylan. That summer, two teenage girls in the sea in Malta told me that he had been in a car crash and was badly hurt. All I knew was that nobody had announced his death. I still dread that day.

Autumn brought *Blonde on Blonde* to the penitentiary, where I was becoming a confident inmate and was learning to be a wise guy. Our module became thronged with trainee hippies burning incense to 'Sad-Eyed Lady of the Lowlands' until our housemaster banned incense as 'conducive to drugs'. How did he know? Hearing 'Visions of Johanna' completed the alchemical reaction inside me; whatever Dylan was, I wanted to become one too.

It was on the cover of *BOB* that I first heard of Nashville. Come 1967, when Dylan was next spotted in public, he was at a hotel in Nashville, rocking an ear-to-ear beard. I, too, resolved to grow an ear-to-ear beard – which took me another four years – and to go to Nashville, wherever that was. Fifty years later, I was living there.

Like all great influences, Bob Dylan gave me something to aim for and miss; as he did, involuntarily, to thousands of other youngsters in that mythical era. I never suffered from curly hair and sunglasses (as John Lennon put it), nor did I shape a generation, or even sell very many records. I've turned out more like my parents than my teenage self might have wanted, but it's my teenage self who put me here, guided by Bob Dylan. Thank you, Bob – and many happy returns…

Robyn Hitchcock.

Emma Swift

I've Made Up My Mind to Give Myself to You

Bob Dylan Fandom in the Pandemic Era

A cloud of witnesses. To whom? To what?
To the small fire that never leaves the sky.
To the great fire that boils the daily pot.
— Louis MacNeice

I'm sitting on my terrace, lost in the stars
Listening to the sounds of the sad guitars
Been thinking it all over and I've thought it all through
I've made up my mind to give myself to you.
— Bob Dylan

If you had told me at the beginning of 2020 that it would be the year I became part of an extensive internet fan community, the kind with in-jokes and memes and teenage-like obsession over minor biographical details, haircuts and album out-takes, I would have laughed. Surely, at the dud end of my 30s, I was too old for this shit. Surely I had better ways to spend my time. People to see and songs to write and gigs to play. Enter: the pandemic. And suddenly, I'm stuck at home for months on end. And I'm out of work. And I'm craving connection to the outside world, but all I have is four walls and a Twitter account and a lot of time on my hands. Enter: the weird and wonderful of Dylanologists, an extra-ordinary group of people, who, like me, think about Bob Dylan's art in a way that other people would most likely define as maybe, just maybe, a little bit *too* much.

When I first got into Dylan, back in the late 1990s, I was a lonely, nostalgia-obsessed teenager with a bad haircut, purple corduroy flares and a deep desire to disappear into my record collection and never return. My severe fandom, not just of Mr. Dylan, but of Elvis Costello and David Bowie, Ella Fitzgerald and Linda Ronstadt, was a solitary pursuit. And while it inspired me to explore a career in music, it didn't exactly give me a sense of belonging. If anything, it magnified my feelings of being an outsider, of being old before my time, of being born in the wrong decade. But, fast-forward 25 years later and it would appear that in a year where I could have felt a crushing sense of loneliness, instead, I may have finally found my people. Or rather, Bob Dylan found them for me.

It began, as so many things do these days, with a tweet on 26th March 2020:

> Greetings to my fans and followers with gratitude for all your support and loyalty across the years. This is an unreleased song we recorded a while back that you might find interesting. Stay safe, stay observant and may God be with you. Bob Dylan.[1]

The track, 'Murder Most Foul' was a magnificently bleak 17-minute opus, rich in cultural and pop references, delivered without warning and arriving just in time for many of the devoted to have their ears pressed against their speakers from some form of quarantine or lockdown scenario.

'and May God be with you.'

Was this new song, the first new Dylan song in eight years, a sermon? I'm not brave enough to offer an answer for what the famously mercurial author of this tweet did or didn't intend by dropping the 'G' word. But I can tell you, the flock took to singing the praises of 'Murder Most Foul' with evangelistic zeal. Greil Marcus, the rock journalist's rock journalist,

---

[1]   https://twitter.com/bobdylan/status/1243389605451198465

astutely observed in the *LA Review of Books* that the online response to the song was so overwhelming it seemed to have formed its own society (Marcus 2020). And indeed the fans, even the ones who may have wavered over the years, were back praising the Patron Saint of Wayfarers and polka dot shirts and holy reverence for dead poets. And what else could possibly follow next but the rock'n'roll miracle, of course. And so, at age 79, Bob Dylan, the only songwriter to have been awarded the Nobel Prize for Literature, achieved a feat perhaps even less likely, his first #1 single on the Billboard charts.

From this blessing forward, the Dylan-mania sparked online in March continued with a surprisingly youthful fervour, so much so that you could be forgiven for thinking Bob Dylan had become the host body for Harry Styles. From fan-cams to gifs to passionate defences of dubious '80s haircuts and even more dubious '80s production choices, it was extra-ordinary and utterly delightful to witness. The people—the young and the old and those, like me, betwixt the two—still loved Dylan. And in turn, what was perhaps even more special, in a year defined by death and confinement and widespread, perfectly justifiable fear, was that they loved each other.

By the time *Rough and Rowdy Ways* was released in June, I was not merely excited about hearing the new album but I was overcome with anticipation about how my new internet friends would react. Oh, the memes we would chuckle over! The reviews to analyse and memorise! The passionate podcasts! And the songs, we'd cry and laugh and feel comforted, knowing that despite the pervasive and heart-breaking isolation that has blanketed this year like a bitter fog, somewhere, someplace else on earth, there we people just like us—people for whom Bob Dylan is not merely the world's finest songwriter—he is the charming, elusive, sage, handsome, poetic and life-affirming brother, father, uncle and grandfather we never had.

I am, in many ways, forever an adolescent, and my vinyl collection is a place I love to go wandering to and occasionally, okay perhaps more than occasionally, get lost. But online, a place I usually think of as a little bit scary, in a community of strangers with a shared fandom, I found hope, joy, comfort and a remarkable new direction home. I can't imagine how I might have made it through the pandemic without them.

References

Marcus, G. (2020) Real life rock top ten, *LA Review of Books*, 24th April, [Online], https://lareviewofbooks.org/article/real-life-rock-top-10-april-2020/

Emma Swift.

Lucy Boucher

My Bob Dylan Mask
Bob Dylan and the Art of Artifice

Introduction

Bob Dylan is an artist who contains multitudes, an actor switching costumes and stage names, never revealing the man behind the mask. In 2003, Dylan wrote and starred in *Masked & Anonymous*, a film which exemplifies his fascination with masks and personae. The film examines his early career through the self-referential character of Jack Fate—a rock star whose life and music parallels Dylan's own—wryly teasing a removal of the 'Bob Dylan' mask, while remaining anonymous behind the protective shield of the fictional lens. The theatrical mask defines Dylan's artistry. He transforms himself into the protagonists of his song-stories, creating authenticity through artifice. Though he may not be associated with the outlandish physicality of Mick Jagger's peacock strut or Elvis's swivel-hip, he physically inhabits his musical-worlds using costume, props, vocal transformations and masks. In his *Chronicles,* Dylan recalls performing as a Roman soldier in a high school play: 'I liked the costume. It felt like a nerve tonic... I felt... in the center of the planet' (Dylan 2004, 125). In this essay, I will explore the essentiality of the theatrical mask to the authenticity of Dylan's music and how he uses the thespian's tricks to reveal universal truths.

1. The Folk Hero

When Robert Zimmerman arrived in Greenwich Village in 1961, the legend of Bob Dylan was born. The young Zimmerman had experimented with aliases since his high school days in Hibbing, Minnesota, where he performed as Elston Gunn, but it was the carefully crafted 'Bob Dylan' persona that defined him. During his time in Minneapolis, where he ostensibly attended the university but learnt more from the coffee houses where he absorbed the folk music scene, Dylan experimented with different accents, clothes and ways of moving. Bonnie Beecher describes Dylan as 'talking with a real thick Oklahoma accent and wearing a cowboy hat and boots' (Wittman 1991, 20). Influenced heavily by Woody Guthrie, Dylan donned the mask of the folk-hero, costuming himself in the working-man's uniform of engineers' caps, checked shirts and denim jeans.

Dylan created a legend around himself, mythologised in the verse-poem 'My Life in a Stolen Moment', where he described a childhood spent hopping freight-trains, getting into bar brawls and being (falsely) jailed for armed robbery. This fabricated backstory was not a cynical media manipulation strategy. As Oscar Wilde once declared, if you give a man a mask, he will tell you the truth. The mask of 'Bob Dylan' has allowed the artist to reveal universal truths through the characters of his lyrical narratives. Embodying the role of the blue-collar hero, Dylan critiqued a capitalist and consumerist society that he had seen failing the working classes of his hometown of Hibbing. It was not just political songs, such as 'Masters of War', that captured the 1960s zeitgeist. His itinerant wanderer persona give meaning to lyrics such as 'I'm leaving tomorrow but I could leave today' ('Song to Woody', 1962) and captured the spiritual restlessness of a generation who couldn't hop freight-trains but could roam the landscapes of Dylan's worlds seeking shelter from the existential threats of 'a world gone wrong'.

Onstage Dylan was often accompanied only by his acoustic guitar and harmonica, but the low-key nature of these performances belied their theatricality as he inhabited the role of the 'rambling hobo'. This artifice was essential. Dylan's costume of faded shirts and cowboy boots allowed his audience to suspend disbelief and engage with the character of 'Bob Dylan'. Voice was an essential part of his theatre. The *New York Times* critic, Robert Shelton, described Dylan singing with the 'rusty voice' of 'an old farmhand folk singer' (Shelton 2011, 84).

Dylan's vocal transformations accompany his shifts in personae and musical styles—illustrated in the contrast between the rock'n'roll rasp of *Highway 61 Revisited* and the mellifluous tenor of *Nashville Skyline*—and are a testament to the importance of performance in Dylan's art. The costume, the voice and the insouciant physicality all played into the idea of Dylan as a wandering folk troubadour. In performances and interviews his physicality was infused with a nervous energy. In a 1964 appearance on *The Steve Allen Show*, he shifted in his seat and bowed his head, giving the impression that he was ill at ease in the spotlight. The nerves evaporated with the opening chords of 'The Lonesome Death of Hattie Carroll' and he directed his piercing gaze directly at the camera. The contrast between his awkward speech and his strident performance, wielding the prop of his guitar, reinforced the character of 'Bob Dylan' as a reluctant anti-hero.

The folk music scene was rooted in the ethos of authenticity, rejecting the artificial veneer of the 'straight' world, but it wholeheartedly embraced Dylan because the Dylan persona granted a middle-class Jewish boy a passport into the musical world of an itinerant folk hero. His fictitious biography was not a cynical exploitation of working-class culture, but a way to bring his music, and message, to life for his audience.

2. The Rock Star

By 1965, Dylan felt that his image had been co-opted by the folk movement and wrested from his control. He had become the poster-boy for the 1960s folk scene but felt artistically constrained by the genre's limitations. Like a type-cast actor, Dylan needed to don a different mask, fashioning himself into the antithesis of his 'protest singer' role. With the release of 'Like a Rolling Stone', a new character stepped onstage.

It is hard to tell what incensed the folk movement most about the new Dylan—his electric guitar or his expensive clothes. Dylan's embrace of popular music and dandified wardrobe was a blatant signifier of his rejection of the collectivist folk-ethos for the individualist, thrill-seeking vision of the world that came to define the atomised era of the 1960s. Wearing the mask of the avant-garde rock star, Dylan's lyrics shifted from the finger pointing of earlier records to an abstract symbolism inspired by Rimbaud and the Beat poets. The costume of the Carnaby Street rocker was a polka dot shirt, slim-fit tailored trousers, Cuban heels and pointed boots. His ever-present dark shades became an iconic mask which made the man as inscrutable as his lyrics. His new flamboyance mirrored his interest in the French symbolist poets. His decadent dress and experimentation with illicit substances allowed him to play the part of a modern-day Rimbaud whose poems advocated excess as the path to enlightenment. Lyrics such as 'motorcycle black Madonna / Two-wheeled gypsy queen' ('Gates of Eden', 1965) would have been discordant coming from the lips of Woody Guthrie. To enter this new musical world, Dylan needed a new disguise. The costume change was the first part of Dylan's transformation act. The next was his voice.

The 'rusty' voice of the weathered old farmhand that had impressed Robert Shelton was transformed on the records following 1965. On *Highway 61 Revisited* and *Bringing it All Back Home*, Dylan rejected his image as a young man old before his time, adopting an adenoidal snarl. The braying cadence of his words was delivered in a higher and more youthful register than his folk records, playing into the persona of the young Beatnik, hungry for kicks.

This vocal shift was augmented by a new physicality. In reviewing footage of this time, Christoph Lebold (2010) observes Dylan's 'uncannily puppet-like' physicality which 'actively turn the heroic character of the early sixties into a "puppet" Dylan'. This idea is underlined by the 1966 Paris press conference where Dylan told the assembled press through the mouthpiece of a ventriloquist dummy that he wasn't 'going to be anyone's puppet'. In his *Chronicles,* Dylan (2004, 120) writes of his attempts to escape the fixed image the media, record executives and fans had constructed of him as 'the Big Bubba of Rebellion' through theatrical acts intended to 'create some different impressions', such as pouring whiskey over his head and walking into a department store 'acting pie-eyed' (Dylan 2004, 120).

3. Rolling Thunder Shaman

Dylan has always been a consummate actor, disappearing into the role of his lyrical characters. Though his transformations shocked fans and critics, they could be viewed as the natural evolution of an artist experimenting with form and style. In the mid-70s Dylan sought to reveal the artifice inherent in performance. The prophet of the 1960s counterculture was reborn as the shaman of the *Rolling Thunder Revue,* leading a ramshackle troupe of gypsies bedecked in oriental scarves and silks, flowers tucked into their hatbands.

On 31st October 1964, Dylan told an audience at the Philharmonic Hall in New York that he was wearing his 'Bob Dylan mask'. A decade later, Dylan appeared on stage in Plymouth, Massachusetts, wearing a semi-transparent mask—rumoured to have been of Richard Nixon—the footage of which was used in Dylan's cinematic exploration of identity, *Renaldo & Clara*. Sam Shepard (1977, 114), the playwright and actor, recording the experience for his *Rolling Thunder Logbook*, wrote: 'it's a frightening act… The audience is totally bewildered.'

Rolling Thunder's use of elaborate costumes, masks and greasepaint owes a debt to German playwright and director Bertolt Brecht, who sought to alienate his audience from the play's action through deliberately challenging their suspension of disbelief. His actors would break the fourth wall, step out of character and call attention to stage cues. This disruption of audience expectation served to expose the contrivances of the theatre and the same mechanisms at play in society. By making the familiar strange, the audience were forced to look critically at social structures which they had complacently accepted. Dylan had been introduced to Brecht's work during his Greenwich Village days by Suze Rotolo who was an assistant at the Sheridan Square Playhouse during a staging of *Brecht on Brecht* in 1963. The young Dylan was captivated by the performance. Over a decade later, the *Rolling Thunder Revue* revealed the immense debt that Dylan owed to Brecht's influence.

Though Dylan had always toyed with ideas of authenticity in art, *Rolling Thunder*, with its elaborate costumes and theatrical stage make-up, was an overt expression of the illusory nature of art. The stage shows from this era stand in sharp contrast to the pared down performances of the early 1960s which fostered an artificial sense of intimacy. The surrealist anarchy of the *Rolling Thunder* circus, with its grand spectacle, created an aesthetic distance between Dylan and his audience which allowed Dylan to be more open, working through a period of personal upheaval during his divorce from Sara Lownds, behind the mask of a shamanic gypsy-king, whilst simultaneously revealing universal truths to his audience about life, love and heartbreak, in songs such as 'Isis' and 'Sara' (*Desire*, 1976).

Conclusion

Throughout his career, Dylan has used the tools of an actor—masks, props, personas, accents and costumes—to embody the characters that populate his musical worlds. His performances are far from a confidence trick. In *becoming* his lyrical narrators, Dylan reveals universal, social and personal truths. Dylan's ability to inhabit his characters' emotional landscapes, and subsequently those of his audience, is the hallmark of Dylan's art and longevity. The masks and personae that have defined Dylan's career are not outright rejections of his previous alter-egos, but the evolution of an artist who contains 'multitudes'. From strident youth to timeless old age, Dylan continues to defy audience expectations, using masks as a form of self-revelation, and consequently unmasking his audience's own most intimate truths, desires and fears. This is why Dylan, at 80, in his latest incarnation as the timeless voice of the American past, replete in Mississippi gambler knee-length coats and cowboy boots, remains one of the most important figures, on stage or in literature, today.

References

Dylan, B. (2004) *Chronicles: Volume One*, London: Simon & Schuster.

Lebold, C. (2011) The traitor and the stowaway: Persona construction and the quest for cultural anonymity and cultural relevance in the trajectories of Bob Dylan and Leonard Cohen, *IASPM JOURNAL*, 1 (1), pp. 1–17.

Shelton, R., Thomson, E. & Humphries, P. (2011) *No Direction Home: The Life and Music of Bob Dylan*, London: Omnibus Press.

Shepard, S. (1977) *Rolling Thunder Logbook*, New York: Viking Press.

Wittman, M. (1991) The girl from the north country, in Bauldie, J. (ed.) *Wanted Man: In Search of Bob Dylan*, pp. 18–25, New York: Citadel Press.

Hard Rain—the first television special Dylan starred in (NBC Television, public domain).

Jessica Hundley

The Man with No Name

A master of self-creation—chameleonic, charismatic, a shapeshifter adept at adapting to the many whims of his own fanaticism—Bob Dylan has occupied a multitude of guises. Born a rather tepid 'Robert Zimmerman', it is safe to say his first major foray into reinvention was his transformation into the multifaceted 'Bob Dylan' himself, the wandering bard and travelling salesman boasting a name that embodied a romantic anonymity. It was moniker that gave nod to a great Welsh poet, yet was also slyly Americanised in a classic Eisenhower-era way, an appellation that might feel at home emblazoned on the back of a Major League baseball jersey. Like 'Ty Cobb' or 'Babe Ruth', 'Bob Dylan' hinted at glory but in a humble, easily pronounceable way. It could be the name of be any number of mythic Americans, of any era—the two words easily adaptable into whatever complex persona Mr. Zimmerman might wish to occupy.

And there were to be many.

To kick it off, of course, he channelled Guthrie. Emerging first as the folk hero of the 1960s, he howled Dust Bowl protest songs revamped for a new and inflammatory era—his guitar locked and loaded and ready to kill all fascists. Later there were flirtations with identities as far flung from his true origins as a young 'Zimmerman from Minnesota' could get—a delve into Christian myth and revival, a long and fertile romance with the South, a dive into Appalachian Blue Mountain gothic. Dylan's affinity for folk eventually led him down the red dirt road to country—an inspired love affair that remains ongoing. It was a backyard bonfire first lit, in large part, by the legend of J.R. Cash. The inferno finally flickered into high flame when Dylan arrived at a Nashville studio, in 1966, to pay his tribute to the Man in Black, weathered Stetson humbly in hand.

Johnny Cash and Dylan may have seemed an unlikely pairing at the time, but in retrospect it all makes sense. Both were renegades, neither suffered fools, and neither were keen to follow anything but their own instincts when it came to making friends and enlisting collaborators. Cash is said to have liked his Bob's *Freewheelin'*, digging that album so much he is rumoured to have sent out a fan letter. Apparently the two then became pen pals (where are those letters now?), later meeting live and in the flesh at Newport's esteemed Folk Festival. By the time Dylan arrived in Music City, Tennessee, to record *Blonde on Blonde*, he and Johnny had become fast friends, brothers in musical arms.

In Nashville, Dylan would jam alongside veteran session players like Charlie McCoy, Hargus 'Pig' Robbins, the celebrated drummer W.S. Holland and Charlie Daniels, long before 'Devil Went Down to Georgia' made him a crossover superstar. In an interview with *Billboard* magazine in 2015, Daniels remembers of the experience, 'He did things his way and wasn't concerned with meter, tuning, singing. What he wanted it to be was what it turned out to be. He demonstrated a great freedom in how he went about writing a song. It didn't have to be four verses and a bridge. It was about how you were feeling and expressing his self.'

Amid the blood brotherhood in the studio, the allegiance of Cash and the Music City scenesters that supported subsequent albums Dylan recorded there—*John Wesley Harding* (1967) and *Nashville Skyline* (1969)—Zimmerman began to mutate once again. *Blonde on Blonde,* with backwoods foot stompers like 'Most Likely You Go Your Way (and I'll Go Mine)' and the wistful haunted holler ballad, 'Sad-Eyed Lady of the Lowlands', would mark the formation of a new era, the first shine of fresh skin. Each subsequent Nashville album would ultimately add another layer to the lush pelt of an entirely new animal; Dylan the Outlaw, the Cosmic Cowpoke, the Dust-Blown Stranger. In *Harding* he was the brooding Searcher, in *Skyline,* the bright-eyed and playfully mischievous Cowboy Kid. With a wide-armed embrace of both country music and the myth of the Old West, Zimmerman slipped into his new role with unexpected ease, strolling into unknown territory with the tobacco spit strut of a seasoned gunman at high noon.

This Dylan would eventually evolve into the sun-blasted traveller of *Desire* and the wild-eyed carnie and sideshow barker peddling miracle elixirs with his Rolling Thunder Revue. On 1978's *Street Legal* he would explore the Old West in historic context in the track 'Señor (Tales of Yankee Power)'. A poetic country-rock ramble, the song references 19th-century conflicts between Mexico and the US and features Dylan in the guise of saloon balladeer, the man at the player piano when the gunfight starts. But in perhaps its most poignant and complete incarnation, Dylan as cowboy would reach an apex in his work alongside Sam Peckinpah, in the latter's much-maligned and ultimately triumphant meta-Western, *Pat Garrett and Billy the Kid*.

The screenwriter Rudy Wurlitzer originally wrote the movie for his friend Monte Hellman to direct, the two having had a hit with the existential road movie *Two Lane Blacktop*. Instead, Peckinpah got the gig, the director looking to complete his triumvirate of revisionist Westerns that had begun with 1962's *Ride the High Country* and hit full stride in 1969 with *The Wild Bunch*. By the time production on *Pat Garrett* began in Durango, Mexico, however, Peckinpah was on the frontline in his lifelong battle with alcohol. While shooting, the film was plagued with issues, sparked in part by Peckinpah's volatility, as well as a bout of influenza which spread among cast and crew and the usual bluster and chaos of a Hollywood production swooping into rural Mexico, with all its baggage in tow.

An auteur turned self-proclaimed 'whore' (as he called himself in an infamous *Playboy* interview) by the early 1970s, Peckinpah was ready to go wherever Hollywood told him. But Wurlitzer's script was a stunner and the film would ultimately serve to redeem Peckinpah—albeit only after a long battle over edit and a re-release of a director's cut nearly two decades later.

But that is another story.

As production started in 1972, the movie had all the makings of great cinema—not only in the script and talent at the helm, but in the cast as well. Peckinpah had hand-picked a collection of tried and true character actors, all veterans of Westerns past. As his leads, he had matched the always formidable James Coburn as a rangy and rugged 'Garrett' to play opposite Kris Kristofferson as pretty boy 'Billy the Kid'. The latter was just about to take his meteoric ride to the top of both the film and music industry, but at the time was a relative unknown. Rumour has it that it was Kris and screenwriter Rudy, both already friends of Dylan, that helped to bring Bob onboard. Peckinpah claimed he had never heard of Dylan, but despite this confessed ignorance, the director hired him on the spot to both write the soundtrack and appear in the film as the character 'Alias'. It would be Bob's first time on the big screen, in a role that would neatly allow for full incarnation of his Frontier Outlaw aspirations. In the movie, 'Alias' arrives mysteriously on the scene in a battered stove-pipe hat with rakish feather, a knife-throwing rambler whose name slyly contains all of Dylan's many alter-egos. 'Alias' — what could be more fitting? It was name infuriatingly wry, an homage to all the mysteries that had been making the man since his inception. When we first meet 'Alias' onscreen a character called 'Denver' inquires, 'What's your name, boy?'

> Alias: Alias.
> Denver: Alias what?
> Alias: Alias, anything you please.
> Denver: What do we call you?
> Alias: Alias.
> Beaver: Hell, let's call him Alias!
> Alias: That's what I'd do.
> Denver: Alias it is.

Who is Alias? Who is Dylan? These are queries that contain a multitude of replies, depending on the time and place asked. Yet what remains from this moment in Dylan's continual metamorphosis is not so much his appearance in the film (he holds his own), but his evocative and completely unexpected score. Primarily instrumental, the tracks feel both nostalgic and fresh, a ghost town sound that would echo in the music of Dylan's co-star Kristofferson and later in the Texas sky ache of artists like Townes Van Zandt and Terry Allen. Written partly while Dylan was on set, the soundtrack to *Pat Garrett and Billy the Kid* was recorded in early 1973, at studios in Burbank, California and Mexico City. On hand for both sessions were some of Dylan's most talented collaborators — former Byrd Roger McGuinn on guitar as well as (under the alias 'Jolly Roger') on banjo, Booker T. Jones on bass, the legendary Carol Hunter on twelve string and the illustrious Jim Keltner on drums. The latter remembers (in an interview for Howard Sounes' Dylan bio, *Down the Highway*) the sessions as 'monumental', in particular the recording of the track 'Knockin' on Heaven's Door'. 'It was such a touching song; it was the first time I actually cried when I was playing.'

In the film, the first chords of 'Knockin'' can be heard just as Sheriff Colin Baker, played by the unforgettable Slim Pickens, is dispatched in a chaotic gunfight amid blasts of silver six-shooters. Baker's wife kneels weeping and watches as her husband stumbles back into a slow-moving river, the sky beyond streaked with sunset, Baker's big grin marking a life lived without regret. The scene contains that most perfect of cinematic moments, when music and image combine to hit us all straight in the heart.

The song, written for the film, eventually took a life of its own, becoming perhaps one of the greatest, in Dylan's legacy of nearly infinite greats. Over the decades it has been reinterpreted by artist across genres, from Gram and Emmy Lou to Guns n' Roses. At once anthemic, plaintive and timeless, 'Knockin' on Heaven's Door' is one of the few songs on the soundtrack boasting vocals, it's lyrics now an oft-repeated mantra of romantic melancholia. The narrative thread within the song is simple. There are only two verses, one dedicated to Billy and the other to Pat — both describing a laying down of arms and calm acceptance of coming death. It is a Zen kaon of a song — pulling back the veil between worlds in a way that references the finest of American poetry — the visceral gusto of Whitman cut through with the Dickinson spareness.

Although the soundtrack was panned when it was released, it has since emerged as one of Dylan's previously unsung successes — his first experiment in film scoring, effortlessly aligning with Peckinpah's raw and violently beautiful cinematic story. Ultimately it has become not just the soundtrack to the movie, but to a particular time place and Dylan persona. 'Alias' is Dylan. Dylan is an alias.

In Zimmerman's dream of the West, the landscape is tumbleweed strewn and elegiac, populated by men in the midst of reinvention, discarding old identities for characters imbued with the armour of impenetrable mystery. It is a place where the past is abandoned and forgotten, left on the eastern edge of the Mississippi, a world where anonymity is the key to evolution. In other words, exactly the kind of transitory territory where a young Zimmerman might feel most at home. In a brief, cathartic scene in *Pat Garrett and Billy the Kid*, there is a revelatory moment when James Coburn's world-weary 'Garrett' asks the stranger, 'Alias' — 'Who are you?'

And Dylan grins, replying as both his character, and as himself. 'That's a good question.'

Dylan's 12th studio album and first soundtrack LP (1973, public domain).

Barb Jungr

Tangled Up In Blue
Dylan And Love

I'm sitting on my terrace, lost in the stars
Listening to the sounds of the sad guitars
Been thinking it all over and I've thought it all through
I've made up my mind to give myself to you.

Playing the *Rough and Rowdy Ways* collection recently, I was held in suspension, mid-air, by the directness of 'I've Made Up My Mind to Give Myself to You'. It had the same sense of clarity, purity and place as 'If Not for You' whilst being clearly many years further along in time and experience. There was no cynicism, none of the 'take me or leave me' that characterises so many of his early songs of love and the fickle heart. Inspired, I began work on an arrangement of it with my arranger Jenny to have a crack at singing it. Because it's only when I sing the songs that I start to grasp their own internal logic, it is then the song slips into view at the corner of the mind's eye. And sure enough when we *found* the musical shape, found our feet with it, I was at once transported into a landscape of empty desert roads, in a balladic American mythic world populated by lone men and women drinking tequila in bars as the neon flickers on and off on the shabby motel in the distance.

And then I wondered to whom Bob Dylan was addressing this private inner statement of heartfelt, heart-broken, heart-patched-up-again intensity? Was this a general statement of the way he feels while looking at the sun going down from his porch in Malibu (from where he once told Mavis Staples he could see Hawaii before they sang a gospel song together)? Or was it a question posed to someone intimate, someone who once walked alongside him and features in his work? Was he thinking of his 'Sad-Eyed Lady of the Lowlands', the muse of muses and Dylan's first wife, Sara Lowndes Dylan? Or the cast-aside Joan Baez, for whom he has retained, indeed both have for each other, that near-psychic bond musicians share whatever might have happened between them. Or Suze Rotolo, perhaps the inspiration for 'Boots of Spanish Leather'? When I'm singing the song, it feels as though it is to someone who was once very close. And maybe, because it is Bob Dylan writing, it's no one, or it's Mavis Staples herself; after all, he always had a penchant for Mavis. Because it's never clear, and that's what makes the love songs so interesting. In Dylan's illuminating autobiography, *Chronicles*, there are two partners mentioned at different points in time, named 'my wife'. But we know that those two wives are different women. As there are slips, beats in time and place, so there are slips and beats of the heart. Thus something has clearly shifted since the casual insouciance of having your cake and eating it in 'Lay lady Lay'.

My own sense of the towering magnitude of Dylan's work comes from the intuition and, to use a Dylan-type word, learning, that comes from singing the songs over and over again. Letting the songs speak through the voice gives me an insight that literary analysis of the texts can sometimes miss. The music, the melody, illuminates beyond and below the words; and the unique binding of music and lyric releases emotions that a cold reading of the words may not unlock so easily. Dylan's love songs do everything that all of Dylan's other songs do, when they're working at their peak. They tap into our own inner workings, at a near-Jungian inner, deep-sea depth, and so we all understand, for ourselves, in ourselves, each in our way, whatever we need to, from the text. Through that they have achieved a universality found in musical artworks like *Fiddler on the Roof* or the songs of The Beatles. We know what we were doing when we first heard them. The playwright and gay activist Noël Greig once recalled in detail returning from the record shop with his precious newly released copy of *New Morning*, recounting how he sat with his flatmates in the sunshine at the kitchen table as they played that album together, over and over again, until day turned to dusk. Is it any surprise that works of this creative magnitude stamp themselves onto our personal musical DNA? Across continents both physical and inner, these deep, multifaceted songs meander across gender, age and outlook, filtering into our psyches and ringing bells of recognition. So Dylan's love songs tell us about ourselves. They track all kinds of love through all of life's vicissitudes, from young, open, wild and free meadow sex and sawdust; through cityscapes, myriad lovers, children, divorce, loss, misunderstanding and pain; through romantic delusion, realisation and occasional wistful regret; and then finally, to understanding.

I don't think I can bear to live my life alone.

Written in 1974, 'Tangled Up In Blue' is a song I've performed for twenty-plus years now and I'm still blown away every time I sing it. That self-prophetic vision of a person's life spread out ahead of them. A remembered love affair that became a marriage, a life lived across a continent, meetings and partings, a woman in a bar later who opens a poetry book which spills its guts into the heart of the singer until finally the realisation that, after everything, 'I'm going back again, I got to get to her somehow.' Finally the writer tells us the only way it can be, to 'keep on keeping on like a bird that flew' since he's 'still on the road heading for another joint'. Because what else is there for a musician? It's what we do. It's all we do. The Never Ending Tour is completely understandable to any artist. It's not logical. And Dylan is no stranger to the things that lie beyond comprehension, leaving fact and science in their wake. The fortune tellers, the arcane, dark-haired, dark-eyed women who read palms and cards, stars and fate, all lie watchful in the shadows falling across his canon. He is awake to the mysterious connections of fate and chance; where life hinges and changes on a dime, or a flip of the dice or the turn of a tarot card, like a fickle, faithless, faithful heart. Because 'We always did feel the same, we just saw it from a different point of view, Tangled Up In Blue.'

The earlier love songs of Bob Dylan take us from 'If Not for You' with its deceptively sweet paean to romance, pinned like a butterfly to a board by the emotionally pivotal 'without your love I'd be nothing at all, I'd be lost if not for you', through to the bitter accusation of 'Don't Think Twice' which is a love song in as much as it is an exorcism of the rejected lover from the wounded, angry heart, and everything in between. 1975 and 1976 bring *Blood on The Tracks* and *Desire* and yield their heartsore bounty with 'Isis' and 'Sara', 'Abandoned Love', released years later, comes from the same time and from the same wounds and is equally revealing. 'Won't you descend from the throne, from where you sit? Let me feel your love one more time before I abandon it.' 'Shelter from the Storm' echoes 'Tangled Up In Blue' in its scope, complex subtlety and compression of time and experience, and like 'Tangled' projects from the personal through the mythic to the philosophical. But the awareness of what's been lost is emerging. 'If I could only turn back the clock to when God and her were born.'

Time Out of Mind in 1997 allows Daniel Lanois' production to paint watercolour in sound and, depending on your taste, succeeds, or doesn't, in serving Dylan's vision. While 'Make You Feel My Love' lent itself to so many relationships of the time ('It's our song,' said a friend, 'we play it to remind ourselves of the time we fell in love'), it's the extraordinary 'Not Dark Yet' that peels away the paint and rhinestones of The Rolling Thunder past to reveal the stark white bones of love and loss beneath. 'I ain't looking for nothing in anyone's eyes' is about as blunt as it gets. And a new path becomes visible only in the moonlight. 'Your charms have broken many a heart and mine is surely one', he says in 'Sugar Baby', from 2001's revelatory *"Love And Theft"*. In 'Mississippi', 'I'm gonna look at you 'til my eyes go blind', and the mix of philosophy and desire, love and loss, bind together and like tumbleweed in the Arizona desert blow across dusty mindscapes.

Tempest brings hope that it's not all over, that there's love to come and love to renew, and gives us a love song that parallels 'I'll Be Your Baby Tonight' in 'Soon After Midnight', where although 'it's soon after midnight' 'my day has just begun', ending with the telling 'and I don't want anyone but you'. Those three albums form an arc of a world-weary romantic's heart like a rainbow to travel along.

Triplicate, the Dylan detour (or is it?) into The Great American Songbook, brings songs as important and deeply personal as all the self-penned love songs. Watching from the front row of the balcony at the London Palladium, it was Bob Dylan's interpretations of Mercer's 'Autumn Leaves' and Jimmy Dorsey's 'All Or Nothing At All' that brought me to tears. Shredded. I'd never experienced that before, in that way, at a Dylan concert. The combination of the lived experience in his now extraordinary timbre and the way that his unusual, stylised vocal technique manacled itself uniquely to those jazz standards blew the songs out of their familiar water and resonated with something as deep and fathomless, committed and faithless, as every love song he'd carved from his own heart.

And so to where we began: Dylan at 80, and his *Rough and Rowdy Ways*. The colour-tinted cover art shows couples dancing on a strangely lit wooden floor in a long-gone underground club on Cable Street in Whitechapel. There's the past and it's been subtly altered in the present. 'I Contain Multitudes' has at times an almost Cohen-esque quality to the sentiments expressed. 'I'll drink to the truth and the things we said, I'll drink to the man that shares your bed.' The musings that occupy this new collection seem to tie together so many of the threads floating in the blowin' wind of the past.

Dylan and love: sex, spiritual connection, love as moon, spoon, and June. Love for men who arrive in long black coats and sweep you off your feet. Love for men who enter bars with a hidden agenda and ride off with wild women. Love that never ends. 'Yes, and only if my own true love was waitin' / Yes, and if I could hear her heart a-softly poundin' / Only if she was lyin' by me / Then I'd lie in my bed once again.' For surely, 'Tomorrow Is a Long Time'.

With the confidence of youth and that near-brash piercing intelligence, one could have levelled an accusation of cynicism, but as the morning light has given way to starlight, so the easy one-night stand of 'I'll Be Your Baby Tonight' has turned to the deeper commitment of 'I've Made Up My Mind to Give Myself to You'. The musical changes accompanying have been significant. The self-producing has brought forth a mellow Americana that evokes memory and place, the sound of the train coming through the station at night calling to mind Dylan's paintings of lonely station platforms, of orange mountains and red skies, and of women, voluptuous and self-contained. There's something beautifully direct in the quiet certainty of purpose of every track of *Rough and Rowdy Ways*. Dylan at 80 understands this world and his inner world, as we all would hope we would our own. Moreover, he understands his own heart, and all the people who've lodged in there, or passed by, every scar and wound, every dusty trail of lust, every drunken awakening and hurtful slur. If 'Don't Think Twice' is the past, the then, so this is the here, and now. One of the major love songs of his canon, 'I've Made Up My Mind to Give Myself to You' expresses a quality of the weariness of acceptance that can only perhaps be understood fully by an ageing heart. At 80 Dylan remains the romantic he always was:

I've traveled from the mountains to the sea
I hope that the gods go easy with me
I knew you'd say yes, I'm saying it too
I've made up my mind to give myself to you

Barb Jungr (photograph by Steve Ullathorne).

Harrison Hewitt

Only Change

Once upon a time I was sitting on a park bench, wearing a shirt with Bob Dylan's face on it, when a gentleman approached me to express his displeasure. 'I can't stand Bob Dylan!', he said. With my épée at home, I was ill-prepared for a duel, so I nodded my head to signal that I'd registered his objection, and the gentleman—having unburdened himself of bile—marched along to wherever it is people go when they've fulfilled their obligations to an anecdote. I can't say it was a new experience: as any Dylan diehard knows, there's a critic in every park. Still, no matter how many times it happens, and no matter how much I believe that people have the right to say silly things, whenever somebody announces an aversion to Bob Dylan, there's a part of me that can't process the concept. You don't like Bob Dylan? Which one?

There are so many versions of Bob Dylan that saying you're a fan of the man is like saying you're a fan of sports. Are we talking about Brazilian jiu-jitsu or bowling? A lot of stuff fits under that umbrella. Similarly, saying you don't like Bob Dylan is like saying you don't like vegetables. You might hate squash, but why should that preclude you from enjoying green beans? Plant even the most fervent faultfinders in front of the buffet that is Bob Dylan's discography and eventually they will find something they can swallow. At least they will if they don't want to starve.

Whether we want to consider bootlegs or just take the official releases, there's one indisputable fact about Dylan's body of work, and that is this: it's big. Really big. The man has been doing what he does for a long, long time. Bob Dylan recorded his first album in 1961. That's almost as close to the 19th century as it is to the moment I'm writing this. Here are some things that had not yet been invented when Bob Dylan's first album, *Bob Dylan*, was recorded: the cordless telephone, buffalo wings, the sport of snowboarding, the handheld calculator, the Heimlich manoeuvre, the Post-it note, the digital camera, microwave popcorn bags, paintball, light beer, the space shuttle, the internet, zip codes, tilt-and-roll luggage, and the self-wringing mop. When it comes to time and its long-standing relationship with Bob Dylan, there are a lot of facts that can be hard to believe: like the fact that Dylan's most recent album, *Rough and Rowdy Ways*, is more than twice as far removed from Dylan's first album as Dylan's first album was from the recordings of Robert Johnson. Or the fact that *Rough and Rowdy Ways* is as distant from *Time Out of Mind* as *Time Out of Mind* is from *Blood on the Tracks*, which doesn't seem right no matter how many times I run the numbers. Or the fact that Dylan was a Traveling Wilbury in the first half of his career.

How has he made it this far? How has he stayed good? So many artists from Dylan's generation, and from generations before and after, have seen their wells run dry. Why hasn't his? And just where in the heck is his well anyway? These are easy questions to ask, but they're not easy to answer. After all, if there were a formula for Dylan's continued success, artists the world over would be cribbing it. They aren't, which means there probably isn't. Either that or Dylan is hiding the formula, perhaps somewhere inside his well.

Leonard Cohen was fond of saying, 'If I knew where the good songs came from, I'd go there more often.' It's foolish to try, but if I were forced to offer up an explanation for Dylan's creative endurance, I would suggest it has a lot to do with how he views the arc of his life. Reviewing Dylan's memoir *Chronicles: Volume One*, the writer Catherine Nichols observed: 'The tone of his worldview changed as he got older; as that older self writing his younger self, he didn't make any corrections. He writes each version of himself with equal weight, without condescending to the young self from the perspective of someone who has learned to see things differently.' This is something Dylan does in interviews, too. In 2017, Dylan was asked by Bill Flanagan what he sees when he watches footage of himself performing 40 or 50 years ago. He responded: 'I see Nat King Cole, Nature Boy—a very strange enchanted boy, a terribly sophisticated performer, got a cross section of music in him, already postmodern. That's a different person than who I am now.' A different person, but not a lesser person. There's an innocence to the way Dylan describes his younger self and in the matter-of-fact way he admits that he's lost touch with that person. There's no elation or regret, there's just a clear-eyed acknowledgment of reality. As Nichols notes, Dylan's memory doesn't seem to get hung up perceiving 'patterns of improvement or decay'. Rather, one gets the sense that he sees his artistic life as a story of change, and change only.

In a 1984 interview with MTV's Martha Quinn, Dylan expressed annoyance at those who seek to impose order upon his discography: 'They go from this [album] to that and say, "Because this one was here, this one's here. You know, and this one's here and, oh yeah, well, this is a logical extension of that and, all right, well, okay, this don't fit in but this one does, and this is connected to that," and so it all makes sense.' Dylan has never felt that his work needs to make sense, and the absence of this impulse has freed him up to take chances. This freedom is then enhanced by his not standing in judgment of anything he's done after the fact. As Dylan explained to Randy Anderson in 1978, he doesn't believe in regrets: 'Regrets just keep you chained to the past. You gotta make peace with the past. There's no reason to regret it. You've done it, just make peace with it.' Asked if he is at peace with the past, Dylan replied: 'I am, yeah. I try to be, yeah. I always try to keep my past and my present and my future all on the same level.'

Although Dylan doesn't pit the different periods of his career against one another, he does draw a distinction between the songs he wrote in the infancy of his career and the songs he's written since. As he told Jonathan Cott in 1978: 'Right through the time of *Blonde on Blonde* I was [writing songs] unconsciously. Then one day I was half-stepping, and the lights went out. And since that point, I more or less had amnesia. It took me a long time to get to do consciously what I had used to be able to do unconsciously.' Dylan returned to the topic in 1987, telling Kurt Loder: 'As I look back on it now, I am surprised that I came up with so many of [those early songs]. At the time it seemed like a natural thing to do. Now I can look back and see that I must have written those songs "in the spirit," you know? Like "Desolation Row" —I was just thinkin' about that the other night. There's no logical way that you can arrive at lyrics like that. I don't know how it was done.' In 2004, during an interview with Ed Bradley for *60 Minutes*, Dylan quoted the opening lines of 'It's Alright Ma (I'm Only Bleeding)' —'*Darkness at the break of noon / Shadows even the silver spoon / The handmade blade, the child's balloon*' —then said: 'Try to sit down and write something like that. There's a magic to that, and it's not Siegfried and Roy kind of magic, you know? It's a different kind of a penetrating magic. And, you know, I did it. I did it at one time.' Asked by Bradley if he could do it again, Dylan shook his head no. When Bradley followed up to ask if that disappointed him, Dylan suggested it did not: 'You can't do something forever. I did it once, and I can do other things now.' Another statement devoid of judgment. No progression, no regression. Only change.

> Things are going to happen whether I know why they happen or not. It just gets more complicated when you stick yourself into it. You don't find out why things move. You let them move; you watch them move; you stop them from moving: you start them moving. But you don't sit around and try to figure out why there's movement. (Bob Dylan to Nat Hentoff, 1966)

After Dylan was awarded the 2016 Nobel Prize in Literature, he was criticised in certain circles for taking two weeks to make a public statement of thanks, and then again for not attending the Banquet. I felt this reaction was unfair, because I take Dylan at his word when he says that his early songs, so often celebrated, were written 'in the spirit'. If he feels that he was guided in writing those songs by a force beyond his control, it naturally follows that he would be uncomfortable taking the credit for their creation. By eschewing celebrations of his talent, and downplaying his own agency, Dylan shows that he's grateful for the gifts he's been given—gifts, not awards—and he's grateful to the giver of those gifts. (For his 2018 art exhibit *Mondo Scripto*, Dylan handwrote the lyrics to 60 of his most famous songs. In contrast to many of his later songs, which he freely and in some cases drastically revised, I was struck by how he left the lyrics to his early to mid-sixties songs—written 'unconsciously'—almost entirely intact. It's as if he felt he didn't have the authority to monkey around with them.)

Unconscious. Conscious. Contrasting methods, but not competing methods. Dylan differentiates, but he doesn't waste time or energy trying to get back what's lost, because he knows he can only do what he's able to do when he's able to do it. He doesn't create a conflict within himself where no conflict is necessary. He just keeps moving.

I never think in terms of growth. I'll tell you what I do think, though: You never stop at anywhere. There's no place to stop at. You know them places at the side of the road where you can stop? They're just an illusion. You got to get back on the road. And that's all them places to stop are, that's all they are [are illusions]. I mean, you may want to stop, but you can't stay there. (Bob Dylan to Bert Kleinman, 1984)

References

Anderson, R. (1978) An interview with Dylan, *Minnesota Daily*, 17th February.

Bradley, E. (2004) *60 Minutes* video interview, [Online], https://www.cbsnews.com/news/60-minutes-bob-dylan-rare-interview-2004/

Cott, J. (1978) *Bob Dylan: The Rolling Stone Interview, Part 2*, [Online], https://www.rollingstone.com/music/music-news/bob-dylan-the-rolling-stone-interview-part-2-173545/

Flanagan, B. (2017) *Q&A with Bill Flanagan*, [Online], https://www.bobdylan.com/news/qa-with-bill-flanagan/

Hentoff, N. (1966) Playboy interview: Bob Dylan, *Playboy*, March.

Kleinman, B. (1984) Dylan on Dylan, *Westwood One radio special*.

Loder, K. (1987) *The Rolling Stone 20th Anniversary Interview: Bob Dylan*, [Online], https://www.rollingstone.com/music/music-news/the-rolling-stone-20th-anniversary-interview-bob-dylan-194911/

Nichols, C. (2016) *How I Changed My Mind About Bob Dylan*, [Online], https://jezebel.com/how-i-changed-my-mind-about-bob-dylan-1785914944

Quinn, M. (1984) MTV video interview, *YouTube*, [Online], https://www.youtube.com/watch?v=_wvFN92WQAo

Bob Dylan, Joan Baez and Santana, Hamburg, May 1984 (Heinrich Klaffs, under the Creative Commons Attribution-Share Alike 2.0 Generic license CC-BY-SA 2.0).

Keith Frankish

Getting There

'I love you, Bob!', a voice behind me yelled as Bob Dylan walked on stage in Sheffield in 1998. It was a deep male voice with a strong South Yorkshire accent. Not the sort of voice you might expect to express emotion easily, but it was professing love, and there was a sob in it. I knew how the speaker felt. We feel that know Bob Dylan, that we love him. After all, he often sings in the first person — about himself, his loves, his anger, his heartbreak, his despair. And we feel that he knows us, too. He's been through tough times, like us; he knows what it's like and he expresses it with an intensity and beauty that transforms the pain and makes it seem all right.

Of course, few of us know Bob Dylan the man — the musician and songwriter born in Duluth in 1941 and now in his eightieth year. Dylan is a creative artist who uses the first person as a dramatic device and expresses himself through a variety of personas. But it's just this that forges the tight connection to our hearts. Dylan draws on a vast range of sources, musical and literary, which he refines and transmutes into songs that are both distinctively his and deeply rooted in tradition. When he sings, he is channelling a thousand other voices who have sung before. Like Walt Whitman, he contains multitudes, and it's his multitudinousness that enables him to speak to us so intimately. We can each find a Dylan who speaks to us — our reflection in the man's multifaceted brilliance.

Dylan also keeps renewing himself artistically. As he exhausts the potential of one persona, he goes back to his sources, returning with new materials, new techniques and new voices. And so, unlike many other popular musicians, he has been able to remain creatively active throughout his life, singing songs of midlife and old age that are as moving and potent as those of his youth. Nothing better illustrates this than the way he has sung about mortality. Here's how it goes. Or rather, here's how it goes with *my* Dylan, the one that speaks directly to me.

Death has always been a presence in Dylan's work. On his debut album the twenty-year-old Dylan was singing about fixing to die and raucously pleading that his grave be kept clean—asserting his place in a folk tradition occupied with the bitter realities of life. But the young Dylan sings of death with a detachment that only a youth could maintain. Death is often terrible and cruel, but it doesn't touch him personally:

> There's seven people dead
> On a South Dakota farm
> There's seven people dead
> On a South Dakota farm
> Somewhere in the distance
> There's seven new people born
>
> —'Ballad of Hollis Brown'

Even when he sings of his own death, it is as one who sets the terms and is in control of the situation:

> I will not go down under the ground
> 'Cause somebody tells me that death's comin' 'round
> An' I will not carry myself down to die
> When I go to my grave my head will be high
>
> —'Let Me Die in My Footsteps'

He will meet death actively, like an outlaw taking one more cup of coffee before setting out to meet his fate, or a wounded sheriff knocking on heaven's door:

> It's gettin' dark, too dark [for me] to see
> I feel like I'm knockin' on heaven's door
>
> —'Knockin' On Heaven's Door'

In Dylan's Christian period, death assumes a different guise. It won't do to bemoan it or fight it; we must answer the question it poses:

> Are you ready to meet Jesus?
> Are you where you ought to be?

Will He know you when He sees you
Or will He say, "Depart from Me"?

Are you ready, hope you're ready
Am I ready, am I ready?
Am I ready, am I ready?

—'Are You Ready'

But though the question is peremptory, it's not frightening. The gospel-infused songs of this period burst with energy and conviction. Dylan is surfing a wave of faith, and nothing can stop him, not even death. He's still in control. The mood dissipates in the following years, but enough of it survives to produce the serene and uplifting 'Death is Not the End', from the 1988 album *Down in the Groove*.

Then, in the nineties, things change. At a creative dead end and with his voice failing, Dylan went back to his roots to renew himself, producing two albums of spare, increasingly dark folk covers. The reinvention culminated in 1997's *Time Out of Mind*, where he debuted a new persona, the shipwrecked midlifer battered by love and loss, and a new voice, broken, vulnerable, painfully expressive, and perfectly suited to darker, less secure themes. In this persona he sang about death very differently, expressing the cruel change of perspective that age brings. In 'Trying to Get to Heaven', he's no longer a hero knocking dramatically on heaven's door, but a sick and disillusioned man trying to get through the door before it's shut upon him:

Gonna sleep down in the parlor
And relive my dreams
I'll close my eyes and I wonder
If everything is as hollow as it seems
When you think that you've lost everything
You find out you can always lose a little more
I been to Sugar Town, I shook the sugar down
Now I'm trying to get to heaven before they close the door

The song speaks to everyone who has been hit by the brutal midlife realisation that the window for achievement or redemption is remorselessly closing. 'Not Dark Yet' develops the theme. Death is not abstract

now, and it's not under Dylan's control. It is setting the terms, and he is
going to have to adjust to them:

> Shadows are falling and I've been here all day
> It's too hot to sleep, time is running away

The realisation leaves him stalled and disorientated. The wave of faith has
withdrawn, and night is coming:

> I was born here and I'll die here against my will
> I know it looks like I'm moving, but I'm standing still
> Every nerve in my body is so vacant and numb
> I can't even remember what it was I came here to get away from
> Don't even hear a murmur of a prayer
> It's not dark yet, but it's getting there

As our time runs out, so does our freedom, a point made with laconic
resignation in the opening lines of another song from the *Time Out of
Mind* sessions, the majestic 'Mississippi', later rerecorded for 2001's "*Love
And Theft*":

> Every step of the way we walk the line
> Your days are numbered, so are mine
> Time is pilin' up, we struggle and we scrape
> We're all boxed in, nowhere to escape

Yet loss brings release, too, and forgiveness:

> Well my ship's been split to splinters and it's sinking fast
> I'm drownin' in the poison, got no future, got no past
> But my heart is not weary, it's light and it's free
> I've got nothin' but affection for all those who've sailed with me
>   —'Mississippi'

Time Out of Mind is a sombre album, but it closes on a different note, with
the long, dreamlike 'Highlands'. Here we find Dylan wandering around,
lost and confused. He flirts with a waitress, dodges a mangy dog, looks
with envy at the young lovers in the park ('Well, I'd trade places with any
of them / In a minute, if I could'), and wishes someone would push back

the clock for him. But all the while he's got a vision of a better place, a land of healing, the Highlands ('gentle and fair / Honeysuckle blooming in the wildwood air'). He doesn't know how to get there, but he's working on it:

Well, my heart's in the Highlands at the break of day
Over the hills and far away
There's a way to get there and I'll figure it out somehow
But I'm already there in my mind
And that's good enough for now

How do you find your promised land? If you're Dylan, you search in your past. In the two decades since *Time Out of Mind*, Dylan has continually returned to his sources. Not to his folk roots this time, but further back, back to the songs of his childhood — Christmas carols, Sinatra classics and the American standards he heard on the wireless back in Duluth. He has produced albums of these songs — *uncovering* them, as he puts it: 'Lifting them out of the grave and bringing them into the light of day' (Greene 2014). And in revitalising the songs, he has revitalised himself and his creative imagination too. The result has been another creative peak, *Rough and Rowdy Ways*, released in 2020.

The album reveals another new Dylan, an aged crooner, with a sweeter voice, a playful attitude to life, and breath-taking assurance. Mortality is still a theme, but it's handled with a new ease — not the ease of detachment now, but the ease of acceptance. There's a door again, with a sinister Black Rider guarding it:

Black Rider Black Rider tell me when — tell me how
If there ever was a time then let it be now
Let me go through — open the door
My soul is distressed my mind is at war
                                    — 'Black Rider'

But Dylan's seen through this bogeyman. He's a con, like Monty Python's Black Knight:

Don't hug me — don't flatter me — don't turn on the charm
I'll take out a sword and have to hack off your arm

Dylan can disarm him with a song, pension him off:

> Some enchanted evening I'll sing you a song
> Black Rider Black Rider you've been on the job too long

Dylan's made it through the lonesome valley of 'Trying to Get to Heaven'. He's back in control, not of death itself, but of his attitude to it.

As for himself, Dylan knows what to do now. He's going to do with himself what we must do with everything in the end. In the almost unbearably poignant 'I've Made Up My Mind to Give Myself to You', he sings about letting go, about giving oneself to another. He's singing to a lover, and to posterity too. His legacy is himself—the multitudinous Dylan he has created—and he's giving it to us:

> I've traveled from the mountains to the sea
> I hope that the gods go easy with me
> I knew you'd say yes, I'm saying it too
> I've made up my mind to give myself to you

And, finally, he's found that visionary land he was looking for. It's not in the highlands after all, but down in the flatlands, at the southern end of Route 1, way down in Key West:

> Key West is the place to be
> If you're looking for immortality
> Key West is paradise divine
> Key West is fine and fair
> If you lost your mind, you'll find it there
> Key West is on the horizon line
>
>   —'Key West (Philosopher Pirate)'

Dylan knows how to get there now. He knew all along really. He just has to tune in to that pirate radio station that has been playing in his head for eight decades and keep on the road ('Stay on the road / follow the highway sign'). He's heading to a place of old songs, old rituals and old stories, of gaudy flowers and intoxicating plants. It's never winter there, and you can hide out 'under the sun / Under the radar—under the gun'. It is a place for outsiders like him, 'Like Ginsberg, Corso and Kerouac / Like Louie and Jimmy and Buddy and all of the rest'. It's a place that contains multitudes. It will be a while before he gets there, we hope, but he's in the clear now.

I love you, Bob.[1]

References

Greene, A. (2014) Bob Dylan will 'uncover' Frank Sinatra classics on new album, *Rolling Stone*, 9th December, [Online], https://www.rolling stone.com/music/music-news/bob-dylan-will-uncover-frank-sinatra-classics-on-new-album-52143/

Bob Dylan and his band in Buenos Aires, Argentina, 27th April 2012 (photograph by Adrian Lasso, licensed under the Creative Commons Attribution-Share Alike 2.0 Generic license CC BY-SA 2.0).

---

[1] The author thanks Constantine Sandis for his comments on an earlier draft of this piece.

Natalie Ferris

'Cold Irons Bound'
Bob Dylan, Sculpture and Surreality

In 2013, Bob Dylan decided to exhibit a series of iron sculptures that had never been intended for public view. The show 'Mood Swings', at the Halcyon Gallery, London, marked the first time Dylan exhibited his sculptural work, displaying a selection of intricately crafted iron forms assembled alongside pastiches of covers of iconic American magazines, such as *Life* and *Rolling Stone*.[1] Up until 2013, objects such as these had been reserved as gifts for friends or made for his own simple enjoyment, but when approached to put together a show Dylan demurred, and spent three years producing the works made available to the exhibition. It is only in the last decade that Dylan's artistic career has found an audience. Of course, Dylan drew the cover art for The Band's 1968 LP *Music From Big Pink* and his 1970 double album *Self Portrait*, and his affinity with Surrealist art and literature is well-documented, but for most of his professional career he kept his artwork private. In recent years he has opened himself up to galleries and spectators around the world, showing work as part of the celebrated Drawn Blank series in Chemnitz, Germany, at the Kunstsammlungen in 2007, the Brazil Series at the Statens Museum, Copenhagen in 2010, Revisionist Art at New York's Gagosian Gallery in 2012, and in his 2016 exhibition of American Landscapes at the Halcyon Gallery in London.

---

1   The 'Mood Swings' exhibition was on show between 16th November 2013 and 25th January 2014.

Situated alongside a sequence of metal tables and a folding screen, eight flat door-shaped frameworks of welded metal took central focus, displayed at interstitial points between rooms or mounted onto the white walls of the gallery. Dylan named the sculptures his 'gates': 'Gates appeal to me', Dylan said, 'because of the negative space they allow. They can be closed but at the same time they allow the seasons and breezes to enter and flow. They can shut you out or shut you in. And in some ways there is no difference' (Dylan 2013). His gates are full of gaps and holes between their overlapping materials, preventing passage but allowing one to see what lies behind them. Notably, Dylan's gates take on this additional meaning, as portals of near talismanic importance, in terms of the carefully selected objects that feature in their decoration. The eight gates feature wrenches, roller skates, meat grinders and lawn tools, as well as more pictorial devices, such as a silhouetted bird, a guitar and a treble clef. Each sculpture is devised of a flat iron framework, onto which numerous separate metal objects are welded with globs of bronze that look like glue, testament to the fact that Dylan made these sculptures himself without relying on a team of professional assistants. These small glimpses of amateurism are arguably part of their workaday charm.

Suspended, these ordinary objects take on a symbolic quality, read in sequences or patterns across the surface of the work. Dylan's gates are interesting exercises in composition, drawing together disparate elements to speak to one another or transforming these objects into new collisions to form new shapes, new shadows, new resonances. This prompts the question: what significance do these objects hold for Dylan? Like a magpie, Dylan has picked at the curiosities that litter the roads and farmlands of Minnesota and that are scattered throughout the landscapes of his travels while touring across the US, discerning amidst the detritus those elements that will communicate something of their origins. Over many decades, he amassed a vast collection of found materials, everything from farm equipment, children's toys, kitchen utensils, antique firearms, vintage scrap metal and industrial artefacts, to chains, cogs, axes, wheels, bolts, nails and so on. Many of these collected objects have now been transferred to his studio in Los Angeles, in which he has built an adjoining storehouse of used metal.

This medium speaks to his own history: 'I've been around iron all my life ever since I was a kid', Dylan explained in his catalogue note, 'I was born and raised in iron ore country [Hibbing, Minnesota] where you could breathe it and smell it every day. And I've always worked with it in one form or another' (Dylan 2013). Indeed, it is nothing new in Dylan's creative universe: in 1978 he told the *Minnesota Times* that when he returns to his home state, 'I like to blast sculpture out of metal'. Hibbing is the part of Minnesota known as the 'Iron Range', and during his childhood Dylan was surrounded by the influence of heavy industry: the hulking machinery and constant stream of labourers going to and from the mines; the truckloads of taconite rock and rust-coloured haematite ore driven down to the port. These are the kinds of images that made their mark on an impressionable young mind—images of a world where raw materials and manmade objects were animated by a dynamic atmosphere of production. 'He's drawing from an industrial past, a working man's past', Paul Green, director of the Halycon, claimed in the exhibition materials. 'It's partly about looking back but it's also about resurrecting these items and the physical act of putting these objects together' (quoted in Dylan 2013). As an act of collage, then, scrapbooks of scrap materials, they document the history of the artist and the history of the found objects. The gallery couches this in language of a noble industrial past—in which men worked the land, forged new matter in the furnaces, sweated in the mines. Faced with the relentless, clean march of technology, Green suggests, Dylan's faith is still in the soil and the hand and the tool.

To what extent do the gates play with our ready-made assumptions about Dylan and the myth of his origins? There is something of a nostalgic turn in these sculptures, and in the simplicity of their surrounding discourse, from an artist now approaching his eighties. Most of the critical reviews of the show speak of an artist entering a late period characterised by a presiding wistfulness, that reproduces the working class heroes and 'free-born' travels of his past. Indeed, his recent exhibition of American landscapes reproduced open roads, city lights and rolling hills from memory or from old tour photographs. These gates, however, are more ambiguous than simple acts of remembrance—there is something more whimsical at play. Dylan's gates shine with a silvery finish, in spite of what one might assume of discarded industrial objects, as if each of the objects have been scrubbed of the rust, oil and blemishes of their past, or have been covered over with a brightly coloured veneer. Each sculpture features a small metal buffalo, marked with the sign Black Buffalo Iron

Works and followed by Dylan's signature, and several contain small, embedded allusions to Dylan's relationship to music — treble clefs, notes, instruments. These elements contribute to an overall impression of an unassuming body of work — a set of associations easy to fathom and symbols easy to grasp — tools pointing to labour, nature, creativity. Friendly, warm and light of touch, the gates are composed of hardware that has lost its aggressive edge — there is little sense of the toil that characterises the industrial era to which Dylan seemingly alludes.

Even the more playful elements cannot animate the gates, as there is no sense of the speed at which the welded cogs, springs or machine parts once moved. They are static, lacking in dynamism — indeed, many of them are mounted and immobilised — they cannot swing, be pushed, pulled or invite passage. The sculptures bear nothing of the complex optical effects enacted by William Bowie's abstract metal wall sculptures, nor do they have any of the surrealism of Maddy LeMel's 'scavenger poetics', nor do they achieve the magnetism of Eduardo Paolozzi's mechanical sculptures and screenprints. Perhaps it is unfair to attempt to situate Dylan's sculptures within a broader art historical context, particularly as these works do not emerge from a modernist regard for the accelerating potential of the machine, but emerge at a millennial moment in which such machinery is losing relevance. Dylan's gates could be thought of as documenting this passage — indeed the styling of the sculptures has a postmodern flavour in the staginess of the chosen objects, primary colouring and exaggerated symmetry. They celebrate craftsmanship. As with his music, Dylan appears to have confounded critical comment: reviewers appear to have been unable to understand whether these gates and assorted ironworks are serious or playful.

By way of extension of this line of questioning, Dylan's most recent ironwork commission took an unexpected turn, realised on a grander, more extravagant scale than in the gallery. Last year, his fascination with welding, gateways and passages found further expression in the elaborate 'Portal' in Maryland, an iron-worked archway of 26 x 15 feet that now acts as entrance to MGM's sprawling National Harbour Resort casino, close to Washington DC. This is his first permanent public work of art. It's an incongruous setting — all twinkling artificial lights and marble — for this kind of industrial sculpture. Now, we may be perplexed by Dylan's motivations here, an unlikely project by a man known for some of the sharpest indictments of materialism and commercialism known to modern music ('who gotta serve somebody'), and yet considering his work with multinationals and advertising in recent years it is perhaps all simply part of the evolving Dylan continuum. However, perhaps there is something more complex at work here. When these works are sold for amounts as high as any modernist masterpiece—each gate was sold on the opening night of the 2013 exhibition for half a million pounds—we must ask by what criteria we are to judge Dylan's work in the visual arts?[2]

Perhaps the most appealing way of thinking through Dylan's sculpture and how it may alter our sense of his contribution to 20th-century culture is to consider it through the lens of his music. Indeed, this kind of critical anchorage is unavoidable as his governing mode of expression, and frequent mention is made to his established lyrical career as a selling point in gallery press releases. In the main, comparisons between language and sculpture take part in the field of literary scholarship, when considering Dylan's work as poetry. There have been a number of critical accounts made of Dylan's writing and music-making as resembling modern sculpture—Rona Cran writes eloquently about Bob Dylan as a collagist, Paul Williams asks for Dylan's music to be approached as 'sound sculptures' and Peter Balakian speaks of a tangible, material voice that carries with it the 'sediment of American culture' (Balakian 2015; Cran 2014; Williams 2009). These connections are made, however, in allusion to Dylan's complex stacking of socio-political, cultural and geographic references, erecting songs that at once communicate a moral poignancy and an ironic detachment. The items that compose the gates are static in the same way as words on a page, our eyes are required to pass from item to item, albeit in a non-linear way, in an attempt to read the sculpture. However, the clean, apolitical nature of the sculptures—their lack of critical bite—is perhaps all the more apparent when considered alongside his music and poetry.

Although there is not the space or time here to fully explore the relationship between Dylan's music and sculpture, I can close by offering

---

2   This controversy reached new heights in 2019 when the US State Department purchased one of Dylan's gates for $84,375 during the US government shutdown, when more than 800,000 federal workers were going unpaid. See Neuendorf (2019).

an example that I feel may help to unpick a little of what is at stake in Dylan's gates. Dylan's backlist is littered with references to the materials of his sculptural work, steel and iron. We might think of songs such as 'Never Say Goodbye' (1974) in which Dylan wails 'My dreams are made of iron and steel', or 'Not Dark Yet' from 1997, with the line, 'Feel like my soul has turned into steel'. However, Dylan's intriguing comments on the nature of gates as portals that can shut you out or shut you in, as negative space, as points of transition have particular resonance with the well-known song 'Gates of Eden' (from *Bringing it all Back Home* — 1965), which is instructive when thinking through this sequence of works and his new commission 'Portal'. Each of the nine verses of the song end with a line that approaches, lies inside or finally remains outside the gates of Eden:

> All except when 'neath the trees of Eden
> No sound ever comes from the Gates of Eden
> Heading for the Gates of Eden
> All except inside the Gates of Eden
> There are no kings inside the Gates of Eden
> And there are no sins inside the Gates of Eden
> It doesn't matter inside the Gates of Eden
> And there are no trials inside the Gates of Eden
> And there are no truths outside the Gates of Eden

Considered one of Dylan's most surreal songs, the song's dream imagery is thought to have been influenced by the cut-ups of William Burroughs and reminiscent of William Blake's hypnotic *The Gates of Paradise* and 'The Keys of the Gates', contrasting flawed humanity with the false promises of paradise. Allen Ginsberg acknowledged the 'surrealistic conjunction, concatenation' achieved in the song (Hersch 2017). The song lists, verse after verse, the common delusions of mid-century America, themes that persist throughout Dylan's oeuvre to the present day: about obedience and authority, about false religions and idols, about possession and desire, about sexual repression and conformity, about high-toned intellectualism. It closes with a lover's attempt to communicate her dreams, but in failing to do so effectively, prompts the realisation that the only truth is that there is no truth. The ability to distinguish what is real and what is not is not, what is true and what is not, debilitated by the shimmering possibility of what might or might not lie beyond the gates, has become impossible for all of us. By passing under Dylan's gate into the dazzling lights of the monumental MGM casino, a 1.4 billion dollar temple to the seductions of possible fortune, where do we find ourselves? A space governed by a logic wildly different to the one we have left behind? Entitled 'Portal'—which by definition means an opening that connects two locations, dimensions or points in time, essentially two separate realities—Dylan wants those that pass through this gate to see, recognise, feel, sense that shift. At the same time, he cannot prescribe to the notion of such a one-directional exchange—for Dylan gates are 'negative space'—an invitation to non-space. Back and forth, inside or outside, as Dylan suggested, 'in some ways there is no difference'. These gates are poised to swing between different worlds.

References

Balakian, P. (2015) *Vise and Shadow: Essays on the Lyric Imagination, Poetry, Art and Culture*, Chicago, IL: University of Chicago Press.

Cran, R. (2014) *Collage in Twentieth-Century Art, Literature and Culture*, London: Routledge.

Dylan, B. (2013) *Mood Swings, Iron Works and Original Works on Canvas*, London: Halcyon Gallery.

Hersch, C. (1998) *Democratic Artworks: Politics and the Arts from Trilling to Dylan*, Albany, NY: State University of New York Press.

Neuendorf, H. (2019) 'It strikes me as excessive': A Bob Dylan sculpture cost one US Embassy almost $90.000 during shutdown, *artnews*, 5th February, [Online], https://news.artnet.com/art-world/bob-dylan-embassy-1457062

Williams, P. (2009) *Bob Dylan Performing Artist: 1986–1990 and Beyond*, London: Omnibus Press.

Dylan by Stefan Kahlhammer, 2011 (published under the terms of the GNU Free Documentation License, Version 1.3).

Katharine A. Craik

Writing Hard
The Poetics of Candour
in Dylan and Shakespeare

Bob Dylan was awarded the Nobel Prize for Literature in 2016, the year which marked 400 years since the death of William Shakespeare. Dylan mentioned Shakespeare in his acceptance speech, which was delivered by Azita Raji, US Ambassador to Sweden, at the Nobel Banquet on 10th December: 'I began to think about William Shakespeare, the great literary figure. I would reckon he thought of himself as a dramatist. The thought that he was writing literature couldn't have entered his head.' Dylan goes on to describe Shakespeare's attentiveness to the more mundane matters involved in making art: 'Is the financing in place? Are there enough good seats for my patrons? Where am I going to get a human skull?' Dylan reminded his audience that he, like Shakespeare, is shackled by everyday chores such as finding the right musicians, choosing a recording studio and figuring out whether songs are in the correct key. For both artists, the pressing question is not 'is it literature?' but how to keep pushing past the practical obstacles which are always threatening to prevent the work from reaching an audience. As Dylan concluded, 'Some things never change, even in 400 years' (Dylan 2016).

Shakespeare was indeed a pragmatist and a businessman as well as a playwright, and no doubt a resourceful prop-hunter when he had to be. And it's true that the term 'literature' meant more or less nothing when *Hamlet* was written, not least because plays were regarded in Shakespeare's time as ephemera in much the same way that popular songs are in ours. Dylan claimed in his speech that the main credential he shared with Shakespeare was a willingness to graft. At the same time, he made clear that the calibre of his own work was on a par with that of the western world's most famous dramatist. Dylan's songs contain many direct and indirect references to Shakespeare's plays, especially the late tragedies, and he said in a 2015 interview with Robert Love that he had been 'trying for years to come up with songs that have the feel of a Shakespearean drama'. Dylan's acceptance speech certainly created some drama, and the line about finding a human skull packed a particular punch. Suddenly the assembled company found themselves alongside Hamlet in the graveyard, looking death straight in the eye. Taking this moment as its starting point, the present chapter considers Shakespeare and Dylan not as 'literary greats' but instead as writers who embrace the strangeness and discomfort which can be found in language. It does so by reading Shakespeare's Sonnet 66, first published in 1609, alongside the lyrics of the 1962 song which Patti Smith performed at the Nobel Banquet in Dylan's honour and absence: 'A Hard Rain's A-Gonna Fall'.

Dylan has rightly emphasised that Shakespeare's plays are best encountered in performance, just as his own songs are meant to be heard rather than read. At the same time, he has pointed out that the act of reading involves musicality when the inner ear is properly attuned. In an interview with *Time* magazine in 1985, he remarked that 'if I read poems, it's like I can always hear the guitar. Even with Shakespeare's sonnets I can hear a melody because it's all broken up into timed phrases so I hear it' (Muir 2019, 357). Recent recording artists including Rufus Wainwright have found inspiration in the sonnets, several of which invite musical interpretation since they talk so directly about melody, singing and even keyboard playing. But while Shakespeare's sonnets are remarkably melodious in form (fourteen lines, three rhyming quatrains, one rhyming couplet) they are not uniformly melodious in content. Instead their language, like the language of Dylan's songs, finds multiple ways into unease. Through unexpected juxtapositions of words, stripped-back expression and extraordinary candour, both writers find ways of saying what was previously unsaid or unsayable. Whether or not Shakespeare's sonnets provided Dylan with a direct source, both artists certainly know how to disturb any easeful acceptance of the way things have to be.

Like many of Dylan's best-loved songs, Shakespeare's sonnets deal with youth, age, death, memory and the passing of time. And like Dylan, who often responded at the start of his career to earlier folk artists,

Shakespeare was working intensively with lyric traditions which pre-
ceded his own. Sonnets had been circulating since the 13th century, but
Shakespeare rewrote the rules of this traditional, courtly form by writing
about the humiliations involved in erotic infatuation, jealousy, rejection
and despair. Meanwhile 'A Hard Rain' draws on the question-and-
answer form of the traditional Scottish ballad 'Lord Randall' while
expanding this pared-down, domestic story of a lover's betrayal into a
powerful song about existential threat and the possibility of action. Sonnet
66 in particular has many formal similarities with 'A Hard Rain'. Both
work through repetition, and both have the directness of a spoken conversation. Each verse of 'A Hard Rain' starts out by addressing the 'blue-
eyed boy' and 'darling young one' who, in the lines which follow, tells
where he has been, what he has seen, what he has heard, whom he has
met—and, finally, what he will do. Shakespeare's addressee is less clear,
but most readers agree that the first 126 sonnets are addressed to a
beautiful young man. In Sonnet 66 and the sonnets immediately preceding, Shakespeare thinks about how the beauty of a beloved youth may
be harmed by, or may persist through, the devastating effects of time
passing. But neither 'A Hard Rain' nor Sonnet 66 devotes much attention
to these young men. Instead they both offer a wake-up call, through
repeated acts of witnessing, to a world which is terribly depleted by
untruthfulness, prejudice, carelessness, cruelty and neglect.

'A Hard Rain' is, among other things, a song about innocence
confronting the worst of the world. Its power lies in the straightforward
clarity of its vision:

> I saw a newborn baby with wild wolves all around it
> I saw a highway of diamonds with nobody on it
> I saw a black branch with blood that kept drippin'
> I saw a room full of men with their hammers a-bleedin'
> I saw a white ladder all covered with water
> I saw ten thousand talkers whose tongues were all broken

Innocence encounters menace in a series of tableaux sketched in vivid,
stark colours (black, white, red). The images keep multiplying, and
become increasingly threatening as they capture the banal power of
multitudes ('ten thousand talkers') who are bluntly indifferent to the
vulnerable. The speaker's own innocence is captured through the

plainness of his expression: 'I saw... I saw... I saw...' He simply says
what he sees, and seems completely alone in these acts of beholding. Even
the landscape has disintegrated: the highways are crooked, the forests are
sad, the oceans are dead. While the song surely evokes something of the
calamitous political context in which it was written, including the Cuban
missile crisis which escalated the Cold War, its compass seems more
generally existential. The poet is dead in the gutter, and the clown is
crying in the alley—but the young one keeps demonstrating the force and
intensity of telling the truth.

Now let's turn to Sonnet 66 which, like 'A Hard Rain', expresses a
ruined world through a cascade of stark images:

> Tired with all these, for restful death I cry:
> As to behold desert a beggar born,
> And needy nothing trimmed in jollity,
> And purest faith unhappily forsworn,
> And guilded honour shamefully misplaced,
> And maiden virtue rudely strumpeted,
> And right perfection wrongfully disgraced,
> And strength by limping sway disablèd,
> And art made tongue-tied by authority,
> And folly (doctor-like) controlling skill,
> And simple truth miscalled simplicity,
> And captive good attending captain ill.
> Tired with all these, from these would I be gone,
> Save that to die I leave my love alone.
>
> —Burrow (2002, 513)

Senseless folly has seized control, and those who are most deserving will
stay as beggars. Everything that is pure in private or public life has fallen
into corruption. Again it is the mindless multitude which destroys
precious things—especially art and truth—by strumpeting forth, and by
exerting banal forms of disciplinary control. The complexities of skill and
virtue are resolved into meaningless similitude, so that even straightforward truth-telling looks tarnished: 'simple truth [is] miscalled simplicity'. Here the sonnet calls to mind not only 'A Hard Rain' but also
another early Dylan song, 'My Back Pages', where life's rich complexities

are flattened by a dishonest form of speaking which seems akin to death itself: 'Lies that life is black and white spoke from my skull.'

'A Hard Rain' is a young man's song, written when Dylan was around twenty-one. Sonnet 66 is an older man's poem, probably written when Shakespeare was in his mid-thirties. At its conclusion, this sonnet turns inwards as the speaker contemplates 'restful death'. The awkward final rhyme (gone/alone), and the sonnet's sinking back into its own early phrase 'Tired with all these', suggests that even the act of speaking has become exhausting. The sonnet's weariness chimes with Dylan's more recent, reflective 'Not Dark Yet' where 'I can't even remember what it was I came here to get away from.' 'A Hard Rain' on the other hand keeps its focus outwards, on the wider world, expressing the possibility for change — or at least for a more accurate vision of things. The young one is 'a-goin' back out 'fore the rain starts a-fallin'' with a determined sense of what has to be done. In the final verse, set in 'the deepest black forest', the scene is bleak as poison floods into water, home blends into prison and nothingness spreads over everything. And yet the candid voice persists:

> And I'll tell it and think it and speak it and breathe it
> And reflect it from the mountain so all souls can see it
> Then I'll stand on the ocean until I start sinkin'
> But I'll know my song well before I start singin'
> And it's a hard, it's a hard, it's a hard, it's a hard
> It's a hard rain's a-gonna fall.

Like Sonnet 66 which deplores 'art made tongue-tied by authority', 'A Hard Rain' ends with the difficulty of expression. It will take a messianic miracle to keep speaking, against the odds ('I'll stand on the ocean') — and the coupling of 'I start sinkin'' with 'I start singin'' suggests the risk that such expression involves. Telling the truth seems both unstoppable and precarious in a vast and always indifferent world.

In 'Stuck inside of Mobile with the Memphis Blues Again', Dylan evokes an over-familiar Shakespeare 'in the alley / With his pointed shoes and his bells'. But Shakespeare has always meant more to Dylan than cosy English heritage. All avant-garde art is vulnerable to being co-opted by the establishment, as both Dylan and Shakespeare knew, and perhaps this was why it was impossible for Dylan to attend the Nobel Banquet in person. But these two writers have more in common than their sheer prominence in western culture. Sonnet 66 and 'A Hard Rain' draw on a shared set of formal features including repetition, poem-as-drama, and direct speech. Both candidly address the ruinous state of the world. Both think hard about the precarity of youth. And both reflect on the difficulties involved in writing and singing, achieving virtuosic self-expression even as they describe being tongue-tied—or of sinking while singing. Perhaps both writers, as the Nobel Prize committee would have it, were creating 'literature'. But if they were, both seem mindful that any such creation is difficult, risky and cannot last. As Hamlet laments, in the episode Dylan evoked in 2016, 'That skull had a tongue in it, and could sing once.'

References

Burrow, C. (2002) *William Shakespeare, Complete Sonnets and Poems*, Oxford: Oxford University Press.

Dylan, B. (2016) *The Nobel Prize in Literature 2016—Bob Dylan Banquet Speech*, [Online], www.nobelprize.org/prizes/literature/2016/dylan/speech/ [23rd February 2021].

Muir, A. (2019) *Bob Dylan and William Shakespeare: The True Performing of It*, London: Red Planet Books.

William Shakespeare, associated with John Taylor, oil on canvas, feigned ova circa 1600–1610 (National Portrait Gallery, public domain PD-ART/ PD-OLD-100).

Fleur Jongepier

Unselfing in Bob Dylan and Iris Murdoch

The artist is the analogon of the good man,
and in a special sense he *is* the good man:
the lover who, nothing himself, lets other things be through him.
   —Murdoch, *The Sublime and the Beautiful Revisited*

It's never been my duty to remake the world at large,
Nor is it my intention to sound a battle charge.
   —Dylan, 'Wedding Song'

Questions about the identity and authenticity of Bob Dylan/Robert Zimmerman—about where his person ends and his personae begin—has excited many a Dylan fan and has excited more than a few philosophers and scholars of (American) music and literature. The existential question interests me very little. In fact, trying to get answers to these existential questions is, I believe, to miss much of the point of Dylan's work.

Despite not wanting to be a moral exemplar, Dylan I believe sets an example in teaching us something important about morality. Not because, as Ian Bells puts it in *Once Upon a Time*, 'politics in the broadest and deepest sense' would never disappear entirely from his music, though that is no doubt true as well. Rather, because his work teaches us something about a certain activity: about a selfless way of attending to the world. With a little help from Iris Murdoch we can see why this might be so. And with a little help from Bob Dylan we can recognise a distinctly Dylanesque and paradoxical method of unselfing.

Unselfing in Murdoch

Dylan a moral exemplar? Nonsense. Indeed nonsense, at least if we hold onto a modern yet narrow conception of morality and what might constitute moral inspiration. A distinctly modern conception of morality is to think of it as being about making explicit moral choices: to engage in protest, to be a donor, to help a stranger. Morality thus understood is confined to Maggie's farm, Hattie Carroll, Oxford Town, cannonballs flying and hard rain falling.

Murdoch had a broader outlook. In her essays published in 1970 as *The Sovereignty of the Good,* she writes that morality and virtue cover 'the whole of our mode of living and the quality of our relations with the world'. Morality isn't something that can be 'switched off' in between the making of concrete moral choices. It is something that 'goes on continually' also in between the making of such choices. Likewise, virtue can be expressed in ways that might not at first strike one as distinctly 'moral'. For example, being 'a good man' can also be expressed by 'taking delight in flowers and animals', even if 'people who bring home potted plants and watch kestrels' would be 'surprised at the notion that these things have anything to do with virtue'.

If bringing home potted plants or observing hovering kestrels can have an important connection to virtue, then so might being fully immersed in 'Visions of Joanna', 'I Shall be Released', or 'Key West (Philosopher Pirate)'. The key Murdochian thought here is that activities like these allow us to pay selfless attention to the world. For Murdoch, selfless attention is the 'characteristic and proper mark of the active moral agent'. Here, she sees a crucial role for nature and art, or beauty more generally. Enjoying the beauty of art or nature allows one to forget about oneself in quite a literal sense. In the enjoyment of art and nature, she writes, 'we discover value in our ability to forget self, to be realistic, to perceive justly'.

It's common to think that moral growth is achieved through rigorous self-reflection; critically reflecting on the question of who we (really) are and what (truly) moves us. Murdoch, however, warns us that self-reflection can, and often does, stand in the way of virtue. As she puts it, the 'self is such a dazzling object that if one looks *there* one might see nothing else'. The self certainly seems to have dazzled Dylan, and he often looked elsewhere.

It's tempting to think that looking at the world, rather than oneself, and seeing reality for what it is, must be easy. But it's not. A clear perception of the world is typically obscured, often without our realisation, by our own desires, fears and longings. So the trick is — or better, virtue resides in — unegoistic or selfless perception. That is difficult, especially if we are, as Murdoch thinks, 'naturally selfish'; and if in 'moral life the enemy is the fat relentless ego'. Most people, except perhaps for Buddhists, cannot help but think that everything is in one way or another about them, that it resolves around them, praises them, harms them, threatens them. So it is, as Murdoch puts it, 'a *task* to see the world as it is' (her emphasis).

Murdoch's work lends itself quite naturally to a broadly Buddhist interpretation, which is no surprise because Murdoch herself was inspired by Buddhism. There's room for easy misunderstanding, though, which stands in the way of the Murdoch–Dylan alliance I'm after. Murdoch's notion of unselfing can — though should not — be taken to mean that the goal is to reach tranquility, to simply escape, to be liberated from hectic tumult, or simply *not to be present*, similar to the way in which the Buddhist notion of *anatman* or mindfulness is sometimes (mis)understood.

But that isn't the goal. Murdoch points out that we use our imagination and faculty of attention 'not to escape the world, but to *join* it' (emphasis added). Interestingly, the Japanese Zen Buddhist Daisetz T. Suzuki (who also had an influence on figures such as Allen Ginsberg, Jack Kerouac and J.D. Salinger) discusses the relation between Zen and love of nature, stressing that the point is not tranquility at all. As Suzuki writes in *Zen and Japanese Culture*:

> Nature is always in motion, never at a standstill; if Nature is to be loved, it must be caught while moving and in this way its aesthetic value must be appraised. To seek tranquility is to kill nature, to stop its pulsation, and to embrace the dead corpse that is left behind.

What does any of this have to do with Bob Dylan? Well, at least two things. One is that loving art and loving Dylan in particular likewise requires not trying to figure out who he "really" is, because the aesthetic value lies in trying to catch him whilst moving, which means being content with never quite catching him at all. Trying to get answers to existential questions is to kill his music, to stop its pulsation. Second, I think Murdoch and Suzuki in their own ways are trying to get the message across that unselfing is best achieved by seeking *connection* with the world and immersing oneself in its flux, rather than detaching oneself from it. And here I think Dylan is king.

Lessons from Bob Dylan: Unselfing Through Selfing

Dylan's songs are worlds—small worlds full of real, fictious and quasi-fictitious protagonists. If Murdoch is right that attention to the world is connected to virtue, that one might 'grow by looking', and if she's right that enjoyment in art is a particularly strong means to accomplish that, then Dylan's work offers an intriguing, though slightly paradoxical, method of unselfing. Paradoxical, because Dylan's work is anything but selfless: it's shot through with selves. Dylan's work—certainly not all of it, but a substantial chunk of it—invites us to engage in what we might call unselfing through selfing.

'Unselfing through selfing' may sound like a pretentious intellectual phrase, but what I have in mind is really rather simple: that one might lose oneself—in a Murdochian sense—by temporarily identifying with other people, real or imagined. This need not take the shape of an act of empathy *per se*—of trying to feel what others feel—but is in the first instance the simple act of recognition of there being other people, other lives, other feelings, other outlooks, other egoistic perspectives on the world. And then to return to oneself, sitting next to vinyl spinning on a turntable, and then not necessarily to feel an urge to *do* anything or behave differently, but just to have one's world expanded, one's vision altered. As Murdoch puts it: to realise, if only for a short while, that something other than oneself is real.

This form of unselfing is, I think, one that can be experienced when listening to Dylan's music, though it also resonates with some of the things Dylan writes about in his *Chronicles* and elsewhere (for whatever Dylan's self-reflections are worth). In any case, he coins a neat term when he writes about how his songs weren't 'commercial':

> [M]y style was too erratic and hard to pigeonhole for the radio, and songs, to me, were more important than just light entertainment. They were my preceptor and guide into some altered consciousness of

reality, some different republic, some liberated republic. Greil Marcus, the music historian, would some thirty years later call it "the invisible republic".

Greil Marcus no doubt meant something else by it when he used the term to write about the *Basement Tapes*, and who knows how Dylan understood the term (assuming Dylan himself even knew) but still, "the invisible republic" nicely cashes out the distinct experience when listening to Dylan as a figure speaking *to*, speaking *as* and speaking *with* members of some community, be those members forgotten, imagined or invisible. A distinct feature of Dylanesque unselfing, then, is that it isn't meant to overcome or somehow go beyond the social world, but that the social world is part of the very way in which unselfing can be achieved.

In fact, in her essay *The Sublime and the Beautiful Revisited*, Murdoch points at just this "social" type of unselfing or the 'realization of a vast and varied reality outside ourselves' which in its most important form comes from 'gazing not at the Alps but at the spectacle of human life'. She laments the type of art that is overly concerned with the individual, such as novels in which the struggles of all other protagonists are in reality nothing more than struggles of the central figure. In such a case, Murdoch says we have lost persons and have ended up only with a self-centred individual. Virtue is concerned with really apprehending that other people exist, which, she adds, is the most important thing that *art* can reveal. Ultimately, she says, 'we judge the great novelists [and songwriters, FJ] by their quality of their awareness of others.' If the artist is a good man because he 'lets other things be through him', then Bob Dylan is a good man.

There's an urge, at this point and at many other points in which persons who are also academics listen to and then *reflect on* Dylan's work, to tease out and clarify whichever connections one discerns. But that's the beauty of art (and the tragedy of philosophy, but that's another essay): that it can enrich lives in ways that resist systematic analysis. There's also an urge to know: to what extent was Dylan aware of the virtue of revealing that other people are real in giving voice in his lyrics to people like Jimmy Reed, Johnny in the Basement, or Frankie Lee and Judas Priest? Perhaps he was, perhaps he wasn't. Maybe all of Dylan's protagonists in the end are simply all about Dylan himself, and his career is one big self-expressive exercise. This actually seems rather likely. The idea that Dylan expresses himself through other selves is also something which the film *I'm Not There* has powerfully expressed. To that extent, Dylan may well be overly egoistic in Murdoch's sense. But that doesn't matter, because it doesn't stand in the way of unselfing. Quite the contrary: Dylan teaches us that precisely self-expression *through* selfing — by being other people, adopting different roles — can lead to unselfing. Dylan's exercises in selfing help us realise that 'other people are real', as Murdoch puts it, even if the artist's own intention was possibly, as it were, a lot more self-bound. One does not have to consider oneself a moral exemplar to be one.

So it doesn't matter what Dylan's own views are, or whether his intention was ever to invite us to engage in unselfing or help us realise the vast and varied reality outside ourselves — it doesn't matter whether that was ever *the point* of it all. Giving in to that existential urge would be to regard him as some sort of leader or authority figure in unselfing. But we've each got to do our own unselfing. For some it's bringing home potted plants, for others it's reaching lonely mountain tops or travelling on subways in Tokyo. For others it's *Blood on the Tracks*. So it's best we all listen to Bob Dylan: 'Don't follow leaders, watch the parkin' meters' ('Subterranean Homesick Blues').[1]

---

1   Many thanks to Gary Browning and Constantine Sandis for comments on an earlier version.

Iris Murdoch.

Ray Foulk

The Rockstar of Painting and the Picasso of Rock
The Improbable Similarity Between Bob Dylan and Pablo Picasso

Having moved among fans and afficionados of Picasso and Dylan, and authored books on both, it has long since surprised me how their striking resemblance seems to have received little attention.

If a single cultural colossus bestrode the first half of the 20th century, it was the painter, sculptor, ceramist who invented Cubism. From Pablo Ruiz Picasso's precocious attendance, aged nineteen, at the 1900 Paris *Exposition Universelle* with a painting representing Spain, to his death in 1973, he informed the very look of the century like no other. His singular work, *Les Demoiselles d'Avignon* (1907), was the precursor of 20th-century modernism, percolating through all the visual arts, advertising, cinema and architecture. The very look of the century was cast with this one painting of five passive-aggressive prostitutes staring down the viewer from its eight-foot square canvas.[1] No single practitioner in the visual arts has since compared with the change-making capacity of the gifted Andalusian. Some say none before, either. Development has always been incremental throughout the long history of art. But there was nothing incremental about the explosion of *Les Demoiselles* and the jettisoning of

---

[1]   Held by the Museum of Modern Art, New York.

perspective as a prerequisite to painting—at least not since Giotto in the 14th century and the invention of perspective.

To find another artist *in any medium* with comparable influence and power of longevity, one need look no further than the dominant change-maker in the second half of the century: the singer-songwriter, rock star, Nobel literature laureate Minnesotan, Robert Allen Zimmerman, alias Bob Dylan.

I unhesitatingly concede that patently these assertions are subject to challenge. I have argued my corner for decades past with many who dispute such an absolutist stance. But I always ask, if not these two giants of the arts, then who? My thesis is not about how much one likes their work (what's 'like' got to do with art appreciation anyway?) or who is best. My own measure of greatness ultimately focuses on how *influential*. How much of a change-maker is the artist? By this test, if Picasso was not the most influential force in 20th-century painting, then who was? And, if Dylan was not the most influential practitioner in the rock genre, if not its inventor, then who was? I would discount (others would not) e.g. Warhol; Pollock; Duchamp, whose famous innovative work was so much easier since Picasso had first crashed through the ramparts. And the same with, say, the Sex Pistols or David Bowie, regarding Dylan.

My introduction to the two 20th-century giants began with first-hand experience of the enormity of Bob Dylan's extraordinary stardom, when, as a young man, I brought him to England to headline the 1969 Isle of Wight Festival—since chronicled in my *Stealing Dylan from Woodstock*, (Medina Publishing, 2015). The enormity of Woodstock was in part attributable to an expectation that Bob Dylan might appear—given his residency in the eponymous town. At that time, he was unassailably the greatest individual artist in the still young rock genre, having led his generation into issue-based rock music and its essential function within the sixties counterculture. When we drew up lists of potential acts for the festival, categorising them for 'pulling power', there were just three in the top 'superstar' (today we would say megastar) class: the Beatles, Elvis Presley and Bob Dylan. The Rolling Stones and Pink Floyd, to name the top acts in the next category, were not remotely in the same league as the top three. Elvis, of course, was not a festival act and was certainly passé to the current generation. The Beatles, yes, were on a par with Dylan, if not above, but they were four musicians. Individually, they would not have compared with Dylan for drawing a large audience across the water. When Dylan appeared, he attracted followers from across the world, including three of the Beatles and several Rolling Stones. No other artist (except perhaps Elvis) would have attracted the kind of media attention afforded Bob Dylan.

My embrace of the Picasso phenomenon began two decades later when, at Cambridge reading architecture, I discovered the unprecedented pivotal role the originator of Cubism had played in changing the course of art. I spent the next twenty years researching the spectacular story, culminating in my recent book, co-authored with my daughter Caroline, *Picasso's Revenge* (Medina Publishing, 2019).

With their inventiveness, longevity, global fame and success, the artists tower as the two tallest poppies among 20th-century change-makers in the arts. Inevitably, therefore, some comparisons may readily be drawn. Beyond the obvious, however, there are more subtle and structural technical attributes informing their work. In choice of subject matter — though scarcely unusual among artists — they both plundered the world of what they saw around them. Baudelaire influenced Picasso with his 'Painting of Modern Life', while folk and the blues influenced Dylan in singing about everyday life, and both, moreover, extended their observations to what they *felt*, frequently subordinating what it looked, or sounded, like. Combined with this, their work was often, if not usually, self-revelatory, regardless of how unflattering.

While Picasso's Cubism portrayed multiple and overlapping views or angles of an object or scene, many Dylan songs represented multifaceted elements of a dismantled and reassembled narrative or landscape. Obvious examples include, 'A Hard Rain's A-Gonna Fall' (is this Dylan's *Guernica*?), 'Desolation Row', 'Mr. Tambourine Man', 'Brownsville Girl', 'Sad Eyed Lady of the Lowlands' and 'Lilly, Rosemary and the Jack of Hearts'. And of course, with both artists, the listener/spectator is left to work it all out, with no further help from the authors. Unlike most artists, happy and even eager to talk about their art, these two titans have famously steadfastly refused to do any such thing. Self-denying resolution only reinforced their mystique, as too was their obtuse attitude, playing games with the press and critics — and they were particularly good at it!

Famously, both men were rebels in their lives and artistic production, deftly dipping into previous art for material. Unjust (in my humble opinion) allegations of plagiarism are often levelled at Dylan and Picasso, the latter proudly claiming, 'bad artists copy, great artists steal.' Borrowing from history, both men fluently switched between classical and modern abstract. Similarity is also derived from fearlessness and avoidance of following trends. Risk-taking is a common trait, and significantly, when they pushed at the boundaries of convention, breaking the limits, they invariably escaped not just unscathed, but emerged triumphant.

Given the extraordinary longevity of their productive careers, during which they have mostly remained at the top of their game, their respective voluminous bodies of work are divisible by distinctive periods. Picasso had his Blue Period, Rose Period, African Period, Cubism, Neoclassicism and Surrealism, and so on. For Dylan it was folk, protest, electric folk-rock, country, American roots, gospel/Christian.

Picasso could draw like Raphael but chose to discard classical representation, showing that art was not so much about craft skills as ideas and content. Similarly, although Dylan could not croon like Tony Bennett, he demolished the convention that a singer must have fine vocal delivery to succeed. One redefined the painter's skills in art, while the other redefined the vocalist's function in contemporary performance. In fact, jettisoning entrenched convention helped polarise opinion about them both. People have always loved or hated Picasso's art, especially at the time of its greatest innovation. His liberties with visual representation engendered the strongest reactions. Similarly, people love or hate Bob Dylan's voice. With sheer strength and power of the image or the vocal, they could bypass the need for traditional refinement, carrying the work through to a successful conclusion.

Women feature strongly in the lives and work of both men. Picasso used his wives and lovers as essential muses throughout much of his career, inseparable from his art. Bob Dylan is a little different although there are many masterpieces wrought from relationships. The fourth side of *Blonde on Blonde*, 'Sad Eyed Lady of the Lowlands', is about Sara Lownds, whom he married shortly before the recording in February 1966. Nine years later, the next real milestone album, *Blood on the Tracks*, was largely inspired by the marriage breakup. A year later the track 'Sara' appeared on the next album, *Desire*. Think also of, 'Ballad in Plain D' (1964) and 'Just Like a Woman' (1966), and many more classics. Both men are branded as womanisers, although the singer has managed his personal relationships a little more discretely than the painter.

We may also consider how the two artists related to God. Aside from Dylan's gospel phase, in which he became a born-again Christian and produced three religious albums, he had brought God into his work much earlier (e.g. the ironic 'With God on Our Side', 1964). I never cease to be moved by the line at the end of the much later 'Tempest' (2012). After the Titanic has gone down with the Grim Reaper taking sixteen hundred:

> They waited at the landing
> And they tried to understand
> But there is no understanding
> On the judgement of God's hand.

Picasso endured a complicated relationship with God, after blaming Him for the childhood death of his sister. This and other tragedies in his early life profoundly informed his art and is the subject of *Picasso's Revenge*. As their work evolved over such lengthy careers, it often deepened with age due to a religious dimension.

Both launched into arts beyond their primary repertoire. Picasso ventured into printmaking, playwriting, film and photography. Dylan also involved himself in film. He is a successful and prolific painter in oils and acrylics with canvases selling for six figures in fashionable galleries. Most unusual is his sculptural prowess, welding virtuoso iron gates and furniture from salvaged farm machinery and equipment; highly regarded and again commanding eye-watering gallery prices. In their respective careers, it not being enough to be just a prolific painter or singer-songwriter, there has remained a great well of creativity bursting to be released. From their earliest days a burning restlessness drove them on. If any artists were ever entitled to rest on their laurels it would be these two with their phenomenal successes, but never have they done so. Consider Picasso's 50,000 works of art, and the more than 450 songs written by Dylan, and his 'Never Ending Tour', now over 30 years with more than 3,000 shows. As though prefiguring his career, he aptly closed his second album in 1964 with 'Restless Farewell'.

It is also worth noting a difference in their early impacts. Whereas the painter changed the course of art with a single move—Cubism—the singer changed the course of rock with a two-pronged assault. Firstly, popularising folk music with contemporary issues, capturing the zeitgeist with songs like 'The Times They Are A-Changin'' and 'Blowin' in the Wind', and then 'going electric' with issue-based songs, normally belonging to the idiom of folk: the alchemy of rock.[2] The Newport Folk Festival, 1965, amounted to Bob Dylan's *Les Demoiselles*.

None of this is to exaggerate and argue that our two artists single-handedly changed the world. But each instigated and influenced great change. Their radical art fed into popular culture filtered through their peers. Once Picasso launched Cubism, every young painter in Paris followed suit with various manifestations. Full propagation was via his peers. Even Henri Matisse, twelve years Picasso's senior and the leading modern painter in Paris in 1907, was furiously scathing about *Les Demoiselles* when he first saw it but was himself practising a form of Cubism within a few years. If Picasso could be said to be the Pied Piper of modern art, so could Dylan of rock when he 'went electric'. Many artists made chart hits with his songs but more significantly, rock—electrified issue-based songs—became the standard in this first phase of the genre and has remained the staple of what is loosely termed 'rock music' ever since.

The uniqueness of the two artists in our cultural milieu places them in a class of their own (the Beatles were four people and endured for less than a decade). Many, many great artists have arguably produced comparable if not superior work to Picasso or Dylan, but no others have been such change-making forces and have endured with such profound and prolonged influence. I have so far not resorted to the word 'genius', but if ever it was justified, it would be here. The most obvious similarity of all.

As to why we might be interested in these uncanny similarities, perhaps it will help us better understand what propelled one or other or both these gifted individuals to the summit of artistic achievement.

---

[2] My own working definition: rock is not rock'n'roll, nor is it pop. It is a broad genre invented in the mid-sixties and has remained the main staple of modern music since, albeit with myriad sub-genres.

Dylan with Ray Foulk, 1969.

Isle of White Festival, 1969.

Roger Dalrymple

'I Know the Score'
Musical Echoes in
Dylan's Live Performances

Early in Act II of Conor McPherson's *Girl from the North Country*, a violin and acoustic guitar launch into the opening phrase of a mid-seventies Dylan classic. Ripples of recognition animate the audience as they pick out the introduction to 'Hurricane', the lead track from *Desire* (1976). Before the exclamatory opening line is even sung ('Pistol shots ring out in the barroom night') we recognise the song; we know the score.

Famously, this kind of musical echo of a song's recorded version is rare in Dylan's own live performances. Dylan's fast-moving and restless approach to the studio leaves scant room for fixed arrangements to take root, let alone survive into the rehearsal room or onto the touring stage. But there are some exceptions to this rule and, where they occur, they are often charged with resonance and meaning. That violin line from 'Hurricane', Mike Bloomfield's double-stop guitar licks on 'Like A Rolling Stone', Al Kooper's opening Hammond organ phrase on 'Positively Fourth Street'—these are distinctive musical echoes which, when reproduced live, can carry us briefly back to our first listen to a beloved song, or even summon up a life stage to which it served as soundtrack. In this chapter I'd like to explore how audience pleasure in these rare musical echoes is evidently shared by Dylan's collaborating musicians, while Dylan's own attitude towards them is harder to fathom. My examples focus on three periods of the Never Ending Tour (NET) which were particular highpoints for Dylanesque echoes and two of which I was lucky enough to witness in person: the GE Smith era of 1988–90; the "*Love*

And Theft" band era of the early 2000s; and a brief window in late 1995 when Dylan joined Patti Smith for seven duets steeped in musical echoes.

Echoing the Thin, Wild, Mercury Sound:
The GE Smith Era

'Lit from behind, he looked the perfect image of the skinny, one-time folky who had upset his early fans by moving to the amplified rock field… When he started playing, there was a lively, noisy wash of sound which developed into the '66 song from *Blonde on Blonde*, "Stuck Inside of Mobile with the Memphis Blues Again"' (*The Guardian*, 5th February 1990). The sense of 'flashback' captured in this review of the opening night of the Hammersmith 1990 residency was indeed palpable; as an audience member on that cold February evening, I remember well the crowd's roar of excitement as the silhouetted Dylan took the stage. But our vociferous cheer also had a specific musical stimulus — the signature descending pentatonic riff from the studio recording of 'Stuck Inside of Mobile' (E-D-B-A-G-E), now played with particular urgency and attack by guitarist GE Smith and then repeated in unison as the rhythm section piled in behind him. If there was a sense of time-travel in the opening moments of that gig, its medium was sound as much as vision.

The original guitarist on the NET, Smith was particularly alert to the musical signatures inscribed on *Highway 61 Revisited* and *Blonde on Blonde* by Mike Bloomfield, Joe South, Robbie Robertson and the other session guitarists from this era of Dylan's 'thin wild mercury sound'. Smith's playing on such iconic songs as 'Like A Rolling Stone' and 'Most Likely You Go Your Way' would nod back to these signatures, colouring and balancing the otherwise wholly contemporary sound that he and the band crafted with Dylan to bring the songs equally into the present moment.

Smith recalls that these echoes entered the arrangements organically, even subconsciously, in the absence of specific musical direction from Dylan: 'I got the feeling that he just wanted to let the music happen. Because of my many years spent listening to his records prior to joining the band I guess it was inevitable that I would quote or at least allude to some of the great guitar playing on those records that had influenced my playing so much' (Smith 2021).

These classic echoes blended powerfully with the high-energy garage band sound Dylan cultivated on this phase of the NET, creating a sound-scape that mixed memory and the present moment, the then and the now.

Echoing *Nashville Skyline*:
The *"Love And Theft"* Band Era

Where Smith excelled at channelling the classic mid-60s Dylan sound, the *"Love And Theft"* band of the late 1990s and early 2000s showed a particu-lar affinity for the country-tinged Dylan of the *Nashville Skyline* era. Led by multi-instrumentalist Larry Campbell, this phase of the NET saw the rediscovery of some of the soundscapes of *Nashville Skyline*. Into the set came 'Lay Lady Lay', 'I Threw It All Away' and even the raucous 'Country Pie' (the first ever performance of that 1969-vintage song arriving in early 2000). These renditions were notably closer to the studio templates than the majority of songs in the set. On 'Lay Lady Lay', for example, drummer David Kemper resurrected Kenny Buttrey's dis-tinctive cowbell percussion from the record while, on steel guitar, Larry Campbell faithfully reproduced Pete Drake's licks from 1969. The ascending coda or 'outro' to the song, long missing from Dylan's live renditions, was also added back into the arrangement. The same treat-ment was afforded the other *Nashville Skyline* tracks with not only guitar parts but even period-specific guitar *tones* ringing from the guitars of Campbell and second guitarist Charlie Sexton.

Yet, as we might expect, Dylan's own engagement with these musical echoes was of a more mercurial, 'push-pull' variety. His rendering of the vocal melodies was in no way evocative of his *Nashville Skyline* 'croon' and, instead of adding the gentle strum of acoustic guitar as per the studio template, he would play a third electric guitar, contributing lead phrases which showed little regard for any distinction between sung and instrumental passages. Indeed, in this period, Dylan's lead guitar playing was a central focus of his performances. Based, as his book *Chronicles* relates, on a repetitive three-note system, the approach was designed to take the songs into a new space which would deliberately disrupt audience expectations: 'Of course, some of them would still only con-centrate on the lyrics and they might be dismayed because the two-beat strum they'd been used to for so long would now be off rhythm, refocused and rushing the songs into the heart of unimagined territory'

(Dylan 2004, 161). The effect he sought is clearly in evidence on renditions of the *Nashville Skyline* songs of this era where the contrast between the smooth, template-focused backing band and Dylan's restless and staccato guitar licks plays out with varying degrees of synergy (the version of 'Tell Me That it Isn't True' that I witnessed at Stirling Castle in 2001 being one particularly tense example).

Two musicians' insights from this era reveal the complexity of Dylan's approach to these echoes. On the one hand, Larry Campbell has mentioned that, when he revived Dylan's original Travis-picking pattern on 'Don't Think Twice', 'he would always want me to play that acoustic guitar part' while in all other respects 'he would try to change everything about that song' (Campbell 2015). On the other hand, keyboardist Augie Myers was steered away from evoking a comparable echo when recording *"Love And Theft"* (2001):

> [Dylan]: 'I've heard that sound on "Like a Rolling Stone."'
> And I said, 'Yeah. That's where I came from.'
> He said, 'Yeah, well we gotta do something different.'
> (Margotin et al. 2015, 1051)

The 'Dark Eyes' Duets

Deepening the enigma of Dylan's take on these echoes, our final example finds him giving seven highly structured and disciplined duet performances of a song which might itself be seen as one long musical allusion. 'Dark Eyes', the final song on the mid-80s album *Empire Burlesque*, stands apart from the rest of that synth-heavy and overdub-rich album, being a solo acoustic track recorded in a continuous take—an echo of Dylan's original recording practice at Columbia Records in fact. In his duets with Patti Smith in December 1995 this sense of flashback to a template sound is magnified with moving results. Smith (who had chosen the song for the duet slot) sings half solo, half in tandem with its composer. Smith thus leads the performance, standing, uniquely, in Dylan's shoes at centre stage, while he plays uncharacteristically soft and spare acoustic guitar by her side. Smith's solo delivery of the first two lines of each stanza is impassioned, and scrupulously respectful of the original melody, only with a more legato smoothing of the syllables:

Oh, the gentlemen are talking and the midnight moon is on the riverside
They're drinking up and walking and it is time for me to slide.

Dylan and Smith's 'Dark Eyes' duets—artwork by Melissa O' Brien (2021).

Dylan joins in for the second two lines of each stanza, his vocal a combination of harmony and unison singing of the melody. Over the seven performances, hints of his fluid approach surface as he experiments with slight variations of harmony and timbre, but Smith's dominant vocal serves as a lodestone, drawing his vocal back into close harmony based on the third of the scale.

Performed in this way, the song's poignancy is conveyed with renewed force, not least in the lines evoking the narrator's isolation: 'I live in another world'; 'I can hear another drum'; 'I feel nothing for their game'; 'All I see are dark eyes.' Meanwhile, Smith's visceral delivery summons up the song's cast of lonely characters as if she can dimly make out their forms on the other side of the footlights: 'another soldier's deep in prayer'; 'Some mother's child has gone astray'; 'The French girl, she's in paradise.' It's perhaps Smith's total immersion in the song that prompts Dylan to accede to a much more faithful rendition than he would normally proffer, following her lead on melody, intonation and phrasing, acknowledging the echo.

Happily, live recordings of these exquisite 'Dark Eyes' duets continue to circulate and I'd recommend seeking all of them out. Each duet is distinguished by the focused discipline of the performers, the reverential audience hush, and the precise and soulful accompaniment from Tony Garnier's upright bass and Bucky Baxter's ethereal steel guitar. A real singularity, these seven performances give us renditions of a Dylan song *as we already knew it,* only magnified.

The warmth and remarkable power of the duets was recollected by Patti Smith in an interview with *Rolling Stone* magazine: 'I really felt an extreme amount of dignity and happiness singing with him. I allowed myself to think about how important he's been to me, and what a hero, and to glean a certain amount of joy' (Greene 2014). This atmosphere of sustained reminiscence is palpable in Smith's contribution to the duets, and holds out a precious reflective space in which the musical echoes of the performance do their work and the listener is vouchsafed their own rare moment of simultaneously encountering a Dylan song both in memory and in the moment.

Given Dylan's ambivalence towards musical echoes, it bespeaks his admiration for his duet partner that he joined so fully in these faithful renditions of 'Dark Eyes' that December. And it is a nice twist in our tale that, in the final duet, it was Smith rather Dylan who went 'off script' and deviated from the score:

> On the last night, I doubled the end of the last chorus, without saying anything to him. And he looked at me, and said (sardonically), 'Good ending'. (McKay and Elder 2021)

References

Campbell, L. (2015) Personal correspondence.

Dylan, B. (2004) *Chronicles: Volume One*, London: Simon & Schuster.

Greene, A. (2014) Flashback: Bob Dylan sings 'Dark Eyes' with Patti Smith, *Rolling Stone*, 11th November.

Margotin, P. & Guesdon, J.-M. (2015) *Bob Dylan All the Songs: The Story Behind Every Track*, New York: Black Dog & Leventhal.

McKay, A. & Elder, E. (2021) *Alternatives to Valium*, blog, [Online], https://alternativestovalium.blogspot.com/2009/03/dark-eyes-and-sardonic-smile-patti_03.html [26th March 2021].

Smith, G.E. (2021) Personal correspondence.[1]

---

[1] My thanks to Martin Nichols and Rikky Rooksby for help with points bearing on the text, and to Melissa O' Brien for permission to reproduce her painting of the 'Dark Eyes' duets.

James Adams

'Furnish Me with Tape'
The Always Evolving Way We Listen to Live Dylan

Bob Dylan has produced a massive body of art in his eighty years on this earth. Although best known for his single songs and albums of the middle 1960s, Dylan is relentlessly creative and productive as a filmmaker, painter, sculptor, satellite radio host and whiskey distiller. Over the last thirty years, Dylan has probably been most prolific as a performer, giving live concerts with a staggering regularity and frequency. He's done over 3,000 shows since 1988, and many hundreds more before.

Anyone who's been to one of Bob Dylan's concerts knows that the performances heard there bear little resemblance to those on Dylan's commercial recordings. A true performance artist, Dylan uses the stage as a place to experiment with his songs, tinker with them, and allow them to evolve. To Dylan, the songs are living things, and changeable. Sometimes the resulting alterations are minor, such as a slight change in key or tempo. But even minor adjustments can be astonishing. Live perform-ances of 'Mr. Tambourine Man' from 1993 sound strikingly different from those given in 1995.

More significant for a Nobel laureate in Literature, during live per-formances Dylan often alters the lyrics—the words and content, some-times even the meaning—of his songs. Even slight lyric changes are intriguing. Why does the narrator in 'When I Paint My Masterpiece' rush back to his hotel room? In 1971, it's for 'a date with Botticelli's niece'. In 2019, it's to 'wash off my clothes, scrape off all of the grease'. What is the meaning and purpose of that change?

In other instances, the rewrites are more significant and result in dramatic shifts in meaning and narrative arc. For example, some performed versions of 'Tangled Up In Blue' have lyrics that are vastly different from the 1975 album original. The characters in the rewritten song have different goals, concerns and emotions, and may be different characters altogether. Likewise, Dylan's 2019 lyrics for 'Gotta Serve Somebody' are decidedly different from those he used in 1980, and different still from performances in 1990.

Those different versions of Dylan's songs are important precisely because they are different. Because Dylan experimented with their text and language, they are an essential component of the man's art and worthy of closer study and examination (Williams 2004, xiii–xiv). In an abstract sense, those varied performances are akin to manuscript drafts, and evidence of a ceaselessly creative mind at work.

But of course, a concert isn't a manuscript. Live performances are fleeting. They vanish the moment they're given and they're fugitive. There's no infrastructure for their preservation and study. That is, unless they're captured and preserved by those who recognise their significance. Dylan scholars are lucky that intrepid fans, often at some personal risk, have taken it upon themselves to make, save and share recordings of Dylan's live performances. A massive archive now exists, although it lives almost entirely in the shadowy world of tape traders. It's hard to say precisely how large it might be. Ten thousand hours of unreleased recorded Dylan? That is perhaps an underestimate when one considers studio outtakes in addition to concert recordings.

These are not counterfeit or pirated recordings, those illegal copies of legitimate releases. Likewise, these are not commercial bootlegs. That is, concert recordings and studio outtakes sold to a consumer who may be unaware that the product is unofficial. Rather, there are long-standing networks of traders who pass "tapes" from one fan or scholar to another, with no financial consideration. For almost as long as Dylan has performed, his fans have traded these 'field recordings', to borrow a phrase more often used to describe the work of song collectors like Charles Seeger and Alan Lomax. Recordings like the Minneapolis Hotel Tape, made by a friend of Dylan's in December 1961, have circulated for more than fifty years. Sharing the music, and knowledge of Dylan's talents, career and accomplishments, is the overarching goal for the traders.

Although tape trading is now an old hobby, the audio media and method for sharing recordings has evolved over time. Whereas early commercial bootleggers pressed their tapes onto vinyl, then convinced local record shops to carry the illicit wares, non-commercial traders prioritised sound quality and often exchanged reel-to-reel tape recordings. The legendary *Basement Tapes* of Bob Dylan and The Band circulated on reel-to-reel before making the jump to commercial bootleg vinyl (Heylin 1994, 43–44).

The rise of Compact Cassette audio tape in the late 1970s was slow to take hold in tape-trading circles, because early versions of that technology were plagued by comparatively poor audio quality. That trend shifted in the early 1980s, with the introduction of products like Sony's WM-D6C, the 'Walkman Pro', that made high-quality recordings on a portable, more concealable machine. At the same time, home stereo equipment increasingly allowed for the passable duplication of cassette tapes, albeit with incrementally diminished sound quality.

Cassettes were the standard trading format until the early 1990s, when Digital Audio Tape (DAT) became preferable among sound-obsessed traders. Because DATs were digital, dubbed copies did not have lesser sound quality than the master recording. But DATs reigned supreme for only a short time, and some fans never made the transition, as DAT tape and machines were more expensive than their cassette counterparts. Some traders, myself included, skipped from audio cassette to CD-Recordable (CD-R) technology at the end of the century, just as home CD burners became more reliable and affordable. Like many fans, I filled endless ring binders with page after page of discs. Most Dylan concert recordings required two CDs. Some fan-made compilations required a dozen discs, or more.

The internet changed everything. First used by Dylan fans as a chat-room and place to share lists of tapes available for trade, increasing download speeds and hard drive storage ultimately paved the way for sharing recordings online. Initially, MP3 files were favoured because their size allowed for faster transfers and bigger collections. Nowadays, most traders and collectors insist on swapping FLAC, SHN or other lossless audio files that preserve the full sonic range of the original recording in the highest possible quality. Using those file formats, a full Dylan show requires about 750 megabytes of digital storage space. Or, none at all.

That's because many Dylan concert audio recordings have been uploaded to video sharing websites like YouTube. That easy access allows both dedicated fans and the bootleg curious to quickly browse and stream Dylan concert audio from across his performance history. It has never been easier to hear a 'rare' Dylan performance.

But it's all so haphazard and blurry online. Many Dylan scholars and fans don't know how to find high-quality copies of specific concert recordings on the internet, and the specialty file formats require some technical sophistication. Recordings posted on YouTube have degraded audio quality and are very often incomplete or mislabelled. Some YouTube recordings have no descriptive labels or helpful metadata at all, in a deliberate effort by uploaders to avoid running afoul of copyright restrictions that result in file removal.

What's needed—and what's warranted, given Dylan's increasingly recognised importance—is an accessible and comprehensive database of live Dylan recordings, available to scholars, fans and the curious, to allow this significant body of art to be better studied, understood and appreciated.

This is not an original suggestion. In the preface to the second edition of her seminal study, *Performed Literature,* Betsy Bowden imagined the creation of an audio *Complete Works of Bob Dylan,* collecting the 'thousands upon thousands of sound recordings, not words on paper'. 'Right now,' Bowden continued, 'no existing technological tool can give researchers ready access to his entire corpus of work.' Bowden wrote those words in 1997 (Bowden 2001, vii). Things have changed, and not only is the technology available, but Bob Dylan's contemporaries have harnessed it to make their own performance art more accessible.

Take, for instance, the Grateful Dead. Although the band now has a reputation for being 'taper-friendly', that wasn't always the case. Only after years of fruitless pushback did the band and its crew allow fans to tape and trade recordings of their concerts, so long as no money changed hands in exchange for the music. Decades later, those recordings are now freely available to any listener, in a vast but easy-to-use database hosted by the invaluable Internet Archive. The open availability of those recordings has not hampered the Grateful Dead's ability to capitalise on the value of their concert recordings. Representatives of the band routinely select choice concerts from the Grateful Dead's performance history and give those recordings a formal commercial release. Those recordings are popular and routinely sell out their production runs. A subscription service is available for fans to keep up with the release schedule.

Neil Young provides another example. In 2017, Young established an online version of his *Neil Young Archives* music series. For a modest subscription fee, fans and scholars are given open access to the entirety of Young's immense body of work. His studio albums are there, along with outtakes and rarities. The recordings are contextualised with documentary information that lists participating musicians, recording dates and tours, all presented alongside illuminating photographs, videos and relevant ephemera. In 2020, the archive began hosting recordings of Young's live performances, and announced plans to expand the concert database in the future. Although the user interface can be difficult to navigate, the *Neil Young Archives* is already the best place to access and interrogate the whole of the man's art.

With clear models for the required technology, the possibility of a Bob Dylan audio performance database is no longer an abstract thought, but rather a definite possibility, perhaps an eventuality. That's because *The Bob Dylan Center* has nascent plans to create a Dylan listening centre and audio database, including recordings of his concerts, at their archive and museum in Tulsa, Oklahoma (Greene 2017). We must assume that Dylan approved the creation of that database, and thereby the ability of visiting scholars to access his concert recordings.

While admirable, the limitations of such a system are obvious. Not every researcher can make it to Tulsa, particularly as the world of Dylan studies has spread around the globe. Moreover, those who can access the sound stations at the centre will face the challenge of listening to many days', even weeks' worth of relevant material that could quickly overwhelm research budgets and travel time. For scholars who can secure a sabbatical in Tulsa, the rewards will be rich. Everybody else will struggle and scrape.

Perhaps those travel-constrained researchers will fall back on the long-standing networks of Dylan tapes and traders. It's true that much of the concert audio that will be made available in Tulsa also exists in the sometimes-opaque world of digital tape swapping, although not everything is there, and rarely in the same audio quality. And who's to say what preferred audio format those recordings will take next? From reel-to-reel to Compact Cassette, DAT to CD, MP3 to FLAC, and now streaming audio, the formats have changed almost as often as Dylan himself, always shedding off one more layer of skin. With that perspective, it's not the audio format that matters, but rather our ability to access, hear and listen to every mind polluting word.

References

Bowden, B. (2001) *Performed Literature: Words and Music by Bob Dylan*, Lanham, MD: University Press of America. N.B. Although the second edition of Bowden's book was published in 2001, her preface is dated January 1997.

Greene, A. (2017) A look inside Bob Dylan's secret archives, *Rolling Stone*, [Online], https://www.rollingstone.com/music/music-features/exclusive-a-look-inside-bob-dylans-secret-archives-199434/ [7th January 2020].

Heylin, C. (1994) *Bootleg: The Secret History of the Other Recording Industry*, New York: St. Martin's Press.

Williams, P. (2004) *Bob Dylan Performing Artist: The Early Years 1960–1973*, London: Omnibus Press.

The *Great White Wonder* LP — rock music's first notable bootleg album, released in July 1969 (public domain).

Michael Gray

The Finishing End?

The beginning of my interest in Dylan's endings was when I first heard 'Positively 4th Street' — which was when it was new.

What struck me before I registered how that song ends, or how that track ends, was how it begins. 'You got a lot of nerve to say you are my friend.' That extremity of directness, and direct hostility to its addressee(s), was *so refreshing* in 1965, in a pop world of flaccid euphemisms ('I Want To Hold Your Hand') in which every addressee was pined for. Here instead was a song of outspoken animus, heightened by its emerging out of a strong melody and a jaunty musical sound.

It was just as striking a contrast to most 1960s taste in folk music. Folksong tended to be narratives about other people, mostly from long ago or myth, without an 'I' or a personalised 'you', and sometimes beginning with the apparent archaism of '"Twas'.

But 'Positively 4th Street' also *ends* in a way that seemed noticeably unconventional. The "rules" for how to end a popular song are mainly either that you make the pay-off line clear by cranking it up to a declamatory crescendo (a distinctive master of this being Roy Orbison) or else you repeat that last line so that you sing it three times, optionally slowing it down that last time around or using a fade-out. What Dylan does, more effectively, is refuse either formula. His last stanza comes hot on the heels of the one before it, and there is no clue that this is where the lyric will terminate until that affable and catchy music fades out on us fast. Fade-outs can mean many things, but what this one effects is a hasty withdrawing: he's said his piece, turned a corner and vanished up the street.

Two other songs, and in one case its track too, end unlike any pop or folk song I'm aware of. Musically, 'All Along the Watchtower' ends unremarkably, but the import of the lyric leaves it enigmatically open as to whether a rather terrifying full stop is implied by the silence after that last line, 'The wind began to howl', or whether *un*ending nightmare is implied.[1] Rather clearer is the implication at the finish of 'Man Gave Names to All the Animals', a track that suspends its own ending, knowing we'll fill in the line Dylan declines to sing. (Live, instead of trusting the audience, he adds an extra chorus after that absent concluding line of verse.)

He surprises me by other means on the *Nashville Skyline* version of 'Girl from the North Country': he gives Johnny Cash the last word.

When Dylan began his career, there was a Folk Revival idea, quietly prevalent, that recording turned authentic song performance into artificial fixity, and you shouldn't make it worse by any kind of studio trickery. On Dave Van Ronk's first album, for example, every track ends 'properly'. No fade-outs.[2] Dylan's first album sticks to that rule on every traditional song, and 'Baby, Let Me Follow You Down' starts with his Ric Von Schmidt attribution, exactly as if performed to a club audience—but his own 'Talkin' New York' is allowed a fade-out. On *Freewheelin'* he's still keeping fade-outs to a minimum: only 'Corrina, Corrina' and 'I Shall Be Free' fade away. None of the big songs does.

What begins here, though, is a way Dylan develops to *signal* that a song's end is coming: i.e. if a track includes harmonica, the signal is a significant harp break just ahead of the final verse. In live performance, for some decades, this became so prevalent we might have assumed he'd always done it: that tracks like 'Masters of War' and 'A Hard Rain's A-Gonna Fall' must have been that way. In fact, it's introduced on only one *Freewheelin'* song, 'Girl from the North Country' —and appears on just one third LP track too, 'The Lonesome Death Of Hattie Carroll' (and that's the *ninth* track on the album). On *Another Side Of*, he signals this way on just

---

[1]   This was first discussed in a *Village Voice* review by Richard Goldstein and in Gray (1972, 210–11).

[2]   *Dave Van Ronk Sings Ballads, Blues and a Spiritual*, Folkways, May 1959. Henry Diltz (to Sid Griffin 2021, on my behalf): 'Yes! There was a purist element who wanted recordings to be like a club gig… A song ended, you put your banjo or fiddle down, it had ended. Not faded out. No one in our corner was doing production tricks.' But for an interesting, well researched article on the history and usages of fade-outs across different kinds of music, see William Weir, https://slate.com/culture/2014/09/the-fade-out-in-pop-music-why-dont-modern-pop-songs-end-by-slowly-reducing-in-volume.html.

two: 'Chimes of Freedom' and 'Ballad in Plain D'. (On the latter there's no harmonica at all *until* just after the penultimate verse.) By 1965 and *Bringing It All Back Home* he's doubled the frequency of this signalling: it's on four tracks—'Love Minus Zero/No Limit', 'On the Road Again', 'Mr. Tambourine Man' (live performances prompt me to add 'of course') and 'It's All Over Now, Baby Blue'. There's also an equivalent *non*-harp instrumental break ahead of the last stanza on 'Subterranean Homesick Blues'.

By this point, there's also been an increase in how often his album tracks fade out; on this, the first eight use fade-out, so that in this respect Dylan has long since abandoned any loyalty to folk recording traditions. Yet in another way his songs are still constructed like those of old. Not a single song on any of these first five albums has that popular song device, the bridge, or middle eight. We don't get one till the fifth song on *Highway 61 Revisited*, with 'Ballad of a Thin Man' offering the bridge section beginning 'You have many contacts' and running through to 'tax-deductible charity organisations'. And tellingly, when Dylan returns to a "folksier" sound on *John Wesley Harding*, he abandons bridge sections again, with the sole exception of the album-ending country pop of 'I'll Be Your Baby Tonight'.

Four *Highway 61 Revisited* tracks end with that harmonica-solo signal that the end is coming: 'It Takes a Lot to Laugh, It Takes a Train to Cry' (no harp until that point), 'Queen Jane Approximately', 'Just Like Tom Thumb's Blues' and the ten-verse 'Desolation Row', with a whole verse's worth of harp solo where we expect, and another long solo at the end. Three consecutive *Blonde on Blonde* tracks deploys the same signal, and a fourth has a parallel non-harp instrumental interlude. Two *John Wesley Harding* tracks follow the pattern.

A more conventional signal that a song's end is nigh, and which he uses on songs from 'Girl from the North Country' through 'Obviously Five Believers' to 'Key West (Philosopher Pirate)', is to have as the last verse or chorus a repeat of the first. More Dylanishly, on 'From a Buick 6', when the lyric's penultimate line is 'And just like I said', that in itself tells us we're at song's end.

As I've implied, there's a difference between how a song and a track ends, but because Dylan is a great wordsmith, his verbal finales are often the more striking, and they come to count still more when it comes to how an *album* ends: a different thing again, and dependent on the ordering of tracks.

Discounting live albums, compilations and the so-called Sinatra albums, Dylan ends his as follows: thirteen fade out, and four sort-of-fade-out (*Desire* and *Oh Mercy* stop but leave odd tiny noises to fade; a friend complains that *Street Legal* fades out a Billy Cross lead guitar solo he wants to hear more of, but I think this fades down but not out; and "*Love And Theft*" fades only on the reverberating final musical note). The other sixteen albums yield definite endings; they come to full stops.

But what sorts of full stop? What's most marked in the ending of the last song, and thus of the album, on *New Morning*, is how the brief, piano-dominated 'Father of Night' ends so suddenly, with more surprise than ceremony. (Ditto on 'Dear Landlord' on Dylan's previous album: another piano-dominated sudden arrest, though not at album's end.) Only twice does Dylan seem to throw away an album end instead of, as it were, imposing it. Strange that *Freewheelin'* ends with the featherweight 'I Shall Be Free'; less strange that *Together Through Life* ends with the dire 'It's All Good'. As for *Blood on The Tracks*, 'Buckets of Rain', clearly, is not the album's most heavyweight song, yet it gives us a fine album end, its mood so calmly good-humoured and good-natured, and adds that lovely more serious farewell touch, 'All you can do is do what you must / You do what you must do, and you do it well…'

In five important cases an album ends on its longest song: *Highway 61 Revisited* with 'Desolation Row', *Blonde on Blonde* with 'Sad-Eyed Lady of the Lowlands', *Shot of Love* with 'Every Grain of Sand', *Time Out of Mind* with 'Highlands', and *Rough and Rowdy Ways* with 'Murder Most Foul'. You might say that's another Dylan trademark style of ending; however, and who knows why, some albums refuse to comply. *Another Side of* might have achieved a more significant sign-off with 'Chimes of Freedom' or the clear statement of 'My Back Pages'. *Infidels* ends with the indifferent 'Don't Fall Apart on Me Tonight' where it could have finished, rather than begun, with the riches of 'Jokerman'. Most oddly of all, why is the *very* great 'Brownsville Girl' buried in the middle of *Knocked Out Loaded*? How much more favourably that album might have been received had the eleven shining minutes of 'Brownsville Girl' been spot-lit at album's end!

In considering these endings, I also note curious resemblances between the gist of some consecutive albums' final titles. The fourth album ends with 'It Ain't Me, Babe' and the fifth with 'It's All Over Now, Baby Blue'. With an opposite thrust, from *John Wesley Harding* to *Nashville Skyline*, the one signs off with 'I'll Be Your Baby Tonight', the other with 'Tonight I'll Be Staying Here With You'.

In the exceptional case of *Empire Burlesque*, Dylan's ending on the solo acoustic 'Dark Eyes', after the other, remorselessly Bakerised tracks, is an implicit apology: a 'Sorry about all that: does this compensate a bit?'

Then frequently, Dylan ends his albums either with a 'goodbye' or something close to it — *Under the Red Sky* signs off with 'Goodnight my love, and may the Lord have mercy on us all', and *Good as I Been to You* with the cheery kiss-off of 'If you want any more you can sing it yourself' — or with death: death of one sort or another.

Bob Dylan ends with 'See That My Grave Is Kept Clean'; the third album with 'Restless Farewell' ('I'll just say "farewell" and not give a damn'); *Slow Train* ends on the mass death of sinners 'When He Returns', *Saved* with asking 'Are You Ready?' for that same ending, and the last verse of 'Sugar Baby' ends *"Love And Theft"* with 'Look up, look up — seek your Maker — 'fore Gabriel blows his horn.' *Knocked Out Loaded* ends wondering if the singer will 'die of thirst / two feet from the well'; *Oh Mercy* concludes with his watching a shooting star 'slip away'; *World Gone Wrong* ends with the dead 'Lone Pilgrim' singing 'My soul flew to mansions on high / …The same hand that led me through seas most severe / Has kindly assisted me home.' *Christmas in the Heart* ends with that beautifully sung word 'Amen'.

Yet Dylan often questions the very existence of such finalities, so that some of his finest endings *challenge the notion* of endings. Christopher Ricks' essay 'Clichés That Come To Pass' discusses that phrase 'come to pass' and American English's greater capacity to make 'its own transience an acknowledgment and not just an admission'.[3] Dylan uses the phrase as challenging pun, embracing the sense that things arrive only to depart, in 'Seeing the Real You at Last' — 'I don't mind a reasonable amount of trouble / Trouble always comes to pass', that sense of the temporary nicely at odds with the claim to finality of 'at last'; but the phrase is placed

---

3   Ricks (1977, 22–29).

more insistently in ending 'I Pity the Poor Immigrant': '…when his glad-ness comes to pass.' Here too, however, Dylan is doubting that ends occur. The song's first verse includes 'in the end', but the last verse has 'in the *final* end'—a doubling that embodies its own distrust of every apparent end; and it's a doubling he had used four albums earlier, on 'To Ramona', where, piled onto the doubling of 'returning on back', he sings of 'the finishing end'. And his own end to that song enfolds the same distrust: 'Everything passes, everything changes'; these two contradict each other. If something changes, it perpetuates in different form: it doesn't 'pass'.

Dylan's most recent such doubling is this: 'Key West is on the horizon line.' Why not just 'on the horizon'? You can try to draw a line all you like, but the horizon just keeps moving out of reach.

As for Robert Zimmerman's own eventual ending, that will not stop Bob Dylan's work from continuing. As he once sang, death is not the end. How long the work will continue to be valued can't be known until a long time after we are all dead ourselves.[4]

References

Gray, M. (1972) *Song & Dance Man: The Art of Bob Dylan*, London: Hart-Davis-MacGibbon.

Christopher, R. (1977) Clichés that come to pass, in Gray, M. & Bauldie, J. (eds.) *All Across The Telegraph: A Bob Dylan Handbook*, London: Sidg-wick & Jackson.

---

[4]   Special thanks to Sid Griffin, Lucas Hare and Rainer Vesely.

Dylan on harmonica, Finsbury Park, London, 18th June 2011 (photograph by Francisco Antunes, licensed under the Creative Commons Attribution 2.0 Generic license CC BY 2.0).

Lou Majaw

Afterword
The Eastwind Farewell

1965 is the year that was and will always be, the Year of the Light
From the thatched and homely hut in the village where breakfast, lunch
and dinner are just words on an empty table, where kerosene lamps and
candles shine bright enough to guide you to a bigger village of tall
mansions and crowded streets, where the colourful and bright city lights
blind the cold and hungry soul, yet survived.
Songs and music from hotels, restaurants and almost every street corner
fill the air like a healing touch to the lost and lonely soul.
Yes, music was everywhere.
Music to soothe and comfort you,
music to make you feel good,
and music to make you think.
Amidst songs and music of rain, sunshine and rainbows
came the voice of a man who makes you feel what you see and hear.
All of us are indeed blessed to taste and share the fruits from his garden
of hope and wisdom.
Thank You Bob Dylan for enlightening and enriching our lives.
Have a meaningful birthday!
God bless you with health and peace, forever more.
Khublei
Lou Majaw

Lou Majaw.

Receiving the Presidential Medal of Freedom from Barack Obama, 29th May 2012 (NASA/Bill Ingalls; public domain).